Finance & Accounting for Nonfinancial Managers

THIRD EDITION

STEVEN A. FINKLER
Ph.D., CPA

ΛSPEN
PUBLISHERS

1185 Avenue of the Americas, New York, NY 10036
www.aspenpublishers.com

NOTE: This book is not designed to make the reader a financial analyst, accountant, or tax expert. The purpose of the book is to allow you to better understand what such experts are doing, and to better communicate with them. One should not make any financial or tax decisions based on the contents of this book without first consulting an expert in the appropriate fields of accounting, finance, or tax.

© 2003 Aspen Publishers, Inc.
A Wolters Kluwer Company
www.aspenpublishers.com

Printed in the United States of America.

ISBN 0-7355-4604-5

3 4 5 6 7 8 9 0

Includes an interactive CD-ROM!

Finance &
Accounting
for
Nonfinancial
Managers

basic tax
concepts

financial
statements

ratio analysis

internal rate
of return

accountability
& control

personal
finances

glossary

THIRD EDITION

STEVEN A. FINKLER
Ph.D., CPA

ASPEN
PUBLISHERS

Part 4
Financial Statement Analysis

In loving memory of my mother

ABOUT THE AUTHOR

Steven A. Finkler, Ph.D., CPA, is a Professor of Accounting and Financial Management at the Robert F. Wagner Graduate School, New York University. At the Wagner School he is the Director of the Finance Specialization. He holds a bachelor's degree with a major in Finance and a master's degree in Accounting from the Wharton School. His master's degree in Economics and Ph.D. in Business Administration are from Stanford University. Before joining NYU, he was on the faculty of the Wharton School.

An award-winning teacher and author, he has also written six other books on budgeting, cost accounting, and financial management, and over two hundred articles on financial management. He has consulted for numerous organizations around the United States and abroad. He worked for several years as a CPA with Ernst & Young.

Contents

Part 1
Introduction

ONE

TWO

Part 2
The Framework of Accounting

SEVEN

EIGHT

Part 3
Financial Decisions

NINE

TEN

ELEVEN

TWELVE

THIRTEEN

PART 5

Getting Your Own Finances in Order

PREFACE

There was a time when controllers and treasurers served a clear staff function of providing information and support for line managers. Today it often seems to nonfinancial managers that the financial officers are the tail wagging the dog. Financial officers may often appear to be more preoccupied with their own ever-increasing empires than with the provision of timely, useful, understandable information for running the firm efficiently. They certainly don't seem to have the time to translate the information they do generate into a form comprehensible to the average nonfinancial manager.

Yet the nonfinancial manager can no longer avoid financial information. Profit statements, operating budgets, and business plans are a constant part of the manager's day. This book is an introduction to the world of financial management. However, its intent is not to make the reader a financial manager. Rather, it is an attempt to familiarize the nonfinancial manager with what accounting and finance are all about. This book concentrates on providing a working vocabulary for communication, so that the reader can develop an ability to ask the right questions and interpret the jargon-laden answers. Any accountant can bury any nonaccountant in debits and credits. But once you understand a few basics you can fight back and demand information that is both useful and usefully explained.

In addition to vocabulary, this book describes a variety of methods, processes, and tools of accounting and finance. They are not described in sufficient detail for the reader to fire the treasurer or controller and take over the job (how many of you really want to do that?). Instead, there is sufficient detail so that the reader can say, "So that's what LIFO-FIFO is all about? I always wondered why we changed our inventory system," or perhaps, "Hey, we never thought about those advantages of leasing rather than buying; maybe we should give leasing a closer look!"

How many managers are rewarded on the basis of return on investment (ROI) without understanding the difference between ROI and ROE (return on equity) and ROA (return on assets), not to mention RONA (return on net assets)? There's no escaping the fact that all managers are affected by the financial decisions that every firm makes. This book clarifies in the reader's mind what questions are important to the firm's financial management and why.

Who are the nonfinancial managers this book is aimed at? They are presidents and vice presidents and all other managers except for the accountants and other financial experts in the firm. This includes all the engineers, marketing and sales personnel, and production people who have moved up within their firm to the point at which they need more financial lingo to follow what's going on in their communications with the financial officers. It includes those in law and human resources, and others throughout all areas of the firm, who have shifted career paths or who have simply grown with the firm and been promoted to more responsible positions. Sometimes managers need this book simply because the growth of their firm has been so fast that the financial complexity has increased at a more rapid rate than they have been able to keep up with.

Most of the readers of this book will not have attended business school. Surprisingly, however, many business school graduates will pick this book up as an excellent refresher. Frequently, business school graduates who majored in fields such as management, marketing, and industrial organization have commented years later that they would have paid far more attention to their accounting and finance coursework had they realized how valuable that background is to those in responsible positions in industry.

Essentially, this book is for any manager or future manager who comes into contact with elements of the financial process and feels a need for a better understanding of what's going on. This is not a text. The structure of this book is such that the reader can sit down and read it in whole or in part. Although it is not a novel, the material is presented in a prose that should eliminate the need for intensive studying to understand the main points. A once-through reading should provide the reader with a substantial gain in knowledge. As specific financial questions come before the reader at times in the future, the book will serve as a good reference to brush up in a particular area.

The widespread acceptance of the first two editions of this book has been gratifying. When first published, it was selected as the book of the month by Fortune Book Club. Since then it has been featured by a number of other book clubs, and over 165,000 copies have been sold. It has been included in CD business collections, and is the basis for an on-line interactive course in accounting and finance. It has been adopted by a number of colleges and universities that wanted a less technical book for their non-accounting majors. It has been the basis for a number of executive education programs as well. I am most proud of the wide number of individuals who have used it on their own, and then written to thank me because they found it so useful. It has consistently held the number one or two sales position in its category at both Amazon.com and BN.com (Barnes and Noble).

There are a number of changes to this newest edition. Six new chapters have been added, covering basic tax concepts, business plans, capital structure and sources of capital, working capital management and banking relations, accountability and control, and personal finances. An extensive glossary has also been added to the end of the book. Updates for the latest tax and accounting rule changes have been incorporated throughout the book. Within existing chapters, material has been added expanding discussion of sale and leaseback arrangements, T-accounts, the chart of accounts, forecasting, budgeting, benchmarks, and derivatives.

Included with this edition (on the CD at the back of the book) are Microsoft Excel templates that will allow you to immediately apply many of the concepts and techniques discussed throughout the book. Also included is an extensive annotated list of Web sites related to accounting and finance that would be useful for nonfinancial managers.

My thanks go to Stewart Karlinsky for his valuable contributions to the tax sections of this book. Any comments or questions concerning this book may be addressed to me at:

Steven A. Finkler, Ph.D., CPA
Professor of Accounting and Financial Management
The Wagner School, New York University
600 Tisch Hall
40 West 4th Street
New York, NY 10012-1118
or at:
steven.finkler@nyu.edu

List of Excel Templates

To ease your way into the application of the material in this book, a set of computer templates has been prepared. These templates, using Microsoft Excel spreadsheet software, are on the CD that accompanies this book. In each chapter where the material for a template is discussed, there is a box referring the reader to the template. The templates on the CD are:

Part 1

Introduction

One

An Introduction to Financial Management

WHAT IS FINANCIAL MANAGEMENT?

This book focuses on accounting and finance. See Figure 1-1. *Accounting* is a system for providing financial information. It is generally broken down into two principal elements: financial accounting and managerial accounting. *Finance* has traditionally been thought of as the area of financial management that supervises the acquisition and disposition of the firm's resources, especially cash.

The *financial accounting* aspect of accounting is a formalized system designed to record the financial history of the firm. The financial accountant is simply a historian who uses dollar signs. An integral part of the financial accountant's job is to report the firm's history from time to time to interested individuals, usually through the firm's annual and quarterly reports.

The *managerial accountant* looks forward whereas the financial accountant looks backward. Instead of reporting on what has happened, the managerial accountant provides financial information that might be used for making improved decisions regarding the future. In many firms the same individual is responsible for providing both financial and managerial accounting information.

Finance has expanded significantly from the functions of borrowing funds and investing the excess cash resources of the firm. In its broader sense the finance function involves providing financial analyses to improve decisions that will affect on the wealth of the firm's owners. Whereas the managerial accountant will provide the information for use in the analyses, the finance officer often will perform the actual analyses.

3

Figure 1-1. Accounting and Finance

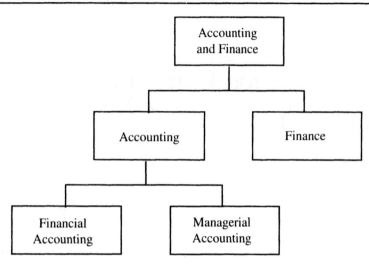

THE GOALS OF FINANCIAL MANAGEMENT

At first thought, one might simply say that the goal of financial management is to aid in the maximization of owner wealth, or more simply, maximization of the firm's profits. Profits are, after all, literally, the bottom line. That's true, but as all managers know, the corporate environment has many other goals—maximization of sales, maximization of market share, maximization of the growth rate of sales, and maximization of the market price of the firm's stock, for example. For not-for-profit organizations maximization of profits may not be a goal at all, although at least some profit is usually necessary to ensure the financial well-being of even not-for-profit organizations.

On a more personal level, managers are concerned with maximization of salary and perks. Such maximization is often tied in with the maximization of return on investments (ROI), return on equity (ROE), return on assets (ROA), or return on net assets (RONA). (See Chapter 22 for a discussion of these terms.) The list of goals within the organization is relatively endless, and our intention is to narrow the range rather than broaden it.

From the perspective of financial management there are two overriding goals: profitability and viability. See Figure 1-2. The firm wants to

Figure 1-2. Organizational Goals

be profitable, and it wants to continue in business. It is possible to be profitable and yet fail to continue in business. Both goals require some clarification and additional discussion because they surface time and time again throughout this book.

Profitability

In maximizing profits there is always a trade-off with risk. See Figure 1-3. The greater the risk we must incur, the greater the anticipated profit or return on our money we demand. Certainly, given two equally risky projects, we would always choose to undertake the one with a greater anticipated return. More often than not, however, our situation revolves around whether the return on a specific investment is great enough to justify the risk involved.

Consider keeping funds in a passbook account insured by the Federal Deposit Insurance Corporation (FDIC). You might earn a profit or return (in nominal terms—we'll talk about inflation later) of about 2 per-

Figure 1-3. Profitability Trade-Off

Profitability
Trade-Off

Risk   versus   Return

cent. The return is low, but so is the risk. Alternatively, you could put your money in a nonbank money market fund where the return might be considerably higher. However, the FDIC would not insure the investment. The risk is clearly greater. Or you could put your money into the stock market. In general, do we expect our stocks to do better or worse than a money market fund? Well, the risks inherent in the stock market are significantly higher than in a money market fund. If the expected return weren't higher, would anyone invest in the stock market?

That doesn't mean that everyone will choose to accept the same level of risk. Some people keep all their money in bank accounts, and others choose the most speculative of stocks. Some firms will be more willing than others to accept a high risk in order to achieve a high potential profit. The key here is that in numerous business decisions the firm is faced with a trade-off—risk vs. return. Throughout this book, when decisions are considered, the question that will arise is, "Are the extra profits worth the risk?" It is, I hope, a question that you will be somewhat more comfortable answering before you've reached the end of this book.

Viability

Firms have no desire to go bankrupt, so it is no surprise that one of the crucial goals of financial management is ensuring financial viability. This goal is often measured in terms of *liquidity* and *solvency*. See Figure 1-4.

Liquidity is simply a measure of the amount of resources a firm has that are cash or are convertible to cash in the *near term*, to meet the obligations the firm has that are coming due in the near term. Accountants use the phrases "near-term," "short-term," and "current" interchangeably.

Figure 1-4. Viability

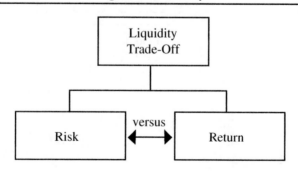

Generally the near-term means one year or less. Thus a firm is liquid if it has enough near-term resources to meet its near-term obligations as they become due for payment.

Solvency is simply the same concept from a long-term perspective. *Long-term* simply means more than one year. Does the firm have enough cash generation potential over the next three, five, and ten years to meet the major cash needs that will occur over those periods? A firm must plan for adequate solvency well in advance because the potentially large amounts of cash involved may take a long period of planning to generate. The roots of liquidity crises that put firms out of business often are buried in inadequate long-term solvency planning in earlier years.

So a good strategy is maximization of your firm's liquidity and solvency, right? No, wrong. Managers have a complex problem with respect to liquidity. Every dollar kept in a liquid form (such as cash, T-bills, or money market funds) is a dollar that could have been invested by the firm in some longer-term, higher yielding project or investment. There is a trade-off in the area of viability and profitability. The more profitable the manager attempts to make the firm by keeping it fully invested, the lower the liquidity and the greater the possibility of a liquidity crisis and even bankruptcy. The more liquid the firm is kept, the lower the profits. Essentially this is just a special case of the trade-off between risk and return discussed earlier.

We mentioned that profitability and viability are not synonymous. A firm can be profitable every year of its existence, yet go bankrupt anyway. How can this happen? Frequently it is the result of rapid growth and poor financial planning. Consider a firm whose sales are so good that inventory is constantly being substantially expanded. Such expansion requires cash payments to suppliers well in advance of ultimate cash receipt from sales.

Consider the hypothetical firm, Expanding Growth Company, that starts the year with $40,000 in cash, $80,000 of receivables, and 10,000 units of inventory. Receivables are amounts its customers owe it for goods and services that they bought, but have not paid for yet. Its inventory units are sold for $10 each and they have a cost of $8, yielding a profit of $2 on each unit sold. During January it collects all of its receivables from the beginning of the year (no bad debts!), thus increasing available cash to $120,000. January sales are 10,000 units, up 2,000 from the 8,000 units sold last December.

Due to increased sales, Expanding Growth decides to expand inventory to 12,000 units. Of the $120,000 available, it spends $96,000 on replacement and expansion of inventory (12,000 units acquired @ $8). No cash is collected yet for sales made in January. This leaves a January month-end cash balance of $24,000.

$ 40,000	Cash, January 1
+ 80,000	Collections during January
$120,000	Cash Available
− 96,000	Purchases of Inventory
$ 24,000	Cash Balance, January 31

During February all $100,000 of receivables from January's sales (10,000 units @ $10) are collected, increasing the available cash to $124,000. In February the entire 12,000 units on hand are sold and are replaced in stock with an expanded total inventory of 15,000 units.

$ 24,000	Cash Balance, January 31
+100,000	Collections during February
$124,000	Cash Available
−120,000	Purchases of Inventory (15,000 units @ $8)
$ 4,000	Cash Balance, February 28

Everyone at Expanding Growth is overjoyed. They are making $2 on each unit sold. They are collecting 100 percent of their sales on a timely basis. There appears to be unlimited growth potential for increasing sales and profits. The reader may suspect that we are going to pull the rug out from under Expanding Growth by having sales drop or customers stop paying. Not at all.

In March, Expanding Growth collects $120,000 from its February sales. This is added to the $4,000 cash balance from the end of February, for an available cash balance of $124,000 in March. During March, all 15,000 units in inventory are sold and inventory is replaced and expanded to 20,000 units. Times have never been better, except for one problem. Expanding Growth has only $124,000, but the bill for its March purchases is $160,000 (i.e., 20,000 units @ $8). It is $36,000 short in terms of cash needed to meet current needs. Depending on the attitudes of its supplier and its banker, Expanding Growth may be bankrupt.

$ 4,000	Cash Balance, February 28
+120,000	Collections during March
$ 124,000	Cash Available
−160,000	Purchases of Inventory
$ (36,000)	Cash Balance, March 31

Two key factors make this kind of scenario common. The first is that growth implies outlay of substantial amounts of cash for the increased inventory levels needed to handle a growing sales volume. The second is that growth is often accompanied by an expansion of plant and equipment, again well in advance of the ultimate receipt of cash from customers.

Do growing companies have to go bankrupt? Obviously not. But they do need to plan their liquidity and solvency along with their growth. The key is to focus on the long-term plans for cash. It is often said that banks prefer to lend to those who don't need the money. Certainly banks don't like to lend to firms like Expanding Growth, who are desperate for the money. A more sensible approach for Expanding Growth than going to a bank in March would be to lay out a long-term plan for how much it expects to grow and what the cash needs are for that amount of growth. The money can then be obtained from the issuing of bonds and additional shares of stock (see Chapter 10), or orderly bank financing can be anticipated and approved well in advance.

Apparently, even in a profitable environment cash flow projections are a real concern. Liquidity and solvency are crucial to the firm's viability. Throughout the book, therefore, we will constantly return to this issue as well as that of profitability. In fact, the reader will become aware that a substantial amount of emphasis in financial accounting is placed on providing the user of financial information with indications of the firm's liquidity and solvency.

The remaining chapter in Part 1 of this book provides a primer on income taxes. Taxes are a complex field. However, all managers can benefit from having at least a broad overview of that area.

Part 2 of this book provides a framework for accounting. It assumes that the reader has relatively little formal financial background. Many readers will find most of it to be new information. Others may find it a good review of material with which they are already generally familiar. Some readers may even find it rather elementary. For those more advanced readers, it might be appropriate to skip Part 2 and proceed directly to Parts 3 and 4.

Part 3 discusses specific areas of interest for financial decision making. It begins with a discussion of business plans, followed by consideration of choices to be made in acquiring long-term financing for the organization. It later gets into the various choices for inventory and depreciation methods, including a discussion of tax implications. It also discusses budgeting, cash and working capital management, leasing, leverage (both operating and financial), cost accounting, and long-term investment decision making. These topics should be of interest to all readers.

Part 4 of the book concentrates on the financial statements as the key to financial analysis. Emphasis is placed on the use of ratio analysis and on understanding the notes to the financial statements.

Part 5, the last section of the book, considers personal finances. Although the primary focus of the book is on finance and accounting for organizations, many readers will find this last section useful for making many of their personal financial decisions.

KEY CONCEPTS

Financial management—management of the finances of the firm in order to maximize the wealth of the firm's owners.

Accounting—the provision of financial information.

a. *Financial accounting*—provision of retrospective information regarding the financial position of the firm and the results of its operations.

b. *Managerial accounting*—provision of prospective information for making improved managerial decisions.

Finance—provision of analyses concerning the acquisition and disposition of the firm's resources.

Goals of Financial Management

a. *Profitability*—A trade-off always exists between maximization of expected profits and the acceptable level of risk. Undertaking greater risk requires greater anticipated returns.

b. *Viability*—A trade-off always exists between viability and profitability. Greater liquidity results in more safety, but lower profits.

Two

A Primer on Taxes

HOW MUCH DO YOU NEED TO KNOW?

Taxation in the United States is incredibly complicated. Starting from a fairly simple basic framework of a graduated income tax, our government has added rules and regulations that have created an intricately complex web. Some of the complexity exists to respond to policy goals. For example, allowing a deduction for individuals for interest paid on their residence is designed to promote home ownership—seen as something society should encourage. Allowing individuals to deduct donations encourages people to make charitable contributions. Similarly, a number of "tax breaks" exist for corporations, to encourage them to undertake activities society sees as being beneficial. Each tax break adds to the complexity of the system.

Not all tax breaks are designed to meet specific policy goals. Sometimes special interest groups lobby for advantageous tax treatment. As a result, some complexity exists because of the loopholes that have been created to lower the taxes paid by some taxpayers. On the other hand, taxpayers can be very creative in making existing rules work to their advantage. As a result, sometimes the tax code becomes even more tortuous as efforts are made to close unintended loopholes.

Providing a full understanding of tax rules and regulations is well beyond the scope of this book. On the other hand, managers must always keep in mind the fact that taxes exist, and that their decisions may result in taxes being higher or lower. Since financial decisions affect taxes, you need to have at least a bare-bones understanding of the tax system. We will focus here and in later chapters on issues related to federal income tax. There are many other types of taxes that managers need to be aware of as well.

Often companies are subject to state and local income or franchise taxes, sales tax, Social Security tax, and real estate tax, in addition to a wide variety of charges and user fees such as sewer levies, motor vehicle charges, and excise fees. These various taxes and fees vary tremendously from one area of the country to another. All companies should seek the assistance of a qualified tax expert who, at a minimum, can review all issues related to compliance with all tax laws. In addition, tax consultants can provide valuable assistance in minimizing your tax obligations.

PERSONAL VS. CORPORATE TAXES

The first and perhaps most important distinction to be made is the difference between personal income taxes and corporate income taxes.

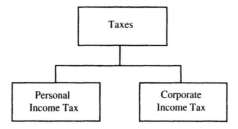

The personal income tax is levied on U.S. citizens and residents. The corporate income tax is levied on entities that have incorporated in the United States. This dual structure affects the decision of whether to run a business as an incorporated or unincorporated business. Businesses can be formed as *sole proprietorships, partnerships, limited liability companies (LLCs),* or *corporations.*

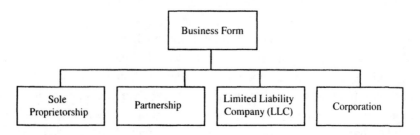

Sole proprietorships, partnerships, and LLCs are unincorporated businesses. A sole proprietorship is owned and run by one person. It is easy to form. The profits of the business are directly profits of the individual and are reported to the government on the individual's own federal tax return (Schedule C). The main drawback is that the individual is personally liable for the debts of the business. If the business loses money, the creditors can legally claim the owner's personal assets.

Partnerships are similar to sole proprietorships, but the business is owned by more than one person. Partners report their share of the business income on their personal tax returns. It is important to have a written partnership agreement. Business situations can quickly turn the best of friends into enemies, and a written understanding of who owns what share of the business and who has the final word on decisions can prevent bitter legal disputes.

The corporate form of business organization is quite common because of two key advantages. Corporations have unlimited lifetimes and limited liability.

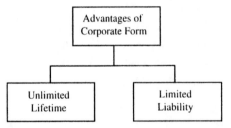

Corporations are considered to be "legal persons." The lives of these legal persons can extend beyond the lives of the original owners. If we are interested in having a business for just a few years, this is not critical. If we are hoping to build a company that will last for many years, this is a clear benefit. Further, corporations have *limited liability*. This means that creditors can come after the valuable resources of the corporation, but they generally cannot claim anything from the owners. If the corporation fails to pay its debts, the owners of the corporation are not personally obligated to pay them (unless they have personally guaranteed them).

Once a corporation is formed, it may sell shares of stock. The money it raises from the sale can be used to buy the resources (e.g., buildings, equipment, and inventory) needed to run the business. Those paying for the stock become the owners, or shareholders, of the company. The shares of stock can later be sold, transferring ownership of the organization to different owners, without affecting the running of the business.

Why aren't all organizations formed as corporations? Corporations are legally harder to form, and may have to comply with more laws than unincorporated businesses. Furthermore, a major factor that dissuades many from incorporating is that corporations pay corporate income taxes. After paying these taxes, when corporations distribute their earnings to their owners, the owners must also pay personal income taxes. This creates an effective *double taxation*. The same profits are taxed twice!

Corporations may temporarily avoid the second layer of taxes, the personal taxes, by retaining their profits rather than distributing them in the form of taxable dividends. A downside of this is that the owners do not receive current distributions from the corporation. A potential benefit, however, is that the retained profits may be invested by the corporation in profitable activities. The profits from those activities make the corporation more valuable. That drives up the value of the stock.

If the owners sell some of their stock at these higher prices, they earn a profit called a *capital gain*. For individuals, capital gains on investments owned for more than one year are taxed at substantially lower rates than ordinary income. Double taxation still exists, but its impact is thus first deferred for a period of time while the profits are retained, and then partially offset due to the lower capital gains tax rate.

Limited Liability without Double Taxation

Clearly, it would be the best of both worlds to have the benefits of limited liability, while paying taxes only once. There are several options that allow companies to gain these benefits. The options are S corporations (Sub-S), limited liability companies (LLCs), and limited liability partnerships (LLPs).

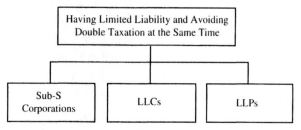

An S corporation is often referred to as an "S corp" or as a "Sub-S" because the rules related to these corporations are contained in Subchapter S of the Internal Revenue Code, which allows corporations to be treated as if they were partnerships for tax purposes. The primary benefit is that the owners have the limited liability benefit of corporate form while avoiding the corporate income taxes. There are a variety of restrictions related to the number and type of shareholders and the need for shareholders to all agree to S corporation treatment.

Note that there may be reasons that some shareholders would prefer not to have such treatment. For example, the owners of an S corp will be taxed on their share of the year's profits each year, the same as if it were a partnership. But if the corporation does not declare a dividend and distribute those profits, some owners may not have the cash they need to pay the taxes on their share of the profits. Also, partnerships, corporations, and foreign investors may not invest in an S corp.

Limited liability companies (LLCs) are neither partnerships nor corporations. They are a type of organization that has the benefits of limited liability for all of their owners. They may elect to be taxed as if they were corporations or partnerships, and they may have an unlimited number of owners, something that is not possible for an S corp. However, in some states LLCs may have their own negative aspects, such as being subject to gross receipts taxes.

The last type of organization that combines these features is a limited liability partnership (LLP). LLPs are partnerships and are taxed as such. In this type of organization partners are liable for their own acts and those of individuals under their direction. However, they are not liable for acts of other partners. This is a common business form for professional organizations, such as public accounting firms. There may be state laws that prevent a professional organization from incorporating or becoming an LLC. In such a case, the LLP form affords some limited liability for the partners.

THE TAX RATE AND THE TAX BASE

For both the personal and corporate income tax, the most essential elements are the *tax base* and the *tax rate*. The tax base defines what is subject to the tax. For individuals, their federal income tax base is their *taxable income.* This taxable income is calculated by applying tax regulations that indicate what must be included in taxable income. For example, wages and most interest are included, but some types of interest (e.g., interest on a municipal bond) may be tax-exempt. Such tax-exempt interest is not part of taxable income. The tax rate is the percentage that is multiplied by the tax base to calculate the tax.

PROGRESSIVE, PROPORTIONAL, AND REGRESSIVE TAX RATES

Tax systems can be *progressive*, *proportional*, or *regressive*.

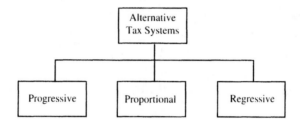

A progressive system has increasing rates as the tax base increases. A proportional tax would maintain one tax rate for all payers regardless of their tax base. A regressive tax is one that has declining rates as the tax base grows.

Our personal income tax structure is based primarily on a progressive basis. This approach is deemed to have a greater degree of equity, because those most able to afford taxes are called upon to pay a larger share.

Proponents of the flat tax support the notion of a proportional tax. They would argue that even under a flat tax, those with a greater tax base pay more taxes. For example, if we had an across-the-board proportional flat tax of 20 percent, someone earning $10,000 might pay $2,000 while someone earning $1,000,000 would pay $200,000. The rich would pay more than the poor. Opponents argue that the rich wouldn't be paying at a progressive or increasing rate. They would argue that, to the person earning $10,000, a tax of just 15 percent or $1,500 might be much harder to bear than a tax of 40 percent or $400,000 for a person earning $1,000,000.

Under the existing graduated tax rates, a person earning $10,000 pays less than $2,000, and the person earning $1,000,000 pays considerably more than $200,000. Or do they? Flat tax proponents argue that rich

Americans can afford to spend a fair amount of money on strategies to avoid taxes. They find loopholes to substantially reduce their taxes. It is possible that some taxpayers earning $1,000,000 would pay more taxes with a flat 20 percent tax with no loopholes than they currently pay, even though tax rates currently are graduated to a higher level than 20 percent. Further, flat tax proponents argue that there could be a floor at a level such as $50,000. Individuals with a tax base below that floor would not be subject to tax at all. They argue that the simplicity of taxes under such a system (they envision a postcard tax return) and the reduction of efforts to avoid taxes would make the system much more equitable in the long run.

Regressive taxes place the heaviest burden squarely on the shoulders of those least able to pay. Your first reaction may be that, in this country, we certainly would never enact such a tax. However, currently the FICA tax for Social Security is 7.65 percent (paid by both the employee and the employer) on wages up to $80,400, and then 1.45 percent on wages above that amount. That is a regressive tax, as the rate is lower for wages over $80,400.

MARGINAL, AVERAGE, AND EFFECTIVE TAX RATES

You should not assume that the taxes paid are all paid at the highest rate the taxpayer might fall into. The lowest portion of a taxpayer's taxable income is taxed at the lowest rate. For example, for a married couple filing a joint return in April 2002, for their taxable income earned during 2001, the tax rate was 15 percent on the first $45,200. The rate then rose to 27.5 percent for additional income up to $109,250. Then it rose to 30.5 percent, then 35.5 percent, and then 39.1 percent. See Table 2-1. Note that new, lower rates are being phased in over time as part of the Economic Growth and Tax Relief Reconciliation Act of 2001.

This gives rise to the distinction between the *marginal*, *average*, and *effective tax rates*.

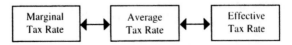

Suppose that you were married and filed a joint tax return for 2001, and you had taxable income of $100,000. Your marginal tax rate is the amount that you will have to pay on additional income that is earned. For

TABLE 2-1.

2001 Tax Rate Schedule for Married Individuals Filing a Joint Return

IF TAXABLE INCOME IS:	THE TAX IS:
Not over $45,200	15% of taxable income
Over $45,200 but not over $109,250	$6,780.00, plus 27.5% of the excess over $45,200
Over $109,250 but not over $166,500	$24,393.75, plus 30.5% of the excess over $109,250
Over $166,500 but not over $297,350	$41,855.00, plus 35.5% of the excess over $166,500
Over $297,350	$88,306.75, plus 39.1% of the excess over $297,350

example, if you earned another $5,000, the marginal tax rate on that $5,000 would have been 27.5 percent, because your income fell into the $45,201 to $109,250 tax bracket. However, what if you earned an extra $20,000 rather than an extra $5,000? Part of that additional income would have been taxed at 27.5 percent. However, with your starting tax base of $100,000, the $20,000 of extra income would have pushed you over the $109,250 point, into a higher tax bracket. The $10,750 earned above the $109,250 level would have been taxed at a rate of 30.5 percent. That would have become your new marginal tax rate. You can then anticipate that additional earnings will be taxed at that rate (or higher if you move into an even higher tax bracket).

Would the $20,000 of additional income have resulted in your paying an average of 30.5 percent on all of your taxable income? No. Even though you were moved into the 30.5 percent tax bracket, that rate is just paid on the amount above $109,250. The first $45,200 would still have been taxed at 15 percent, the next $64,050 at 27.5 percent, and the remaining $10,750 at 30.5 percent. All together the tax would have been $27,673. If we compare this total tax to the tax base of $120,000 we find that the average rate paid would have been 23.1 percent ($27,673 tax ÷ $120,000 tax base = 23.1 percent average tax rate). We can see this average rate is less than the marginal tax rate assessed on the highest portion of taxable income.

Note further that the tax rate is only applied to the tax base. Part of a taxpayer's income is not included in the tax base. For example, taxpayers may not have to pay tax on tax-exempt interest. If we divide the tax of $27,673 by the total income of the taxpayer including the income that is not taxable, the rate would fall further. That rate is referred to as the effective tax rate.

Tax Brackets

There are separate tax rate structures for corporations and individuals. The corporate tax rate structure was designed to ease the tax burden on small corporations. This encourages individuals to incorporate to get the benefits of limited liability, without creating a tremendous tax burden. The corporate tax structure at the time of this writing appears in Table 2-2.

TABLE 2-2.
Corporate Tax Brackets

TAXABLE INCOME	TAX
First $50,000	15% of Taxable Income
Over $50,000 but not over $75,000	$7,500 + 25% of taxable income over $50,000
Over $75,000 but not over $100,000	$13,750 + 34% of taxable income over $75,000
Over $100,000 but not over $335,000	$22,250 + 39% of taxable income over $100,000
Over $335,000 but not over $10,000,000	$113,900 + $34% of taxable income over $335,000
Over $10,000,000 but not over $15,000,000	$3,400,000 + 35% of taxable income over $10,000,000
Over $15,000,000 but not over $18,333,333	$5,150,000 + 38% of taxable income over 15,000,000
Over $18,333,333	35% of taxable income

Even though the rates start out fairly low, this still can pose a substantial burden for a small business owner. Suppose that a business earns $45,000 of profit. The owner may well need all of this money to live on. Retaining it in the business to avoid double taxation may not be a feasible option. Further, there is an excess accumulated earnings tax designed to prevent corporations from retaining earnings to avoid double taxation.

A corporation would have to pay 15 percent tax on the $45,000 of profit, and then the remaining profit could be paid to the owner as a dividend. The owner would then pay tax on the dividend. However, there is a solution to this problem. The owner can also be an employee of the corporation and can be paid a reasonable salary. If $45,000 is reasonable, then the profits of the business would drop to zero after incurring the employee wage expense of $45,000. The owner will have effectively gained limited liability with no increase in taxes. Corporations can also avoid double taxation on payments to pension plans.

The tax rate for more profitable corporations is 34 percent. Notice from Table 2-2, however, that there is a range where the marginal rate is 39 percent and another where it is 38 percent. The purpose of these rates in excess of 35 percent is to eliminate the benefit that corporations with low profits receive. The structure is designed so that for corporations with profits in excess $100,000 the benefits of the 15 percent and 25 percent brackets are phased out, and by $335,000 the corporation is paying 34 percent on *all* of its taxable income, not just on the marginal portion. For corporations with profits in excess of $15,000,000, the benefit of the 34 percent bracket is phased out. By the time we reach $18,333,333 or above, the corporation winds up paying 35 percent on all of its taxable income, rather than just on the income in the top bracket. The marginal and average tax rate would both be 35 percent.

Individual tax brackets are even more complicated. There are separate rate schedules for single individuals, for heads of household, for married filing joint returns, and for married filing separate returns. In addition, tax rates are complicated by capital gains tax rules. As noted earlier, if investments are held more than one year, they often qualify for long-term capital gains tax treatment. The maximum long-term capital gains rate is 20 percent on investments owned for more than one year, and 18 percent on investments acquired after 2000 and held for more than five years. In some cases, owners of small, closely-held businesses may be able to exclude half of their gain, resulting in a maximum tax of 14 percent on the gain on the sale of their investment.

CALCULATING FEDERAL INCOME TAX

The calculation of federal income tax is complicated by a variety of deductions, exemptions, and other factors related to the Internal Revenue Service's rules and regulations. Table 2-3 summarizes the calculation for both individuals and corporations.

TABLE 2-3.
Calculation of Federal Income Tax

Total Income from All Sources	$XXX
Less: Exclusions (items specifically excluded such as interest on some municipal bonds)	– XX
Gross Income	$XXX
Less: Deductions (itemized deductions for individuals or expenses for businesses)	– XX
Less: Exemptions (for individuals only)	– XX
Taxable Income	$XXX
Tax on Taxable Income (computed using Tax Rate Schedules)	$XXX
Less: Tax Credits	– XX
Tax Obligation	$XXX
Less: Prepayments	– XX
Balance Due to Government or Refund Due to Taxpayer	$XXX

Taxpayers must first determine their total income. This includes income on items that may be exempt from tax for some reason. The items that are specifically exempt are then excluded. However, if the exclusions become too great, they are subject to the alternative minimum tax (AMT). The AMT is designed to ensure that all taxpayers (whether individuals or businesses) pay at least some minimum percent of tax on their income. Total income, less exclusions, is referred to as gross income. From this gross income, deductions and exemptions are subtracted. For a business, this refers to the basic expenses of running the business. For an individual this refers to itemized or standard deductions and personal exemptions. The net result is taxable income.

The tax rate schedules are then applied to the taxable income to determine the income tax before consideration of tax credits. Credits are allowed for a variety of reasons. For example, if taxes are paid to a foreign country, the taxpayer is allowed in some circumstances to subtract that foreign tax as a credit.

In some cases foreign taxes can be subtracted as a deduction rather than a credit. Does it matter which way you subtract the foreign tax? Tremendously. A credit is subtracted after the tax has been computed. A one-dollar credit reduces federal taxes by $1. A deduction is subtracted before taxes are calculated. A one-dollar deduction reduces federal taxes based on the marginal tax rate. For example, if your marginal rate is 35 percent, a one-dollar deduction saves you 35 cents, while a one-dollar credit saves you $1. Whenever a choice is available, other things equal, a credit is always preferred to a deduction.

Once credits have been subtracted, the result is the tax obligation to the government. If prepayments of taxes have already been made, those amounts are subtracted to find out the remaining amount that the taxpayer owes to the government or the government owes the taxpayer.

Excel Exercise

Template 1 provides an opportunity to try experimenting with tax calculations. The template is included on the CD that accompanies this book.

OTHER CONCERNS FOR CORPORATIONS

Although the tax brackets may seem straightforward, corporations do not always pay the rate in the table, which is referred to as the *statutory* rate. There are many factors that affect the actual rate paid. Two of the most prominent of these relate to operating loss carryovers and to dividends received.

Operating Loss Carryovers

When a corporation's deductions are greater than its gross income, it has a loss, referred to as a *net operating loss (NOL)*. Corporations are allowed to use this loss to offset profits in other years, thus lowering the tax for those years. The corporation may first carry back the NOL to offset income from two years before the current tax year, then the year before the current tax year; then any remaining balance may be carried forward for up to twenty years until the full NOL is used to offset profits. After twenty years any remaining NOL expires.

Corporations may choose not to carry back the NOL, but instead to only carry it forward. This election would be made if taxes in earlier years were at low marginal tax rates and the corporation expects to be in a higher tax bracket in future years.

Dividends Received

Think double taxation is bad? How about triple taxation? At times corporations invest in the stock of other corporations. If they receive dividends from those corporations, those dividends will be taxable income. The result is that one corporation earns profits and pays tax on the profit. It pays dividends to a second corporation that owns some of its stock. That second corporation must pay tax on that dividend income. When this second corporation pays dividends to its stockholders, the stockholders will pay tax on that same income.

To lessen the impact of this triple taxation, corporations are allowed, subject to some limitations, a dividends-received deduction. The dividends-received deduction works as follows: if a corporation owns less than 20 percent of the corporation paying the dividend, it may deduct 70 percent of the dividends received from that corporation. If the corporation receiving the dividend owns 20 percent or more, but less than 80 percent of the stock of the corporation paying the dividend, 80 percent of the dividend may be deducted. If a corporation owns 80 percent or more of the corporation that is paying the dividend, it may deduct the entire dividend received.

CONCLUSION

This chapter has served as no more than a brief introduction to the complicated world of taxation. It is important for readers to always bear in mind that their actions often have tax implications. There are many opportunities for controlling your tax liability, and it is often worth the cost to have a tax specialist provide input as decisions are made.

KEY CONCEPTS

Limited liability—legal protection of personal assets from creditors.

Business form

> *Sole proprietorships* and *general partnerships* generally have unlimited liability.
>
> *Corporations* have an unlimited lifetime, ownership can be transferred easily, and they have limited liability.
>
> *S corporations, limited liability companies,* and *limited liability partnerships* have the benefit of limited liability and the ability to avoid double taxation.

Tax base—Defines what is subject to the tax.

Tax rate—the percentage that is multiplied by the tax base to calculate the tax.

Tax rate schedule—a chart that shows the percentage of tax that must be paid on different amounts of taxable income.

Marginal tax rate—the percentage of an extra dollar of taxable income that must be paid in tax.

Net operating loss (NOL)—a corporation's loss that may be used to offset income in other years, to lower taxes in those years.

Dividends-received deduction—To reduce the impact of triple taxation, corporations may deduct some or all of the dividends that they receive from other corporations.

Part 2

The Framework of Accounting

Three
Accounting Concepts

In most MBA programs, accounting is required in the first semester of study. Accounting has frequently been referred to as the language of business. The buzzwords you encounter in accounting are used as a normal part of the everyday language of finance, marketing, and other areas of financial management. Receivables, payables, journal entries, ledgers, depreciation, equity, LIFO, and MACRS are a smattering of the terms that you encounter if you have any dealings with the financial officers of your firm. All these terms have their roots in accounting.

Part 2 of this book focuses on introducing the reader to accounting and to many of the terms used by accountants. Specifically, Part 2 emphasizes the financial accounting system, that is, reporting the financial history and current financial status of the firm.

BASICS

Accounting centers on the business entity. An entity is simply the unit for which we wish to account. Entities frequently exist within a larger entity. An entity can be a department, or a project, or a firm. For example, Joe's Chili Dog Stand is a firm that is an entity. However, if it is not a corporation and Joe owns it solely, the Internal Revenue Service considers it to be part of the larger entity, Joe. That larger entity includes Joe's salary, other investments, and various other sources of income in addition to the chili dog stand.

From an accounting point of view there are two crucial aspects of the entity concept. First, once we have defined the entity we are interested in, we shouldn't commingle the resources and obligations of that entity with those of other entities. If we are interested in Joe's Chili Dog Stand as an accounting entity, we mustn't confuse the cash that belongs to Joe's Chili Dog Stand with the other cash that Joe has.

Second, we should view all financial events from the entity's point of view. For example, consider that the Chili Dog Stand buys chili dog rolls "on account." A transaction on account gives rise to an obligation or account payable on the part of the buyer and an account receivable on the part of the seller. In order for both the buyer and seller to keep their financial records, or "books," straight, each must record the event from their own viewpoint. They must determine whether they have a payable or a receivable.

We assume throughout this book that the firm you work for is the entity. Once we establish the entity we want to account for, we can begin to keep track of its financial events as they happen. There is a restriction, however, on the way in which we keep track of these events. We must use a monetary denominator for recording all financial events that affect the firm. Even if no cash is involved, we describe an event in terms of amounts of currency. In the United States, accounting revolves around dollars; elsewhere the local currency is used.

This restriction is an important one for purposes of communication. The financial accountant not only wants to keep track of what has happened to the firm but also wants to be able to communicate the firm's history to others after it has happened. Conveying information about the financial position of the firm and the results of its operations would be cumbersome at best without this monetary restriction. Imagine trying to list and describe each building, machine, parcel of land, desk, chair, and so on owned by the firm. The financial statement would be hundreds if not thousands of pages long.

Yet, don't be too comfortable with the monetary restriction either, because currencies are not stable vis-à-vis one another, nor are they internally consistent over time. During periods of inflation or deflation, the assignment of a dollar value creates its own problems. For example, the values of inventory, buildings, and equipment constantly change as a result of inflation or deflation.

ASSETS

The general group of resources owned by the firm represents the firm's assets. An asset is anything with economic value that can somehow help the firm provide its goods and services to its customers, either directly or indirectly. The machine that makes the firm's product is clearly an asset. The desk in the chief executive's office is also an asset, however indirect it may be in generating sales.

Assets may be either tangible or intangible. Tangible assets have physical form and substance and are generally shown on the financial statements. Intangible assets don't have any physical form. They consist of such items as a good credit standing, skilled employees, and patents, copyrights, or trademarks developed by the firm. It is difficult to precisely measure the value of intangible assets. As a result, accountants usually do not allow these assets to be recorded on the financial statements.

An exception to this rule occurs if the intangible asset has a clearly measurable value. For example, if we purchase that intangible from someone outside of the firm, then the price we pay puts a reasonable minimum value on the asset. It may be worth more, but it can't be worth less or we, as rational individuals, wouldn't have paid as much as we did. Therefore the accountant is willing to allow the intangible to be shown on the financial statement for the amount we paid for it.

If you see a financial statement that includes an asset called *goodwill*, it is an indication that a merger has occurred at some time in the past. The firm paid more for the company it acquired than could be justified based on the market value of the specific tangible assets of the acquired firm. The only reason a firm would pay more than the tangible assets themselves are worth is because the firm being acquired has valuable intangible assets. Otherwise the firm would have simply gone out and duplicated all of the specific tangible assets instead of buying the firm.

After the merger, the amount paid in excess of the market value of the specific tangible assets is called goodwill. It includes the good credit standing the firm has with suppliers, the reputation for quality and reliability with its customers, the skilled set of employees already working for the firm, and any other intangible benefits gained by buying an ongoing firm rather than by buying the physical assets and attempting to enter the industry from scratch.

The implication of goodwill is that a firm may be worth substantially more than it is allowed to indicate on its own financial statements. Only if the firm is sold will the value of all of its intangibles be shown on a financial statement. Thus we should exercise care in evaluating how good financial statements are as an indication of the true value of the firm.

LIABILITIES

Liabilities, from the word *liable*, represent the obligations that a firm has to outside creditors. Although there generally is no one-on-one matching of specific assets with specific liabilities, the assets taken as a whole represent a pool of resources available to pay the firm's liabilities. The most common liabilities are money owed to suppliers, employees, financial institutions, bondholders, and the government (taxes).

OWNERS' EQUITY

Equity represents the value of the firm to its owners. For a firm owned by an individual proprietor we refer to this value as owner's equity. For a partnership we speak of this value as partners' equity. For a corporation we talk of this value as shareholders' or stockholders' equity. This book commonly uses the term *stockholders' equity* whenever the equity of the owners is meant. Except in the rare cases in which a topic is relevant only to corporations, the reader from a proprietorship or partnership can simply convert the term in his or her mind to the appropriate one.

The stockholders' equity of a firm is often referred to as the "net worth" of the firm or its "total book value." Book value per share is simply the total book value divided by the number of shares of stock outstanding.

The equity of the owners of the firm is quite similar to the equity commonly referred to with respect to home ownership. If you were to buy a house for $400,000 by putting down $80,000 of your own money and borrowing $320,000 from a bank, you would say that your equity in the $400,000 house was $80,000.

If the house were a factory building owned by a firm, the $400,000 purchase price could be viewed as the value of the factory building asset, the $320,000 loan as the firm's liability to an outside creditor, and the $80,000 difference as the stockholders' equity, or the portion of the value of the building belonging to the owners.

THE ACCOUNTING EQUATION

The relationship among the assets, liabilities, and stockholders' equity is shown in the following equation and provides a framework for all of financial accounting.

$$\text{ASSETS} = \text{LIABILITIES} + \text{STOCKHOLDERS' EQUITY}$$

The left side of this equation represents the firm's resources. The right side of the equation gives the sources of the resources. Another way to think about this equation is that the right side represent the claims on the resources. The liabilities represent the legal claims of the firm's creditors. The stockholders' equity is the owners' claim on any resources not needed to meet the firm's liabilities.

The right side of the equation is frequently referred to as the equity side of the equation because the liabilities and stockholders' equity both represent legal claims on the firm's assets. Therefore, both can be thought of in an equity sense. Frequently the entire equation is referred to as the firm's assets and equities.

By definition, this equation is true for any entity. Once the firm's assets and liabilities have been defined, the value of ownership or stockholders' equity is merely a residual value. The owners own all of the value of the assets not needed to pay off obligations to creditors. Therefore, the equation need not ever be imbalanced because there is effectively one term in the equation, *stockholders' equity*, that changes automatically to keep the equation in balance. We refer back to this basic equation of accounting throughout this book.

KEY CONCEPTS

Entity—the unit for which we wish to account. This unit can be a person, department, project, division, or firm. Avoid commingling the resources of different entities.

Monetary denominator—All resources are assigned values in a currency such as dollars in order to simplify communication of information regarding the firm's resources and obligations.

Assets—the resources owned by the firm.

a. *Tangible assets*—assets having physical substance or form.

b. *Intangible assets*—assets having no physical substance or form; result in substantial valuation difficulties.

Liabilities—obligations of the firm to outside creditors.

Owners' equity—the value of the firm to its owners, as determined by the accounting system. This is the residual amount left over when liabilities are subtracted from assets.

Fundamental equation of accounting—Assets = Liabilities + Stockholders' Equity

Four

An Introduction to the Key Financial Statements

This chapter is a brief introduction to the key financial statements contained in annual financial reports. We will discuss the balance sheet (or statement of financial position), the income statement, and the statement of cash flows. These statements are crucial to understanding the finances of a firm.

THE BALANCE SHEET

The statement of financial position, more commonly referred to as the balance sheet, indicates the financial position of a firm at a particular point in time. Basically, it illustrates the basic accounting equation (Assets = Liabilities + Stockholders' Equity) on a specific date, that date being the end of the accounting period. The accounting period ends at the end of the firm's year. Most firms also have interim accounting periods, often monthly for internal information purposes and quarterly for external reports.

By default, a firm ends its year at the end of the calendar year. Alternatively a firm may pick a financial or "fiscal" year-end different from that of the calendar year. This choice often depends on making things easier and less expensive. One factor in this decision is the firm's inventory cycle. At year-end, most firms that have inventory have to physically count every unit. If you make shipments on a seasonal basis, the low point in the inventory cycle makes a good year-end, because it takes less time and cost to count the inventory than it would at other times during the year.

Another factor in the selection of a fiscal year is how busy your accounting and bookkeeping staff is. At the end of the fiscal year, many things have to be taken care of by both your internal accountants and your external auditor. An audit must take place, with time-consuming questions and information demands by the CPA. Tax returns must be prepared. Reports to the Securities and Exchange Commission are required for publicly held companies.

Thus, if you can find a time when the accounting functions within the firm are at a slow point, it makes for a good fiscal year-end. For example, many universities end their fiscal year on June 30 because this date gives them all of July and August to get things done before the students start returning to campus.

The basic components of a balance sheet are shown in Exhibit 4-1, which uses the hypothetical Coffin Corporation as an example. The first asset subgroup is current assets, and the first liability subgroup is current liabilities. The terms *short-term*, *near-term*, and *current* are used interchangeably by accountants and usually refer to a period of time less than or equal to one year. Current assets generally are cash or will become cash within a year. Current liabilities are obligations that must be paid within a year. These items get prominent attention by being at the top of the balance sheet. Locating the current assets and current liabilities in this way ensures that the reader can quickly get some assessment of the liquidity of the firm.

EXHIBIT 4-1.
Coffin Corporation
Balance Sheet
December 31, 2002

ASSETS		LIABILITIES & STOCKHOLDERS' EQUITY	
		Liabilities	
Current Assets	$ 5,000	Current liabilities	$ 3,000
		Long-term liabilities	4,000
Fixed Assets	10,000	Total Liabilities	$ 7,000
		Stockholders' Equity	
Investments	3,000	Contributed Capital	$ 5,000
		Retained Earnings	7,000
Intangibles	1,000	Total Stockholders' Equity	$12,000
		TOTAL LIABILITIES &	
TOTAL ASSETS	$19,000	STOCKHOLDERS' EQUITY	$19,000

The long-term (greater than a year) assets are broken into several groupings. Fixed assets represent the firm's property, plant, and equipment. Fixed assets are sometimes referred to as *capital facilities*. Investments are primarily securities purchased with the intent to hold onto them as a long-term investment. Securities purchased for short-term interest or appreciation are included in the current asset category. Intangibles, although frequently not included on the balance sheet, are shown with the assets when accounting rules allow their presentation on the financial statements.

In addition to current liabilities, the firm also typically has obligations that are due more than a year from the balance sheet date. Such liabilities are termed *long-term* liabilities.

The stockholders' equity consists of *contributed capital* and *retained earnings*. Contributed capital (sometimes referred to as "paid-in capital") represents the amounts that individuals have paid directly to the firm in exchange for shares of ownership such as common or preferred stock. Retained earnings represent the portion of the income that the firm has earned over the years that has not been distributed to the owners in the form of dividends.

Retained earnings, like all items on the equity side of the balance sheet, represent a claim on a portion of the assets and are not an asset themselves. Retained earnings of $100,000,000 does not imply that somewhere the firm has $100,000,000 of cash readily available that could be used for a dividend. It is far more likely that, as the firm earned profits over the years, the portion of those profits that was not distributed to the owners was invested in plant and equipment in order to generate larger profits in the future. Retained earnings represents the stockholders' ownership of the plant and equipment rather than a secret stash of cash.

Excel Exercise

Template 2 provides an opportunity to prepare a simple balance sheet for your organization. The template is on the CD that accompanies this book.

THE INCOME STATEMENT

The income statement compares the firm's revenues to its expenses. Revenues are the monies a firm has received or is entitled to receive in exchange for the goods and services it has provided. Expenses are the costs incurred in order to generate revenues. Net income is simply the difference between revenues and expenses. The simplest form of an income statement appears in Exhibit 4-2.

EXHIBIT 4-2.
Coffin Corporation
Income Statement
For the Year Ending December 31, 2002

Revenues	$20,000
Less Expenses	12,000
NET INCOME	$ 8,000

Unlike the balance sheet, which is a photograph of the firm's financial position at a point in time, the income statement tells what happened to the firm over a period of time, such as a month or a year.

The income statement is frequently used as a vehicle for the presentation of changes in retained earnings from year to year. Since maximizing the wealth of the stockholders of the firm is a key goal of the firm, it is important to convey to stockholders the changes in the amount of the firm's income that is being retained for use by the firm. As noted earlier, this use may consist of purchasing buildings and equipment to increase the firm's future profits.

A combined statement of income and retained earnings might appear as in Exhibit 4-3. The year's net income is added to the beginning retained earnings. This combined amount is the total accumulated earnings of the firm that have not been distributed to its owners. Dividends declared during the year are then subtracted because they are a distribution to the owners of a portion of the accumulated earnings of the firm. The resulting balance represents the firm's retained earnings as of the end of the year. Alternatively, changes in retained earnings for the year may be presented in a separate statement of retained earnings, such as the one in Exhibit 4-4. Note that in both Exhibits 4-3 and 4-4, the retained earnings as of December 31, 2002, is the same number that appears on the Balance Sheet (Exhibit 4-1) as of December 31, 2002.

Excel Exercise

Templates 3–5 provide an opportunity to prepare income, retained earnings, and combined income and retained earnings statements for your organization. The templates are on the CD that accompanies this book.

EXHIBIT 4-3.
Coffin Corporation
Statement of Income and Retained Earnings
For the Year Ending December 31, 2002

Revenues	$20,000
Less Expenses	12,000
Net Income	$ 8,000
Retained Earnings, January 1, 2002	4,000
Total	$12,000
Less Dividends Declared	5,000
Retained Earnings, December 31, 2002	$ 7,000

EXHIBIT 4-4.
Coffin Corporation
Statement of Retained Earnings
For the Year Ending December 31, 2002

Retained Earnings, January 1, 2002	$ 4,000
Net Income for the Year Ending December 31, 2002	8,000
Total	$12,000
Less Dividends Declared	5,000
Retained Earnings, December 31, 2002	$ 7,000

THE STATEMENT OF CASH FLOWS

The third major financial statement is the cash flow statement. This statement provides information about the firm's cash inflows and outflows. The current assets section of the balance sheet of the firm shows how much cash the firm has at the end of each accounting period. This can be compared from year to year to see how much the cash balance has changed, but that gives little information about how or why it has changed.

Looking only at the balance sheet can result in erroneous interpretations of financial statement information. For example, a firm experiencing a liquidity crisis (inadequate cash to meet its currently due obligations) may sell off a profitable part of its business. The immediate cash injection from the sale may result in a substantial cash balance at year-end. On the balance sheet this may make the firm appear to be quite liquid and stable. However, selling off the profitable portion of the business may have pushed the firm even closer to bankruptcy. There is a need to explicitly show how the firm obtained that cash.

The statement of cash flows details where cash resources come from and how they are used. It provides more valuable information about liquidity than can be obtained from the balance sheet and income statements. Exhibit 4-5 presents a simplified example of what a statement of cash flows would look like.

Excel Exercise

Template 6 provides an opportunity to prepare a cash flow statement for your organization. The template is on the CD that accompanies this book.

NOTES TO FINANCIAL STATEMENTS

As you continue to read this book, you will find that the accounting numbers don't always tell the entire story. For a variety of reasons, the financial statements tend to be inadequate to fully convey the results of operations and the financial position of the firm.

As a result, accountants require that notes be provided to supplement the financial statements that we have discussed. These notes provide

EXHIBIT 4-5.
Coffin Corporation
Statement of Cash Flows
For the Year Ending December 31, 2002

Cash Flows from Operating Activities	
Collections from Customers	$19,000
Payments to Suppliers	(8,000)
Payments to Employees	(3,000)
Net Cash from Operating Activities	$ 8,000
Cash Flows from Investing Activities	
Purchase of New Equipment	$ (6,000)
Net Cash Used for Investing Activities	$ (6,000)
Cash Flows from Financing Activities	
Borrowing from Creditors	$ 2,000
Issuance of Stock	1,000
Payment of Dividends	(2,000)
Net Cash from Financing Activities	$ 1,000
NET INCREASE/(DECREASE) IN CASH	$ 3,000
CASH, BEGINNING OF YEAR	1,000
CASH, END OF YEAR	$ 4,000

detailed explanations and are included in annual reports as an integral part of the overall financial statements. Notes to financial statements are discussed somewhat further in Chapter 5. Also, a detailed presentation on notes to financial statements is made in Chapter 21.

KEY CONCEPTS

Fiscal year-end—The firm's year-end should occur at a slow point in the firm's normal activity to reduce disruption caused in determining the firm's results of operations and year-end financial position.

The balance sheet—Tells the financial position of the firm at a point in time.

Asset classification—Assets are commonly classified on the balance sheet as current, fixed, investments, and intangibles.

Liability classification—Liabilities are generally divided into current and long-term categories.

Stockholders' equity is divided into contributed capital and retained earnings.

a. *Contributed* or *paid-in capital* is the amount the firm has received in exchange for the issuance of its stock.

b. *Retained earnings* are the profits earned by the firm over its lifetime that have not been distributed to its owners in the form of dividends.

The income statement—a summary of the firm's revenues and expenses for the accounting period (month, quarter, year).

Statement of cash flows—Shows the sources and uses of the firm's cash.

Notes to the financial statements—vital information supplementing the key financial statements.

Five

The Role of the Outside Auditor

The stock market crash of 1929 brought to light substantial inadequacies in financial reporting. Investigations of bankrupt companies showed numerous arithmetic errors and cases of undetected fraud. These investigations also disclosed the common use of a widely varying set of accounting practices. A principal outcome of these investigations was that the newly formed Securities and Exchange Commission (SEC) required that publicly held companies must annually issue a report to stockholders. The report must contain financial statements prepared by the firm's management and audited by a certified public accountant (CPA).

Annual reports are frequently referred to as certified reports or certified statements, although, in fact, it is the outside auditor who has been certified, not the statements themselves. Each state licenses CPAs and in granting the license certifies them as experts in accounting and auditing. The CPA merely gives an expert opinion regarding the financial statements of a company. There is no certification of correctness of the financial statements.

What exactly is the CPA's role in performing an audit? Well, some people consider the CPA to be the individual who walks out onto the field of battle after the fighting has died down and the smoke has cleared and then proceeds to shoot the wounded. CPAs have always been respected individuals, but in their role as auditors they tend to be seen in a rather unpleasant light, as the foregoing analogy indicates. This is largely due to a lack of understanding of what the CPA's role really is. The SEC, in requiring audited statements, was particularly concerned with arithmetic accuracy and the use of a clear, consistent set of accounting practices.

Ultimately the SEC's desire is that a reliable set of financial statements, one that presents a "fair representation" of what has occurred, is given to the users of financial statement information. Those users include stockholders, bankers, suppliers, and other individuals. The CPA's focus is on the financial statements rather than on individual employees in the firm. Errors will occur as long as humans are involved in the accounting process. The CPA has no interest in discrediting individuals. The CPA merely wants to ensure that the most significant of the errors are discovered and corrected.

GENERALLY ACCEPTED ACCOUNTING PRINCIPLES (GAAP)

Achieving a result that everyone would consider to be a fair representation is quite difficult, especially because accounting represents more of an art than a science. In many instances, strong arguments can be posed for alternative accounting treatments. Selection of one uniform set of rules for all firms is not a simple exercise.

For example, consider a firm drilling for oil. The firm buys a tract of land intending to drill 100 exploratory wells. Hypothetically, suppose that statistically for every 100 wells drilled, the industry average is one well with commercially producible quantities.

The firm expects to spend $100,000 on each well it drills and expects to recover $20,000,000 worth of oil from the successful well. After one year, 50 wells have been drilled at a cost of $5,000,000 and no oil has been discovered. Consider how the firm might present this on its financial statements. Exhibit 5-1 provides income statements under three alternative accounting methods. Putting parentheses around a number is an accountant's indication of a negative number.

In all three methods, the net income will be the same for the two-year period. If the firm finds oil, it will receive $20,000,000 in return for a two-year cost of $10,000,000, leaving a profit of $10,000,000. If the firm doesn't find oil, then the combined two years must indicate an expenditure of $10,000,000 with no revenue, or a loss of $10,000,000.

Although the two-year totals are the same under all three methods, oil or no oil, the income reported in each year varies substantially depending on the method chosen. Method One takes things as they come. In Year One no oil is found, so the $5,000,000 spent is down the drain, so to speak. The firm reports a loss of $5,000,000 for the year.

EXHIBIT 5-1.
Alternative Accounting Methods for Oil Exploration

	YEAR ONE	YEAR TWO	
	ACTUAL RESULT	IF OIL FOUND	IF NO OIL
Method One			
Revenue	$ 0	$20,000,000	$ 0
Less Expense	5,000,000	5,000,000	5,000,000
Net Income	$ (5,000,000)	$15,000,000	$ (5,000,000)
Method Two			
Revenue	$ 0	$20,000,000	$ 0
Less Expense	0	10,000,000	10,000,000
Net Income	$ 0	$10,000,000	$(10,000,000)
Method Three			
Revenue	$ 10,000,000	$10,000,000	$(10,000,000)
Less Expense	5,000,000	5,000,000	5,000,000
Net Income	$ 5,000,000	$ 5,000,000	$(15,000,000)

Method Two argues that the $5,000,000 was an investment in a two-year project rather than being a loss. On the basis of the hypothetical oil industry statistics, the firm will likely find oil next year, and it gives an unduly harsh picture of the firm's results to show it as a loss. This method records no revenue or expense for Year One.

Method Three argues that because statistically the firm expects to find oil, and because half of the work is completed by the end of Year One, the firm should report half the profits by the end of Year One. In this method, $10,000,000 of revenue is recorded in Year One, even though oil has not yet been found. If no oil is found in Year Two, the Year One revenue must be eliminated by showing negative revenue in Year Two. Comparing the three methods at the end of Year One leaves the user of financial statements with the information that the firm either lost $5,000,000, or broke even, or made a profit of $5,000,000 during the year.

You may have a favorite among the three methods. Accountants will not allow use of Method Three. It is considered to be overly optimistic, because for a small number of holes drilled, such as 100, there may well (excuse the pun) be no oil at all. Methods One and Two, however, each have strong proponents and substantial theoretical support. Accountants frequently prefer a conservative approach and Method One provides it. On the other hand, accountants like to "match" expense with the revenue it causes to be generated. This preference would support Method Two.

This particular example highlights a major controversy in accounting. It represents only one of a number of situations in which the accounting profession has difficulty selecting one consistent rule and saying that it should be applied across the board to all firms in all situations. There is no true theory of accounting to resolve these dilemmas. The only way to achieve a logical order is by agreement on an arbitrary set of rules.

Comparison of different firms would be simplified if the set of rules selected permitted very little leeway for the firm. However, politically, accountants have not always been able to accomplish this because selection of one method over another will usually help one set of firms and hurt another set. In most instances firms have no choice, but there are a substantial number of situations where alternative rules are allowed.

Then how does that make readers of financial statements any better off now than they were before 1929 and the subsequent establishment of the SEC? First, there are substantial tests of arithmetical accuracy that weren't previously required. Inventory is checked to see that the proper amounts have been recorded. Other audit tests are conducted to verify all of the firm's resources and obligations.

Second and of equal importance are the accountants' rules of disclosure. In 1929, a firm choosing from among alternative methods didn't necessarily disclose which method it had used. Today the firm can choose from only a relatively narrow set of alternative rules. Whenever the firm makes a choice, that choice must be explicitly stated somewhere in the financial statements.

Who makes the rules that firms must follow in their accounting practices? There is a rule-making body called the Financial Accounting Standards Board (FASB). The pronouncements of this board carry the weight of competent authority, according to the American Institute of Certified Public Accountants (AICPA). The AICPA is a body much like the physicians' AMA and has substantial influence with its membership, so much influence that all CPAs look to it to specify the rules their clients must follow. If the CPA chooses not to follow one of the rules, he or she is subject to strong sanctions.

The FASB's (pronounced faz-B) rules are called *Generally Accepted Accounting Principles (GAAP)*. GAAP (pronounced gap) constitute a large number of pages of detailed technical rulings. Following are just a few of the most universally applicable rules. As we go through the book, additional rules relevant to the discussion will be noted.

Going Concern

In valuing a firm's assets, it is assumed that the firm will remain in business in the foreseeable future. If it appears that a firm may not remain a going concern, the auditor is required to indicate that in his or her report on the financial statements. The rationale is that if a firm does go bankrupt, its resources may be sold at forced auction. In that case, the resources may be sold for substantially less than their value as indicated on the firm's financial statements.

Conservatism

The principle of conservatism requires that sufficient attention and consideration be given to the risks taken by the firm. In practice this results in asymmetrical accounting. There is a tendency to anticipate possible losses, but not to anticipate potential gains.

There has been considerable argument over whether this rule actually protects investors. There is the possibility that the firm's value will be understated as a result of the accountant's extreme efforts not to overstate its value. From an economic perspective, we could argue that one could lose as much by failing to invest in a good firm as by investing in a bad one.

Matching

In order to get a fair reflection of the results of operations for a specific period of time, we should attempt to put expenses into the same period as the revenues that caused them to be generated. This principle of matching provides the basis for depreciation. If we buy a machine with an expected ten-year life, can we charge the full amount paid for the machine as an expense in the year of purchase? No, because that would make the firm look like it had a bad first year followed by a number of very good years.

The machine provides service for ten years; it allows us to make and sell a product in each of the years. Therefore its cost should be spread out into each of those years for which it has helped to generate revenue.

Sometimes these principles can conflict with each other. The conservatism principle lends support to using the first method in the earlier oil drilling example. However, the matching principle lends support to the second method. Some of the most difficult reporting problems faced by CPAs arise when several of the generally accepted accounting principles come into conflict with each other.

Cost

The cost of an item is what was paid for it, or the value of what was given up to get it.

Objective Evidence

This rule requires accountants to ensure that financial reports are based on such evidence as reasonable individuals could all agree on within relatively narrow bounds.

For example, if we had bought a piece of property for $50,000 and we could produce a cancelled check and deed of conveyance showing that we paid $50,000 for the property, then reasonable people would probably agree that the property cost $50,000. Our cost information is based upon objective evidence. Twenty years after the property is purchased, management calls in an appraiser who values the property at $500,000. The appraisal is considered to be subjective evidence. Different appraisers might vary substantially as to their estimate of the property's value. Three different appraisers might well offer three widely different estimates for the same property.

In such a case, the rules of objective evidence require the property to be valued on the financial statements based on the best available objective evidence. This is the cost—$50,000! Consider the implications of this for financial reporting. If you thought that financial statements give perfectly valid information about the firm, this should shake your confidence somewhat. Financial statements provide extremely limited representations of the firm. Without an understanding of GAAP, the reader of a financial statement may well draw unwarranted conclusions.

Materiality

The principle of materiality requires the accountant to correct errors that are "material" in nature. Material means large or significant. Insignificant errors may be ignored. But how does one define significance? Is it $5, or $500, or $5,000,000? Significance depends substantially on the size and particular circumstances of the individual firm.

Rather than set absolute standards, accountants define materiality in terms of effects on the users of financial statements. If there exists a misstatement so significant that reasonable, prudent users of the financial statements would make a different decision than they would if they had been given correct information, then the misstatement is material and requires correction.

Thus, if an investor can say, "Had I known that, I never would have bought the stock," or a banker can say, "I never would have lent the money to them if I had known the correct total assets of the firm," then we have a material misstatement. The implications of this are that accountants do not attempt to uncover and correct every single error that has occurred during the year. In fact, to do so would be prohibitively expensive. There is only an attempt to make sure errors that are material in nature are uncovered.

Consistency

In a world in which alternative accounting treatments frequently exist, users of financial statements can be seriously misled if a firm switches back and forth among alternative treatments. Therefore, if a firm has changed its accounting methods, the auditor must disclose the change in his or her report. A note must be included along with the statements to indicate the impact of the change.

Full Disclosure

Accountants, being a cautious lot, feel that perhaps there may be some relevant item that users of financial statements should be aware of, but for which no rule exists that explicitly requires disclosure. So, to protect against unforeseen situations that may arise, there is a catchall generally accepted accounting principle called full disclosure. This rule requires that if there is any other information that would be required for a fair representation of the results and financial position of a firm, then that information must be disclosed in a note to the financial statement.

THE AUDIT

The Management Letter and Internal Control

In performing an audit, the CPA checks for arithmetic accuracy as previously mentioned. In performing this check, the external auditor focuses on the system rather than the individual.

Consider a system in which an individual is issuing invoices to customers based on a shipping document. The individual takes a copy of the shipping document from the in-box, records the amount, issues the invoice, and places the shipping document in the out-box. Again and again, over and over, this same mechanical process is repeated. Occasionally the clerk takes the shipping document, sips some coffee, and puts the document in the out-box without having issued an invoice. Errors do happen.

The auditor will not try to discover every such error. The cost of reexamining every financial transaction would be prohibitive. Instead, by sampling some fraction of the documents processed, the auditor attempts to determine how often errors are occurring and how large they tend to be. The goal is to see if a material error may exist.

What if the accountant feels that the clerk is making too many errors and the potential for a material misstatement may exist? The clerk must be fired and replaced with a more conscientious individual, right? No, wrong. Humans will all make errors and the accountant wants the system to acknowledge that fact. The focus is on what accountants call the *internal control* of the accounting system. Basically, adequate internal control means that the system is designed in such a way as to catch and correct the majority of errors automatically, before the auditor arrives on the scene.

In our example with the clerk, the solution to the problem may be to have the clerk initial each shipping document immediately after he or she processes the invoice. A second individual would then review the shipping documents to see that all have been initialed. Those that haven't been initialed would be sent back for verification of whether an invoice was issued and for correction if need be. Errors can still occur—initialing the document after sipping the coffee, even though the invoice hasn't been processed—but they are less likely and should occur less frequently.

The auditor issues an internal control memo, often called a management letter, which points out the internal control weaknesses to management. Although there may be some expense involved for the firm to follow some of the recommendations, the inducement is that of reduced audit fees. Internal control weaknesses require an expanded audit so that the CPA can ascertain whether a material misstatement does exist. If the internal control is improved, the auditor will feel more comfortable relying on the client's system and less audit testing will be required. The management letter is given to the firm's top management and is not ordinarily disclosed to the public.

Fraud and Embezzlement

In a firm with good internal control, fraud and embezzlement are made difficult through a system of checks and balances. The auditor does not consider it to be a part of his or her job to detect all frauds. In fact, many cases of embezzlement are virtually impossible to uncover.

Although no statistics exist, it is likely that discovered embezzlements in this country amount to only the tip of the iceberg of what is really occurring. It is usually the greedy embezzlers that are caught. The modest embezzlers have an excellent chance of going undetected, especially if collusion among several employees exists.

A common misperception is that embezzlement leaves a hole in the bankbook. All of a sudden we go to withdraw money from our bank account and find that a million dollars is missing. This sort of open embezzlement is really the exception, not the rule.

Consider an individual whose job is to approve bills for payment. Suppose he were to print up stationery for Bill's Roofing Repair and send an invoice for $400 to his company. What happens? He will receive the invoice at work and will approve it for payment. Large payments may require a second approval. Therefore, larger embezzlements may require a partner if they are to go undetected.

Who is likely to question a small repair bill in a large corporation? Or perhaps a series of small bills for office supplies? Our embezzler could be running ten phony companies. One can easily conceive of an employee who, upon retirement after 40 years of apparently faithful service, admits to having charged the firm $1,000 a year for the last 35 years for maintenance and supply for a watercooler in the southern plant, even though the southern plant never had a watercooler.

Doesn't this type of embezzlement cause a cash shortage? No! We record the roofing repair expense or watercooler expense and reduce the cash account by the amount of the payment. Can the auditor issue his report on the financial statements of this company without discovering the fraud? Certainly. But then, doesn't that result in a material misstatement in the financial statements? Probably not, for several reasons.

First, the modest thief, not choosing to draw unwanted attention, would be unlikely to steal a material amount of money. Second, the money is being correctly reported as an expense. From the auditor's viewpoint, there is a misclassification of expense. We are calling the expense a roofing repair expense when, in fact, it should be called miscellaneous embezzlement expense. There would be no impact on the balance sheet nor on the firm's net income if we were to correct this misclassification! The cash account isn't overstated because the account was appropriately reduced when we paid the expense. The income isn't overstated because we did record an expense, even if we didn't correctly identify its cause.

How can the fraud be detected? If we send a letter to Bill's Roofing Repair and ask if their invoice was a bona fide bill, we will likely get an affirmative response, albeit coming from the embezzler himself. If we directly ask the employee if he approved the bill for payment, he will say yes, because he did approve it for payment to himself. In order to really see if this type of embezzlement is going on, we would have to trace each bill back to the individual in the organization who originally ordered the work done or the goods purchased. Unfortunately, the cost of the audit work involved is likely to far exceed the amount likely to have been embezzled.

The result is that the auditor tests some documents in an effort to scare the timid, but it is possible for numerous small frauds to go undetected. The auditor is also likely to suggest in the management letter that large payments require two approvals. This would make embezzlement of large amounts less likely unless there is collusion among at least two employees.

The Auditor's Report

In addition to the management letter, the auditor issues a letter to the top management of the corporation and to its stockholders. This *opinion letter* generally has three standard paragraphs that are reproduced almost verbatim in most auditors' reports. Alternatively, some auditors combine the information from these three paragraphs into one longer paragraph. You might compare the auditor's letter in your firm's financial statement to the following sample letter.

REPORT OF THE INDEPENDENT AUDITORS

To the Directors and Stockholders of Executive Corporation:

We have audited the accompanying balance sheets of Executive Corporation as of December 31, 2002 and 2001, and the related statements of income, retained earnings, and cash flow for the years then ended. These financial statements are the responsibility of the Company's management. Our responsibility is to express an opinion on these financial statements based on our audits.

We conducted our audits in accordance with generally accepted auditing standards. Those standards require that we plan and perform the audit to obtain reasonable assurance about whether the financial statements are free of material misstatement. An audit includes examining, on a test basis, evidence supporting the amounts and disclosures in the financial statements. An audit also includes assessing the accounting principles used and significant estimates made by management, as well as evaluating the overall financial statement presentation. We believe that our audits provide a reasonable basis for our opinion.

In our opinion, the financial statements referred to above present fairly, in all material respects, the financial position of Executive Corporation as of December 31, 2002 and 2001, and the results of its operations and its cash flows for the years then ended, in conformity with generally accepted accounting principles.

Steven A. Finkler, CPA

April 8, 2003

These three paragraphs are the standard *clean* opinion report. The first paragraph is referred to as the *opening* or *introductory* paragraph. The second paragraph is the *scope* paragraph. The third paragraph is the *opinion* paragraph. If there are any additional paragraphs, they represent unusual circumstances which require further explanation.

The opening paragraph serves to inform the users of the financial statements that an audit was performed by the auditor. In some cases auditors perform consulting or other services aside from audits. The opening paragraph indicates explicitly that the company's management bears the ultimate responsibility for the contents of the financial statements.

The scope paragraph describes the breadth or scope of work undertaken as a basis for forming an opinion on the financial statements. This paragraph explains the type of procedures auditors follow in carrying out an audit. Note that just as firms must follow generally accepted accounting principles in preparing their statements, CPAs must follow generally accepted auditing standards in auditing those statements.

The opinion paragraph describes whether the financial statements provide a fair representation of the financial position, results of operations, and cash flows of the company, in the opinion of the auditor. A *clean* opinion, such as this one, indicates that in the opinion of the auditor, exercising due professional care, there is sufficient evidence of conformity to GAAP, and there is no condition requiring further clarification. This paragraph does not contend that the financial statements are completely correct. It does not even certify that there are no material misstatements. The CPA does not give a guarantee or certification. The CPA merely gives an expert opinion.

Note that the opinion of the CPA is that the financial statements are a fair representation of the firm's financial position. This is a somewhat audacious remark. Considering the intangible assets that often are not recorded on the financial statements despite their potentially significant value, and considering that plant, property, and equipment are recorded on the balance sheet at their cost, even though their value today may be far in excess of cost, you have to have a lot of nerve to say the statements are fair.

The key is that the accountant merely says the statements are a fair presentation in accordance with generally accepted accounting principles.

In other words, this *fairness* is not meant to imply fair in any absolute meaning of the word *fair*.

Certainly this creates a problem in that many users of the financial statements are unfamiliar with the implications of GAAP. Such individuals may interpret the word *fair* in a broader sense than is intended. This is why it is vital that in looking at an annual report an individual read the notes to the financial statements as well as the statements themselves. Later in the book we will discuss the notes to the financial statements in some detail.

The auditor may issue an *adverse*, *qualified*, or *disclaimer* opinion, if it is not possible to issue a clean opinion. An adverse opinion is a severe statement. It indicates that the auditor believes that the firm's financial statements are not presented fairly, in accordance with GAAP. A disclaimer indicates that the auditor was unable to compile enough evidence to form an opinion on whether or not the financial statements are a fair representation in accordance with GAAP. A qualified opinion indicates that the financial statements are a fair representation in conformity with GAAP, except as relates to a specific particular area.

In some cases the audit opinion letter will also contain additional paragraphs containing explanations. This is generally the case if there is a significant uncertainty, or a material change in the application of GAAP. Such paragraphs highlight special circumstances that might be of particular concern to the users of the financial statements. An example of a significant uncertainty is a lawsuit of such magnitude that, if the case is lost, it might cause the firm to become insolvent. A material change in GAAP must be reported because it makes the current financial statement no longer completely comparable to the previous ones for the same company. The presence of more than the standard opening, scope, and opinion paragraphs should alert the user to exercise special care in interpreting the numbers reported in the financial statements.

The Management Report

It is common practice for the annual report of the firm to include not only the firm's financial statements and an auditor's report, but also a management report. In contrast to the management letter written by the CPA and given to the firm's management, the management report is written by the firm's management, and is addressed to readers of the annual report.

The management report explains that while the financial statements have been audited by an independent CPA, ultimately they are the responsibility of the firm's management. The report also discusses the organization's system of internal control, and the role of its audit committee. The audit committee, consisting of members of the Board of Directors, has the responsibility for supervising the accounting, auditing, and other financial reporting matters of the firm.

Audit Failures

From time to time a major scandal hits the newspapers because an audit fails to provide users of financial statements with appropriate or timely information. The financial community was finally recovering from the Orange County debacle over the use of derivatives when the Enron bankruptcy occurred, shortly before this book went to press. When events such as these occur, there are four principle issues to be considered: internal accounting systems; disclosure rules; auditor oversight; and ethics.

Internal Accounting Systems

One possible cause of situations such as the Enron bankruptcy is that the accounting systems at Enron were inadequate. Perhaps revenues that were not real were being inappropriately recorded and the accounting system was not designed well enough to pick it up.

Disclosure Rules

A second possible problem is that the existing rules for disclosure have loopholes which do not require all questionable practices to be disclosed. Usually after a highly visible event such as Enron, the disclosure rules will be reviewed, and the FASB and SEC will make rule changes.

Auditor Oversight

CPAs are paid by the organization being audited. Desiring to keep earning their annual audit fees, auditors are sometimes convinced by their clients to allow questionable reporting practices. There is no doubt that the coming years will see changes in oversight of auditors to try to prevent future occurrences similar to Enron.

Ethics

Even with the best internal controls in place, at times auditors don't find everything, or worse yet, may even be in complicity with management in perpetrating a fraud on their stockholders, lenders, employees, and the public. It is necessary to bear in mind that rules and accounting systems can't make up for a lack of ethical behavior on the part of the management or its outside auditor.

Avoiding Future Audit Failures

Clearly, to reduce the likelihood of such failures occurring again in the future, several steps are needed. Auditors need to continue to work to help their clients improve their internal control systems. Regulators need to review and improve their disclosure rules. A better system of auditor oversight is essential. And finally, a culture of ethical behavior must be developed, or individuals will always find ways around the internal control systems and disclosure rules.

KEY CONCEPTS

Audited financial statements—a presentation of the firm's financial position and its results of operations, in accordance with generally accepted accounting principles.

Generally accepted accounting principles (GAAP)—a set of rules used as a basis for financial reporting. Some key GAAP:

a. *going concern*—Financial statements are prepared based upon the assumption that the firm will remain in business for the foreseeable future.

b. *conservatism*—In reporting the financial position of the firm, sufficient consideration should be given to the various risks the firm faces.

c. *matching*—Expenses should be recorded in the same accounting period as the revenues that they were responsible for generating.

   d. *cost*—the value of what was given up to acquire an item.

   e. *objective evidence*—Financial reports should be based on such evidence as reasonable individuals could all agree upon within relatively narrow bounds.

   f. *materiality*—An error is material if any individual would make a different decision based upon the incorrect information resulting from the error than if he or she possessed the correct information.

   g. *consistency*—To avoid misleading users of financial reports, firms should generally use the same accounting methods from period to period.

   h. *full disclosure*—Financial reports should disclose any information needed to assure that the reports are a fair presentation.

The management letter—a report to top management that makes suggestions for the improvement of internal control to reduce the likelihood of errors and undetected frauds or embezzlements.

The auditor's report—a letter from the outside auditor giving an opinion on whether or not the firm's financial statements are a fair presentation of the firm's results of operations, cash flows, and financial position in accordance with GAAP.

The management report—a letter from the organization's management that is part of the annual report.

Six

Valuation of Assets and Equities

One would not expect there to be much controversy over the valuation of balance sheet items. Wouldn't they simply be recorded at what they're worth? Unfortunately, it isn't as easy as that. Consider having bought a car three years ago for $20,000. Today it might cost you $24,000 to buy a similar car. Is your car worth $20,000 or $24,000?

Wait, it's more complicated than that. Your old car is no longer new and so its value has gone down with age. Because the old car is three years old, and generally cars are expected to have a five-year useful life, your car has lost 60 percent of its value, so it's only worth $8,000. However, due to inflation, you could sell the car for $14,000 and you'd have to pay $16,000 to buy it on a used car lot.

What is the value of your car? Is it $20,000 or $24,000, or $8,000, $14,000, or $16,000? Obviously valuation is a complex issue. This chapter looks at how accountants value assets, liabilities, and stockholders' equity for inclusion in financial statements. In addition, several other useful valuation methods that are not allowed for financial statement reporting will be discussed.

ASSET VALUATION

Historical Cost or Acquisition Cost

Financial statements generally value assets based on their historical or acquisition cost. This is done in order to achieve a valuation based on the GAAP of objective evidence. If the firm values all of its assets based on what was paid for them at the time it acquired them, there can be no question as to the objectivity of the valuation.

For example, let's suppose that some number of years ago a railroad company bought land at a cost of $10 an acre. Suppose that 1,000 acres of that land runs through the downtown of a major city. Today, many years after the acquisition, the firm has to determine the value at which it wishes to show that land on its current financial statements. The historical cost of the land is $10,000 ($10 per acre multiplied by 1,000 acres). By historical cost, we mean the historical cost to the firm as an entity. The firm may have bought the land from previous owners who paid $1 per acre. Their historical cost was $1 per acre, but to our entity the historical or acquisition cost is $10 per acre.

Accountants are comfortable with their objective evidence. If the land cost $10,000 and the firm says it cost $10,000, then everyone gets a fair picture of what the land cost. However, one might well get the impression from the balance sheet that the property is currently worth only $10,000.

In fact, today that land might be worth $10,000,000 (or even $100,000,000). The strength of using the historical cost approach is that the information is objective and verifiable. However, the historical cost method also has the weakness of providing outdated information. It doesn't give a clear impression of what assets are currently worth. Despite this serious weakness, historical or acquisition cost is the method that generally must be used on audited financial statements.

For assets that wear out, such as buildings and equipment, the historical cost is adjusted each year to recognize the fact that the asset is being used up. Each year the asset value is reduced by an amount that is referred to as depreciation expense. Depreciation is discussed in Chapter 15.

Price-Level Adjusted Historical Cost

Accountants are ready to admit that the ravages of inflation have played a pretty important part in causing the value of assets to change substantially from their historical cost. The longer the time between the purchase of the asset and the current time, the more likely it is that a distortion exists between the current value of an item and its historical cost. One proposed solution to the problem is price-level adjusted historical cost or PLAHC (pronounced plack). This method is frequently referred to as *constant dollar valuation*.

The idea behind constant dollar valuation is that most of the change in the value of assets over time has been induced by price-level inflation. Thus, if we use a price index such as the Consumer Price Index (CPI) to adjust the value of all assets based on the general rate of inflation, we would report each asset at about its current worth. While this approach may sound good, it has some serious flaws.

Unfortunately, not everything increases at the same rate of inflation. The land in the railroad example may have increased in value much faster than the general inflation rate. There is no way to easily adjust each asset for the specific impact that inflation had on that particular asset, using price indexes such as the CPI.

Where does that leave us? Well, PLAHC gives an objective measurement of assets. However it might allow an asset worth $10,000,000 to be shown on the balance sheet at only $110,000. Perhaps it is better to leave the item at its cost and inform everyone that it is the cost and is not adjusted for inflation, rather than to say that it has been adjusted for inflation when the adjustment may be a poor one.

Net Realizable Value

A third alternative for the valuation of assets is to measure them at what you could get if you were to sell them. This concept of valuation makes a fair amount of sense. If you were a potential creditor, be it banker or supplier, you might well wonder, "If this firm were to sell off all of its assets, would it be able to raise enough cash to pay off all of its creditors?"

The term *net* is used in front of *realizable value* to indicate that we wish to find out how much we could realize net of any additional costs that would have to be incurred to sell the asset. Thus, commissions, packing costs, and the like would be reductions in the amount we could expect to obtain.

This method doesn't seek to find the potential profit. We aren't interested in the comparison of what it cost to what we're selling it for. We simply want to know what we could get for it. In the case of the railroad land, its net realizable value is $10,000,000 less any legal fees and commissions the railroad would have to pay to sell it.

Is this a useful method? Certainly. Does it give a current value for our assets? Definitely. Then why not use it on financial statements instead of historical cost? The big handicap of the net realizable value method is that it is based on someone's subjective estimate of what the asset could be sold for. There is no way to determine the actual value of each of the firm's assets unless they are sold. This always poses a problem from an accountant's point of view. Another problem occurs if an asset that is quite useful to the firm does not have a ready buyer. In that case, the future profits method that follows provides a more reasonable valuation.

Future Profits

The main reason a firm acquires most of its assets is to use them to produce the firm's goods and services. Therefore, a useful measure of their worth is the profits they will contribute to the firm in the future. This is especially important in the case where the assets are so specialized that there is no ready buyer. If the firm owns the patent on a particular process, the specialized machinery for that process may have no realizable value other than for scrap.

Does that mean that the specialized machinery is worthless? Perhaps yes, from the standpoint of a creditor who wonders how much cash the firm could generate if needed to meet its obligations. From the standpoint of evaluating the firm as a going concern, a creditor may well be more interested in the ability the firm has to generate profits. Will the firm be more profitable because it has the machine than it would be without it?

Under this relatively sensible approach, an asset's value is set by the future profits the firm can expect to generate because it has the asset. However, once again the problem of dealing with subjective estimates arises. Here we are even worse off than with the previous valuation approach. At least we can get outside independent appraisers to evaluate the realizable value of buildings and equipment. However, under this method, estimates of future profit streams require the expertise of the firm's own management. Even with that expertise, the estimates often turn out to be off by quite a bit.

Replacement Cost

The replacement cost approach is essentially the reverse of the net realizable value method. Rather than considering how much we could get for an asset were we to sell it, we consider how much it would cost us to replace that asset. While this might seem to be a difference that splits hairs, it really is not.

Suppose that last year you could buy a unit of merchandise for $5 and resell it for $7. This year you can buy the unit for $6 and sell it for $8. You have one unit remaining that you bought last year. Today, its historical cost is $5, the amount you paid for it; its net realizable value is $8, the amount you can sell it for; and its replacement cost is $6, the amount you would have to pay to replace it in your inventory. Three different methods result in three different valuations.

Replacement cost (often referred to as current cost) is another example of a subjective valuation approach. Unless you actually go out and attempt to replace an asset, you cannot be absolutely sure what it would cost to do so.

Which Valuation Is Right?

Unfortunately, none of these methods (see Exhibit 6-1) is totally satisfactory for all information needs. Different problems require different valuations. The idea that there is a different appropriate valuation depending on the question being asked may not seem to be quite right. Why not simply say what it's worth and be consistent?

From the standpoint of financial statements, we have little choice. GAAP requires the use of historical cost information and that restricts options substantially in providing financial statements. You might say, "Okay, the financial statements must follow a certain set of rules, but just among us managers, what is the asset's real value?" Still we respond, "Why do you want to know?" We really are not avoiding the question. Let's consider a variety of possible examples.

First, assume that one of your duties is to make sure the firm has adequate fire insurance coverage. The policy is currently up for renewal and you have obtained a copy of your firm's annual report. According to the balance sheet, your firm has $40,000,000 of plant and equipment. You don't want to be caught in the cold, so you decide to insure it for the full $40 million. Nevertheless, you may well have inadequate insurance. The $40 million merely measures the historical cost of your plant and equipment.

Which valuation method is the most appropriate? In this case, the answer is replacement cost. If one of the buildings were to burn down,

EXHIBIT 6-1.

VALUATION

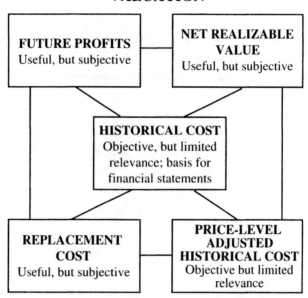

then our desire would be to have enough money to replace it. Other measures, such as net realizable value, are not relevant to this decision.

Suppose we are considering the acquisition of a new machine. What measure of valuation is the most appropriate? We could value the machine at its historical cost—that is, the price we are about to pay for it. This method cannot possibly help us to decide if we should buy the asset. Looking at an asset's value from the point of view of its cost would lead us to believe that every possible asset should be bought, because by definition it would be worth the price we pay for it.

How about using the net realizable value? What would the net realizable value of the machine be the day after we purchase it? Probably less than the price we paid because it is now used equipment. In that case, we wouldn't ever buy the machine. How about using replacement cost? On the day we buy a machine, the replacement cost will simply be the same as its historical cost.

Logically, why do we wish to buy the machine? Because we want to use it to make profits. The key factor in the decision to buy the machine is whether or not the future profits from the machine will be enough to more than cover its cost. So the appropriate valuation for the acquisition of an asset is the future profits it will generate.

Finally, consider the divestiture of a wholly owned subsidiary that has been sustaining losses and is projected to sustain losses into the foreseeable future. What is the least amount that we would accept in exchange for the subsidiary? Historical cost information is hopelessly outdated and cannot possibly provide an adequate answer to that question. Replacement cost information can't help us. The last thing in the world we want to do is go out and duplicate all of the assets of a losing venture. If we base our decision on future profits, we may wind up paying someone to take the division because we anticipate future losses, not profits.

The appropriate valuation in this case would be net realizable value. Certainly we don't want to sell the entire subsidiary for less than we could get by auctioning off each individual asset.

As you can see, it is essential that you be flexible in the valuation of assets. As a manager, you must do more than simply refer to the financial statements. In order to determine the value of assets, you must first assess why the information is needed. Based on that assessment, you can determine which of the five methods discussed here provides the most useful information for the specific decision to be made.

VALUATION OF LIABILITIES

Valuation of liabilities does not cause nearly as many problems as valuation of assets. With liabilities, if you owe Charlie fifty bucks, it's not all that hard to determine exactly what your liability is; it's fifty bucks. In general, our liability is simply the amount we expect to pay in the future.

Suppose we purchase raw materials for our production process at a price of $580 on open account with the net payment due in thirty days. We have to pay $580 when the account is due. Therefore, our liability is $580. The crucial aspects are that our obligation is to be paid in cash and it is to be paid within one year. Problems arise if either of these aspects does not hold.

For instance, suppose we borrow $7,000 from a bank today and have an obligation to pay $10,000 to the bank three years from today. Is our liability $10,000? No, it isn't. Banks charge interest for the use of their money. The interest accumulates as time passes. If we are to pay $10,000 in three years, that implies that $3,000 of interest will be accumulating over that three-year period. We don't owe the interest today, because we haven't yet had the use of the bank's money for the three years. As time passes, each day we will owe the bank a little more of the $3,000 of interest. Today, however, we owe only $7,000, from both a legal and an accounting point of view.

You might argue that legally we owe the bank $10,000. That really isn't so, although the bank might like you to believe that it is. Let's suppose that you borrowed the money in the morning. That very same day, unfortunately, your rich aunt passes away. The state you live in happens to have rather fast processing of estates and around one o'clock in the afternoon you receive a large inheritance in cash. You run down to the bank and say that you don't need the money after all. Do you have to pay the bank $10,000?

If you did, your interest for one day would be $3,000 on a loan of $7,000. That is a rate of about 43 percent per day, or over 15,000 percent per year. Perhaps there would be an early payment penalty, but it would be much less than $3,000. Generally, accountants ignore possible prepayment penalties and record the liability at $7,000.

Another problem occurs if the liability is not going to be paid in cash. For example, perhaps we have received an advance payment for an order of widgets that we intend to fill over the coming year. What we owe is widgets, but we have to make some attempt to value that liability. Take the example one step further. We have received $18,000 for the widgets, but they will only cost us $9,000 to make. Is our liability $18,000 or $9,000?

In cases in which the obligation is nonmonetary in nature, we record the obligation as the amount received, not the cost of providing the nonmonetary item. What if for some reason we cannot provide the widgets? Will the customer be satisfied to receive a refund of $9,000 because that's all it would have cost us to make the widgets? No, the customer needs to get the full $18,000 back, so we must show that amount as the liability. If, over time, we make partial shipments, we can reduce the liability in a pro rata fashion.

VALUATION OF STOCKHOLDERS' EQUITY

The valuation of stockholders' equity is relatively easy. Recall that assets are equal to liabilities plus stockholders' equity. Once the value of assets and liabilities has been determined, the stockholders' equity is whatever it must take to make the equation balance. Remember that the stockholders' equity is, by definition, a residual of whatever is left after enough assets are set aside to cover liabilities. Thus, given the rigid financial statement valuation requirements for assets and liabilities, there is little room left for interpreting the value of stockholders' equity.

On the other hand, might there not be another way to determine the value of the firm to its owners? For a publicly held firm the answer is clearly yes. The market value of the firm's stock is a measure of what the stock market and the owners of the firm think it's worth. If we aggregate the market value of the firm's stock, we have a measure of the total value of the owners' equity.

Is the market value of the firm likely to equal the value assigned by the financial statements? Probably not. The financial statements tend to substantially undervalue a wide variety of assets. Intangible assets that may be quite valuable are not always included in financial statements. Further, historical cost asset valuation causes the tangible assets to be understated in many cases. Thus, the assets of the firm may be worth substantially more than the financial statements indicate. If the public can determine that to be the case (usually with the aid of the large number of financial analysts in the country), the market value of the stock will probably exceed the value of stockholders' equity indicated on the financial statements. Furthermore, stock prices are often dictated by the firm's ability to earn profits. In some cases companies with few assets can still be quite profitable, and therefore have a market value well in excess of the stockholders' equity shown on the balance sheet.

This discussion of valuation of assets and equities has left us in a position to better interpret the numbers that appear in financial statements. Financial statements are the end product of the collection of information regarding a large number of financial transactions. Each transaction is recorded individually into the financial history of the firm using the valuation principles of this chapter. Chapter 7 discusses the process of recording the individual transactions—how and why it's done. Chapter 8 demonstrates how all of the transactions, perhaps millions or even billions during the year, can be consolidated into three one-page financial statements.

KEY CONCEPTS

Asset valuation—There are a variety of asset valuation methods. The appropriate value for an asset depends on the intended use of the asset valuation information.

a. *Historical cost*—the amount an entity paid to acquire an asset. This amount is the value used as a basis for tax returns and financial statements.

b. *Price-level adjusted historical cost*—a valuation method that adjusts the asset's historical cost, based on the general rate of inflation.

c. *Net realizable value*—valuation of an asset based on the amount we would receive if we sold it, net of any costs related to the sale.

d. *Future profits*—This valuation method requires each asset to be valued on the basis of the amount of additional profits that can be generated because we have the asset.

e. *Replacement cost*—Under this method each asset is valued at the amount it would cost to replace that asset.

Liability valuation—The value of liabilities depends on whether they are short-term or long-term and whether or not they are to be paid in cash.

a. *Short-term cash obligations*—Amounts to be paid in cash within a year are valued at the amount of the cash to be paid.

b. *Long-term cash obligations*—Amounts to be paid in cash more than a year in the future are valued at the amount to be paid, less the implicit interest included in that amount.

c. *Nonmonetary obligations*—an obligation to provide goods or services rather than cash, where the liability is generally valued at the amount received, rather than the cost of providing that item.

Stockholders' equity valuation—Given a value for each of the assets and liabilities, stockholders' equity is the residual amount that makes the fundamental equation of accounting balance.

Seven

Recording Financial Information

DOUBLE ENTRY AND THE ACCOUNTING EQUATION

Financial accounting consists largely of keeping the financial history of the firm. In performing financial accounting, the accountant attempts to keep close track of each event occurring that has a financial impact on the firm. This is done in order to facilitate financial statement preparation. By keeping track of things as they happen, the accountant can periodically summarize the firm's financial position and the results of its operations.

In order to keep track of the firm's financial history, the accountant has chosen a very common historical device. In the navy one keeps a chronological history of a voyage by daily entries into a log. For a personal history, individuals make entries in their diaries. Explorers frequently record the events of their trip in a journal. Accountants follow in the tradition of the explorers, each day recording the day's events in a journal, often referred to as a *general journal*. The entries the accountant makes in the journal are simply called *journal entries*. The general journal is often called the *book of original entry*. This term is derived because an event is first entered into the firm's official history via a journal entry.

In recording a journal entry, we need adequate information to describe an entire event. To be sure that all elements of a financial event (more commonly referred to as a transaction) are recorded, accountants use a system called *double-entry bookkeeping*. In order to understand double entry, we should think in terms of the basic equation of accounting, that is:

ASSETS (A) = LIABILITIES (L) + STOCKHOLDERS' EQUITY (SE)

71

Any event having a financial impact on the firm affects this equation because the equation summarizes the entire financial position of the firm. Furthermore, by definition this equation must always remain in balance. Absolutely nothing can happen (barring a mathematical miscalculation) that would cause this equation not to be in balance, because stockholders' equity has been defined in such a way that it is a residual value that brings the equation into balance.

If the equation must remain in balance, then a change of any one number in the equation must change at least one other number. We have great latitude in which other number changes. For example, we might begin with the equation looking like:

$$\begin{array}{ccccc} A & = & L & + & SE \\ \$150{,}000 & = & \$100{,}000 & + & \$50{,}000 \end{array}$$

If we were to borrow $20,000 from the bank, we would have more cash, so assets would increase by $20,000 and we would owe money to the bank. Our liabilities would increase by $20,000. Now the equation would be:

$$\begin{array}{ccccc} A & = & L & + & SE \\ \$170{,}000 & = & \$120{,}000 & + & \$50{,}000 \end{array}$$

The equation is in balance. Compare this equation to the previous one. Two numbers in the equation have changed. The term *double entry* merely signifies that it is not possible to change one number in an equation without changing at least one other number.

However, the two numbers that change need not be on different sides of the equation. For example, what if we bought some raw materials inventory for $15,000 and paid cash for it? Our asset cash has decreased while our asset inventory has increased. The equation now is:

$$\begin{array}{ccccc} A & = & L & + & SE \\ \$170{,}000 & = & \$120{,}000 & + & \$50{,}000 \end{array}$$

The equation appears as if it hasn't changed at all. That's not quite true. The left side of the equation has both increased and decreased by $15,000. Although the totals on either side are the same, our journal entry would have recorded the specific parts of the double-entry change that took place on the left side of the equation.

DEBITS AND CREDITS: THE ACCOUNTANT'S SECRET

It wouldn't be much fun to be an accountant if you didn't have a few tricks and secrets. Part III of this book discusses a few of the more interesting tricks; for now you'll just have to settle for a secret, the meaning of debit and credit.

Earlier an accountant's journal was compared to a navy logbook. That's not the only similarity. Sailors use the terms *port* and *starboard*. Many a time you've watched an old seafaring movie, and in the middle of a fierce storm, with the skies clouded and the winds blowing, the seas heaving and the rains pouring, someone yells out, "Hard to the port!" The sailor at the large oaken wheel, barely able to stand erect in the gusts of wind and the torrential downpour, struggles hard to turn the ship in the direction ordered. Perhaps you thought they were heading for the nearest port—ergo, "Hard to the port." Not at all. The shouted command was to make a left turn.

It seems that port simply stated means left and starboard really means right. Of course, it's more sophisticated than that; port means the left-hand side as you face toward the front of the boat or ship and starboard means the right-hand side as you face the front. Really what port means is debit, and starboard means credit. Certainly we can drape the terms *debit* and *credit* in vague definitions and esoteric uses, but essentially debit means left (as you face the accounting document in front of you) and credit means right.

Perhaps you had figured that out on your own, perhaps not. If you had, then you are potentially threatening to take away the jobs of your accountants and bookkeepers. To prevent that, some rather interesting abbreviations have been introduced to common accounting usage. Rarely will the accountant write out the words *debit* or *credit*. Instead, abbreviations are used. The word *credit* is abbreviated Cr. Got it? Then you can guess the abbreviation for debit: Dr. If you didn't guess it's not too surprising, given the absence of the letter "r" from the word debit. How did this abbreviation come about? Accounting as we know it today has its roots in Italy during the 1400s. Italy is the home of Latin, and were we to trace the word debit back to its Latin roots, the "r" would turn up.

The terms *debit* and *credit* deserve a little more clarification. Prior to actually using the terms debit and credit, accountants perform a modification to the accounting equation (that is, Assets (A) equal Liabilities (L) plus Stockholders' Equity (SE)). Essentially, this modification requires examination of what causes stockholders' equity to change. Chapter 4 said that stockholders' equity (SE) equaled contributed capital (CC) plus retained earnings (RE). So we could think of our basic equation as assets equal liabilities plus contributed capital plus retained earnings, or:

$$A = L + CC + RE$$

In order to find out where we are at the end of a year, we would need to know where we started and what changes occurred during the year. The changes in assets are equal to the change in liabilities, plus the change in contributed capital, plus the change in retained earnings, or:

$$\Delta A = \Delta L + \Delta CC + \Delta RE$$

where the symbol "Δ" indicates a change in some number. For example, ΔA represents the change in assets.

Moving a step further, retained earnings increase as a result of net income and decrease when dividends are paid. Net income consists of revenues (R) less expenses (E). Revenues make owners better off and expenses make owners worse off. Dividends (D) are a distribution of some of the firm's profits to its owners. Therefore, our basic equation of accounting now indicates that the change in assets is equal to the change in liabilities, plus the change in contributed capital, plus the revenues, less the expenses and dividends, or in equation form:

$$\Delta A = \Delta L + \Delta CC + \Delta R - \Delta E - \Delta D$$

The only problem with this equation as it now stands is that accountants are very fond of addition, but only tolerate subtraction when absolutely necessary. The above equation can be manipulated using algebra. We can add the change in expenses and the change in dividends to both sides of the equation. Doing so produces the following equation:

$$\Delta A + \Delta E + \Delta D = \Delta L + \Delta CC + \Delta R$$

Having made these changes in the basic equation, we can return to our discussion of debits and credits. When we say that debit means left, we are saying that debits are increases in anything on the left side of this equation. When we say that credit means right, we are saying that credits increase anything on the right side of this equation. Of course, that leaves us with a slight problem. What do we do if something on either side decreases? We will have to reverse our terminology. An account on the left is decreased by a credit and an account on the right is decreased by a debit.

Debits and credits are mechanical tools that aid bookkeepers. Debits and credits have no underlying theoretical or intuitive basis. In fact, the use of debits and credits as explained here may seem counterintuitive. Cash, which is an asset, is increased by a debit. Cash is decreased by a credit.

If you think about this, it may not quite tie in with the way you've been thinking about debits and credits until now. In fact, what we've said here may seem to be downright wrong. Most individuals who are not financial officers have relatively little need to use the terms *debit* and *credit* in a business setting. We come upon the terms much more often in their common lay usage.

Most of us have come into contact with the terms *debit* and *credit* primarily from such events as the receipt of a debit memo from the bank. Perhaps we have a checking account and we are charged 30 cents for each check we write. If we write twenty checks one month, we will receive a notice from the bank that it is debiting our account by $6. Something here doesn't tie in with the earlier discussion of debits and credits.

If a debit increases items on the left, and assets are on the left, our assets should increase with a debit. But when the bank debits our account, it takes money away from our account. When we make a deposit, the bank credits, or increases, our account. The discrepancy results from the entity concept of accounting discussed in Chapter 3. Under the entity concept, each entity must view financial transactions from its own point of view. In other words, the firm shouldn't worry about the impact on its owners, or managers, or customers; it should only consider the impact of a transaction on itself.

When the bank debits your account, it is not considering your cash balance at all! The bank is considering its own set of books. To the bank, you are considered a liability. You gave the bank some money and it owes that amount of money to you. When the bank debits your account, it is saying that it is reducing an item on the right. The bank is reducing a liability. To you as an entity, there is a mirror image. While the bank is reducing its liability, on your records you must reduce your cash. Such a reduction is a credit. Therefore, receipt of a debit memo should cause you to record a credit on your books or financial records.

Consider returning merchandise to a store. The store issues you a credit memo. From the store's point of view, it now owes you money for the returned item. The store's liability has risen so it has a credit. From your point of view, you have a receivable from that store and receivables are assets. Thus you have an increase in an asset, or a debit.

In other words, about the best way to insult your accountant is to call him or her a credit (that is, liability) to the firm! You'll have to reflect on this new way of thinking about debits and credits for a while if you're not accustomed to it, and if you wish to become fluent in the use of debits and credits. Unfortunately, because the items on one side of the equation increase with debits and the items on the other side decrease with debits, and vice versa for credits, it can take a while before it becomes second nature. Imagine a product manager trying to explain to an accountant that a new product is going to generate extra cash of $100,000. The accountant says, "Okay, debit cash $100,000," and the product manager says, "No, no, I said it *will generate* $100,000, not use it!" Of course the accountant replies, "That's what I said, debit cash a hundred grand!"

If you still find debits and credits to be somewhat confusing, don't be overly concerned. Trying to look at things from a mirror image of what you've been used to all your life isn't easy. Fortunately, debits and credits are simply bookkeeping tools, and you don't need to use them extensively to understand the concepts of accounting and finance.

RECORDING THE FINANCIAL EVENTS

Now we are going to work through an example in which we will actually record a series of transactions for a hypothetical firm, Executive Corporation, for 2003. The purpose of this example is to give you a feel for the way that financial information is recorded, and to show the process by which millions of transactions occurring during a year can be summarized into several pages of financial statements. At the same time, we will use the specific transactions in the example to highlight a number of accounting conventions, principles, and methods.

Exhibit 7-1 presents the balance sheet for Executive Corporation as of December 31, 2002. From this balance sheet, we can obtain information about assets, liabilities, and stockholders' equity for the beginning of 2003. Year-end closing balances will be identical to opening balances for the following year. Our basic equation at the start of 2003 is as follows:

EXHIBIT 7-1.
Executive Corporation
Balance Sheet
As of December 31, 2002

ASSETS

Current Assets:

Cash	$52,000
Accounts Receivable	18,000
Inventory	20,000
Total Current Assets	$ 90,000

Fixed Assets:

Plant and Equipment	60,000
TOTAL ASSETS	$150,000

EQUITIES

LIABILITIES

Current Liabilities:

Accounts Payable	$17,000
Wages Payable	10,000
Total Current Liabilities	$ 27,000

Long-Term Liabilities:

Mortgage Payable	40,000
TOTAL LIABILITIES	$ 67,000

STOCKHOLDERS' EQUITY

Common Stock	$ 10,000
Retained Earnings	73,000
TOTAL STOCKHOLDERS' EQUITY	$ 83,000
TOTAL LIABILITIES & STOCKHOLDERS' EQUITY	$150,000

$$A \quad = \quad L \quad + \quad SE$$
$$\$150,000 \quad = \quad \$67,000 \quad + \quad \$83,000$$

In order to examine financial events during the year, we are interested in the change in this equation. As previously explained, the change in the equation may be stated as follows:

$$\Delta A + \Delta E + \Delta D = \Delta L + \Delta CC + \Delta R$$

Every financial event is a transaction that affects the basic equation of accounting. We will keep track of whether or not each transaction complies with the rules of double entry by examining its effect on this equation. After a journal entry is recorded, placing an event into the financial history of the firm, this equation must be in balance or some error has been made.

The way that accountants actually record journal entries assures that the equation remains in balance at all times. Each journal entry first lists all accounts that have a debit change, and then lists all accounts that have a credit change. The account names for accounts with a debit change are recorded in a column on the left, and the account names for accounts with a credit change are recorded in a column indented slightly to the right. Similarly, the actual dollar amounts appear in two columns, with the debit column to the left of the credit column.

For example, suppose that we buy inventory and pay $5 cash for it. One asset, inventory, goes up by $5, and another asset, cash, goes down $5. In journal entry form this would appear as:

	Dr.	Cr.
Inventory	$5	
Cash		$5
To record purchase of inventory for cash.		

Notice that the word Inventory appears to be somewhat to the left, and the dollar amount on that line appears in the Dr. column. As noted earlier, an increase in an asset is a debit. The word Cash is indented to the right, and the dollar amount on that line is in the Cr. column. A decrease in the asset, cash, is a credit. A brief explanation is often recorded for each journal entry. In this example the explanation is that the purpose of the journal entry was "To record purchase of inventory for cash." The total of all numbers in the Dr. column must equal the total of all numbers in the Cr. column, or the fundamental equation of accounting will not be in balance.

In the example that follows, we will indicate the impact of each transaction on the fundamental equation of accounting, and then show how it would appear in journal entry form.

Executive Corporation 2003 Financial Events

1. January 2. Purchased a three-year fire insurance policy for $3,000. A check was mailed. The starting point for making a journal entry is to determine what has happened. In this case, we have $3,000 less cash than we used to and we have paid in advance for three years worth of insurance. Any item that we would like to keep track of is called an *account*, because we want to account for the amount of that item. Here, the balance in our cash account (an asset) has gone down, and our prepaid insurance (P/I) account (also an asset) has increased. This results in off-setting changes on the left side of the equation, so there is no net effect or change to the equation.

$$\Delta A \quad + \quad \Delta E + \Delta D \quad = \Delta L + \Delta CC + \Delta R$$

Cash − 3,000   = No change on right side

P/I + 3,000

	Dr.	Cr.
Prepaid Insurance	$3,000	
Cash		$3,000

2. January 18. The firm mails a check to its supplier for $15,000 of the $17,000 it owed them at the end of last year. (Refer to Exhibit 7-1 for the accounts payable liability balance at the end of the previous year.) This requires a journal entry showing a decrease in the cash balance and a reduction in the accounts payable (A/P) liability to our supplier.

$$\Delta A \quad + \quad \Delta E + \Delta D \quad = \quad \Delta L \quad + \Delta CC + \Delta R$$

Cash − 15,000   = A/P − 15,000

	Dr.	Cr.
Accounts Payable	$15,000	
Cash		$15,000

Notice that when we look at the impact on the equation, both cash and accounts payable are negative numbers. Each decreases by $15,000. In the journal entry format, negative signs are never needed or used. The decrease in cash is a credit, and appears as $15,000 in the credit column. The decrease in accounts payable results in a debit, and appears in the debit column.

3. February 15. The firm places an order with an equipment manufacturer for a new piece of machinery. The new machine will cost $10,000, and delivery is expected early next year. A contract is signed by both Executive Corporation and the equipment manufacturer. In this case there is no journal entry, even though there is a legally binding contract.

In order for there to be a journal entry, three requirements must be fulfilled. The first is that we know how much money is involved. In this case, we do know the exact amount of the contract. Second, we must know when the transaction is to be fulfilled. Here, we know that delivery will take place early the following year. Finally, the accountant requires that there must have been some exchange, and that the transaction be recorded only to the extent that there has been an exchange. From an accounting point of view, Executive has not yet paid anything, nor has it received anything. There is no need to record this into the financial history of the firm via the formal process of a journal entry.

This doesn't mean that the item must be totally ignored. If an unfilled contract involves an amount that is material, then the principle of full disclosure would require that a note to our financial statements disclose this future commitment. However, the balance sheet itself may not show the machine as an asset, nor show a liability to pay for it.

4. March 3. Executive purchases inventory on account for $15,000. It will be able to sell the inventory for $30,000. The effect of this transaction is to increase the amount of inventory (Inv.) asset that we have and to increase a liability, accounts payable (A/P). Do we record the newly purchased inventory at $15,000 or the amount for which we can sell it? According to the cost principle, we must value inventory at what it cost, even though we might be able to sell it for more than that amount.

$$\Delta A \qquad + \Delta E + \Delta D = \qquad \Delta L \qquad + \Delta CC + \Delta R$$
$$\text{Inv} + 15,000 \qquad\qquad = \text{A/P} + 15,000$$

$$\Delta A \qquad + \Delta E + \Delta D = \qquad \Delta L \qquad + \Delta CC + \Delta R$$
$$\text{Inv} + 15,000 \qquad\qquad\qquad = A/P + 15,000$$

	Dr.	Cr.
Inventory	$15,000	
Accounts Payable		$15,000

5. April 16. Cash of $14,000 is received from customers for purchases from last year. This increases one asset, cash, while reducing another asset, accounts receivable (A/R).

$$\Delta A \qquad + \Delta E + \Delta D \quad = \Delta L + \Delta CC + \Delta R$$
$$\text{Cash} + 14,000 \qquad\qquad = \text{No change on right side}$$
$$A/R - 14,000$$

	Dr.	Cr.
Cash	$14,000	
Accounts Receivable		$14,000

6. May 3. Executive sells inventory that had cost $28,000 for a price of $56,000. The customers have not yet paid for the goods, although they have received them. This is an income-generating activity. Executive has revenues of $56,000 from the sale. It also has an expense of $28,000, the cost of resources used to generate the sale. We can treat this as two transactions. The first transaction relates to the revenue and the second to the expense.

First, we have had a sale of $56,000, so we have to record revenue of $56,000 (Sales). We haven't been paid yet, so we have an account receivable of $56,000. This leaves the accounting equation in balance.

The second transaction concerns inventory and expense. In order to make the sale, we shipped some of our inventory. Thus, we have less inventory on hand. This reduction in inventory represents the cost of the sale, so in addition to reducing the inventory account, we record a cost of goods sold expense (CGS) equal to the decrease in inventory. Once again, this transaction leaves the accounting equation in balance.

	Dr.	Cr.
Accounts Receivable	$56,000	
Cost of Goods Sold	28,000	
Inventory		$28,000
Sales		56,000

7. June 27. Executive places a $9,000 order to resupply its inventory. The goods have not yet been received. In this case there will be no formal journal entry. Our purchasing department undoubtedly keeps track of open purchase orders. However, as in the case of the equipment contract previously discussed, there is no journal entry until there is an exchange by at least one party to the transaction. We haven't paid for the goods and the supplier has not yet supplied them.

8. November 14. Workers were paid $18,000. This payment included all balances outstanding from the previous year. Because we are paying $18,000, cash will decrease by $18,000. Is this all an expense of the current year? No. We owed workers $10,000 from work done during the previous year. Thus, only $8,000 is an expense of the current year. Our journal entry will show that labor expense (Labor) rises by $8,000 and that wages payable (W/P) decline by $10,000. Note that three accounts have changed. Double-entry accounting requires that at least two accounts change. The equation would not be in balance if only one account changed. However, it is perfectly possible that more than two accounts will change. Here we can see that although three accounts have changed, in net, the equation is in balance.

$$\Delta A \quad + \quad \Delta E \quad + \Delta D = \quad \Delta L \quad + \Delta CC + \Delta R$$

$$\text{Cash} - 18{,}000 \quad \text{Labor} + 8{,}000 \quad = \text{W/P} - 10{,}000$$

	Dr.	Cr.
Labor Expense	$ 8,000	
Wages Payable	10,000	
Cash		$18,000

9. December 31. At year-end, Executive makes its annual mortgage payment of $10,000. The payment reduces the mortgage balance by $4,000. It doesn't quite seem correct to pay $10,000 on a liability but only reduce the obligation by $4,000. Actually, mortgage payments are not merely repayment of a debt. They also include interest that is owed on the debt. If Executive is making mortgage payments on its plant and equipment just once a year, then this payment includes interest on the $40,000 balance outstanding at the end of last year (see Exhibit 7-1).

If the mortgage is at a 15 percent annual interest rate, then we owe $6,000 of interest for the use of the $40,000 over the last year. Thus the transaction lowers cash by $10,000, but increases interest expense (IE) (also on the left side of the equation) by $6,000. The reduction of $4,000 on the right side to reduce the mortgage payable (M/P) account leaves the equation exactly in balance.

$$\Delta A \quad + \quad \Delta E \quad + \Delta D = \quad \Delta L \quad + \Delta CC + \Delta R$$
$$\text{Cash} - 10,000 \quad \text{IE} + 6,000 \quad\quad = \text{M/P} - 4,000$$

	Dr.	Cr.
Interest Expense	$ 6,000	
Mortgage Payable	4,000	
Cash		$10,000

10. December 31. A dividend of $3,000 is declared and paid to Executive's stockholders. This creates two changes on the left side of the equation. Cash decreases and dividends (Div) increase. Recall that a dividend is not an expense, but rather a distribution of some of the firm's profits to its owners.

$$\Delta A \quad + \Delta E + \quad \Delta D \quad\quad = \Delta L + \Delta CC + \Delta R$$
$$\text{Cash} - 3,000 \quad\quad \text{Div} + 3,000 \quad = \text{No change on right side}$$

	Dr.	Cr.
Dividends	$3,000	
Cash		$3,000

11. December 31. At year-end, Executive makes an adjustment to its books to indicate that one year's worth of prepaid insurance has been used up. Many financial events happen at a specific moment in time. In those cases, we simply record the event when it happens. Some events, however, happen over a period of time. Technically one could argue that a little insurance coverage was used up each and every day, so the accountant should have recorded the expiration of part of the policy each day, or for that matter, each minute.

There is no need for that degree of accuracy. The accountant merely wants to make sure that the books are up to date prior to issuing any financial reports based on them. Therefore, a number of adjusting entries are made at the end of the accounting period.

One might ask why the accountant bothers to make such an entry even then. Why not wait until the insurance is completely expired? The matching principle would not allow that. In each case of an adjusting entry, the overriding goal is to place expenses into the correct period—the period in which revenues were generated as a result of those expenses.

In the case of the insurance, we have used up one-third of the $3,000, three-year policy, so we must reduce our asset, prepaid insurance (P/I) by $1,000, and increase our insurance expense (Ins) account by $1,000.

$$\Delta A \quad + \quad \Delta E \quad + \Delta D = \Delta L + \Delta CC + \Delta R$$
$$\text{P/I} - 1{,}000 \quad \text{Ins} + 1{,}000 \qquad = \text{No change on right side}$$

	Dr.	Cr.
Insurance Expense	$1,000	
Prepaid Insurance		$1,000

12. December 31. Executive also finds that it owes office employees $3,000 at the end of the year. These wages will not be paid until the following year. This requires an adjusting entry in order to accrue this year's labor expenses. The entry increases labor expense and, at the same time, increases the wages payable liability account.

$$\Delta A \quad + \quad \Delta E \quad + \Delta D = \quad \Delta L \quad + \Delta CC + \Delta R$$
$$\text{Labor} + 3{,}000 \qquad = \text{W/P} + 3{,}000$$

	Dr.	Cr.
Labor Expense	$3,000	
Wages Payable		$3,000

13. December 31. The plant and equipment that the firm owns are now one year older. In order to get a proper matching of revenues for each period with the expenses incurred to generate those revenues, the cost of this plant and equipment was not charged to expense when it was acquired. Instead we allocate some of the cost to each year in which the plant and equipment helps the firm to provide its goods and services. The journal entry increases an expense account called depreciation expense (Depr) to show that some of the cost of the asset is becoming an expense in this period. In this year the expense amounts to $6,000. The calculation of annual depreciation expense is discussed in Chapter 15.

The other impact (recall that the double-entry system requires at least two changes) is on the value of the plant and equipment (P&E). Because the plant and equipment are getting older, we wish to adjust their value downward by the amount of the depreciation.

$$\Delta A \quad + \quad \Delta E \quad + \Delta D = \Delta L + \Delta CC + \Delta R$$
$$P/E - 6{,}000 \quad Depr + 6{,}000 \quad = \text{No change on right side}$$

	Dr.	Cr.
Depreciation Expense	$6,000	
Plant and Equipment		$6,000

These transactions for Executive Corporation give a highly consolidated view of the thousands, millions, or quite possibly billions of transactions that are recorded annually by a firm. These few transactions cannot hope to have captured every individual transaction or type of transaction that occurs in your particular firm. However, in this brief glance you can begin to understand that there is a systematic approach for gathering the raw bits of data that make up the financial history of the firm.

There may be an enormous number of individual journal entries for a firm during the year. Chapter 8 examines how we can consolidate and summarize these numerous individual journal entries to provide useful summarized information to interested users of financial statements.

T-ACCOUNTS

Accountants frequently use a device called *T-accounts* as a form of short-hand when they are considering the financial impact of transactions. For any account that might be affected by a transaction, the accountant draws a large T, and places the name of the account on the top. For example, in the first transaction for Executive Corporation in 2003, Executive purchased an insurance policy for $3,000. This affects both prepaid insurance and cash, and T-accounts would be set up as follows:

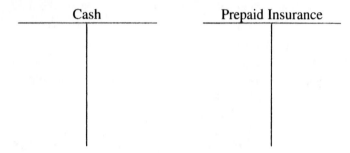

Cash   Prepaid Insurance

Within the T-account, any entries on the left side of the vertical line are debits, and any entries on the right side are credits. The purchase of $3,000 of insurance on January 2, 2003, generates a debit to prepaid insurance and a credit to cash as follows:

Cash

1/2/03 $3,000

Prepaid Insurance

1/2/03	$ 3,000	

Often T-accounts are used to assess the balance that remains in an account after a transaction. From Exhibit 7-1 we see that at the end of 2002, Executive had $52,000 in cash, and no prepaid insurance. We can add this information to the T-accounts, and then summarize the position immediately following the transaction to purchase the insurance as follows:

Cash

12/31/02	$52,000		
		1/2/03	$3,000
Ending Bal.	$49,000		

Prepaid Insurance

12/31/02	$ 0	
1/2/03	3,000	
Ending Bal.	$ 3,000	

Notice that when the beginning debit balance of $52,000 of cash is combined with the $3,000 credit transaction on January 2, the result is a $49,000 debit balance. The $3,000 credit reduces the total amount of the debit balance, in the same way that a negative number offsets a positive number.

The use of T-accounts by accountants for informal discussions and analyses is quite common, even though T-accounts are not generally part of the company's formal accounting system. The biggest problem T-accounts create for nonaccountants is that negative signs are not used. Each part of a transaction, or journal entry, is recorded in a T-account on the left or right side of the T, depending on whether it is a debit or credit, respectively. When you look at a T-account, in order to understand if the account balance is increasing or decreasing as a result of a specific entry, the user needs to be aware of whether each specific account is one that increases with a debit or a credit. Simply keep in mind that assets, expenses, and dividends declared increase with debits and decrease with credits. Liabilities, contributed capital, and revenues increase with credits and decrease with debits.

CHART OF ACCOUNTS

Up to this point we have always referred to accounts by their names, such as accounts receivable or wages payable. In practice, most organizations find it helpful to assign code numbers to each account. This facilities the process of recording journal entries in the computer systems widely used for accounting.

Typically, a company will use a fairly systematic approach to assigning numbers. All asset code numbers might begin with a 1, liabilities with a 2, revenues with a 3, and expenses with a 4, for example. A second and third digit would give more specific information. For example, cash might be represented by 100, while accounts receivable would be represented by 110. Most companies have receivables from many customers. A second set of numbers might provide that detailed information. For example, 110-12850 might refer to accounts receivable from customer number 12850. The company might therefore sell $5,000 of its product to customer 12850 on account. It would record a $5,000 increase in its account number 110-12850.

Charts of accounts can be quite flexible. If a company has five divisions, it can set aside one digit for each division. That digit might come at the beginning or end of the entire account code used for each transaction. Also, the company may choose to use the chart to identify specific programs, projects, departments, or other information. Thus, an account number might look something like 4-110-12850-028. This might indicate that the consulting division (division 4 of the company's five divisions) has an account receivable (110) from customer 12850 related to new venture consulting services (028).

Although this may appear to be complicated, it actually keeps things clear and simple once you know how the company's chart of accounts is set up. The official chart of accounts provides the guide to the system of accounts used by any organization. It will first define the intended purpose of each digit and the meaning of each number contained in each digit. So the first thing you would learn would be that the first digit represents the division of the company, and the specific number associated with each of the five divisions would be listed. Next you would learn the meaning of the second digit, which in this case indicates whether we are looking at an asset, liability, revenue, or expense. If the second digit is 1 in this system, it means we are looking at an asset. The next two digits indicate the specific asset, liability, revenue, or expense. Thus, the 110 after the first hyphen tells us that we are looking at an asset, specifically accounts receivable. And so on.

Generally, in addition to defining the meaning of each digit and providing all data needed to interpret an account number, a complete chart is also maintained. This allows a user to look up any specific account number. Bear in mind, however, that the chart of accounts is a dynamic document. New accounts are frequently added to an accounting system, and it is important to keep the chart of accounts up to date.

KEY CONCEPTS

Double-entry accounting—Each financial event affects the basic equation of accounting. In order for the equation to remain in balance, the event must affect at least two items in the equation, therefore the "double" entry.

Journal—a book (or computer memory file) in which all financial events are recorded in chronological sequence.

Debits—increases in assets, expenses, and dividends declared accounts; decreases in liability, revenue, and contributed capital accounts.

Credits—increases in liability, revenue, and contributed capital accounts, and decreases in asset, expense, and dividends declared accounts.

Timing for recording transactions—Journal entries can be made only if we know with reasonable certainty the amount of money involved and the timing of the event, and if there has been exchange by at least one party to the transaction.

Adjusting entries—Most financial events occur at one specific point in time and are recorded as they occur. Some financial events occur continuously over time, such as the expiration of insurance or the accumulation of interest. Adjusting entries are made immediately prior to financial statement preparation to bring these accounts up to date.

Eight

Reporting Financial Information

Chapter 7 discussed the way that each of the numerous financial transactions affecting the firm can be recorded into the firm's financial history through the use of a journal and journal entries. When we get to the end of an accounting period (typically a month, quarter, or year), we want to report what has occurred. We need some method of summarizing the massive quantity of information we've recorded into a format concise enough to be useful to those who desire financial information about the firm.

Financial statements are used to present the firm's financial position and results of operations to interested users of financial information. As we learned in Chapter 4, the financial statements themselves are only several pages long. How can we process our journal entry information in such a way as to allow for such a substantial summarization? We do it via use of a ledger.

LEDGERS

A ledger is a book of *accounts*. An account is simply any item that we would like to keep track of. Every account that might be affected by a journal entry is individually accounted for in a ledger.

Although today many firms have computerized their bookkeeping systems so that they no longer have a ledger book, you can think of a ledger as if it were simply a book. Each page in the ledger book represents one account. For instance, there is a page for the cash account, and one for the inventory account, and one for retained earnings. Every time we make a journal entry, we are changing the amount that we have in at least two ledger accounts in order to keep the basic equation of accounting in balance.

An immediate benefit of the ledger system is that it allows us to determine how much we have of any item at any point in time. For example, suppose that someone asked us on May 4th how much cash we currently have. One way to provide that information would be to review each and every journal entry that we made since the beginning of the year, determine which ones affected cash, and calculate by how much the cash total has changed. That presents an enormous amount of work.

Using a ledger approach, immediately after making a journal entry, we update our ledger for each account that has changed as a result of that entry. For example, in Chapter 7, the first thing that happened to Executive Corporation in 2003 was a purchase of insurance for $3,000, which was paid for in cash. This expenditure requires us to go to the ledger account for cash and show a decrease of $3,000, as well as go to the ledger account for prepaid insurance and show an increase of $3,000. At the same time, we could update the balance in each account.

The ledger is, in some respects, a more complete picture of the firm than the journal is. Each year the journal indicates what happened or changed during that year. The ledger not only contains this year's events, but also tells us where we were when we started out at the beginning of the year. For instance, Executive Corporation had $52,000 in cash at the end of 2002, according to Exhibit 7-1. Our cash account in the ledger would show $52,000 as the opening balance at the beginning of 2003. Thus, when we purchased our insurance on January 2, 2003, we would be able to determine that our initial balance of $52,000 was decreased by $3,000, and that there is a remaining cash balance of $49,000. This gives a better overall picture of the firm than the $3,000 change alone does.

Essentially, the ledger combines account balances from the beginning of the year with the journal entries that were recorded during the year. All of the beginning balances for this year can be found by looking at last year's ending balance sheet. The balance sheet is the statement of financial position. The firm's financial position at the beginning of the year will be identical to its financial position at the end of the previous year. Therefore, the ledger accounts start the year with balances from the year-end balance sheet of the previous year. During the year, the changes that occur and are recorded as journal entries are used to update the ledger accounts. The year-end balance in each account is simply the sum of the opening balance plus the changes recorded in that account during the year.

EXECUTIVE CORPORATION'S FINANCIAL STATEMENTS

Exhibit 8-1 presents the information from which we can prepare a set of financial statements for Executive Corporation. This exhibit represents a highly abbreviated ledger for the entire corporation for the whole year. All of the journal entries for the year have been recorded. Each column represents one ledger account. The opening balance is recorded for each account, based on information from Exhibit 7-1, Executive Corporation's December 31, 2002 Balance Sheet. The horizontal lines represent the individual numbered journal entries from Chapter 7. A running balance in each account has not been provided in this example.

A number of the ledger accounts in Exhibit 8-1 start with a zero balance. This occurs for one of two reasons. The first reason is simply that there was no balance at the end of last year, so there is no balance at the beginning of this year. Such is the case with prepaid insurance. The second reason is that some items are kept track of year by year rather than cumulatively. The income statement accounts relate specifically to the accounting period. We kept track of our income for 2002. Once 2002 was over and its results reported in our financial statements, we wished to keep track of 2003's income separately from 2002's. Therefore, all of the revenue and expense accounts start 2003 with a zero balance. When we get to the end of this year and ask, "What was our revenue this year?" we want to know the revenue of this year separate and apart from any revenue we made in earlier years.

The revenue and expense accounts are called *temporary accounts* because we will start them over each year with a zero balance. The dividends declared account is also a temporary account. It keeps track of how much in dividends we declared during the entire year. There is a separate permanent account, dividends payable, which would keep track of any dividends we've declared but not yet paid.

The key to conveying financial information is the ending balance of each ledger account. As long as we are using a system in which each journal entry is *posted*, or recorded in the individual ledger accounts involved, we are able to determine the ending balance in each ledger account. Those ending balances provide the information needed for a complete set of financial statements.

EXHIBIT 8-1.
Executive Corporation
Ledger for 2003 (000's omitted)

TRANSACTION	Assets — Cash	Prepaid Insurance	Accounts Receivable	Inventory	Plant & Equipment	Expenses — Cost of Goods Sold	Labor	Interest	Insurance	Depreciation	Div. — Dividends	Liabilities — Accounts Payable	Wages Payable	Mortgage Payable	Stockholder's Equity — Common Stock	Retained Earnings	Rev. — Revenue
Beginning Balance	$52	$0	$18	$20	$60	$0	$0	$0	$0	$0	$0	$17	$10	$40	$10	$73	$0
1	-3	3															
2	-15											-15					
3				15								15					
4	14		-14														
5			56														56
6				-28		28											
7																	
8	-18						8						-10				
9	-10							6						-4			
10	-3										3						
11		-1							1								
12							3						3				
13					-6					6							
Ending Balance	$17	$2	$60	$7	$54	$28	$11	$6	$1	$6	$3	$17	$3	$36	$10	$73	$56

```
┌─────────────────────────────────────────────────────────────┐
│                      Excel Exercise                          │
│                                                              │
│   Use Template 7 to record journal entries, post them to ledger │
│   accounts, and calculate ending balances that can be used to prepare │
│   financial statements. This template is on the CD that accompanies │
│   this book.                                                 │
└─────────────────────────────────────────────────────────────┘
```

The Income Statement

Exhibit 8-2 presents the 2003 Income Statement for Executive Corporation. The income statement for any firm consists merely of a comparison of its revenues and expenses. In order to prepare this statement, we would have to look at the ending balance in each revenue and expense ledger account. The ending balance in the revenue account at the bottom of Exhibit 8-1 shows revenue of $56,000, which is exactly the same as the revenue in the income statement in Exhibit 8-2. You can compare each of the expenses between Exhibits 8-1 and 8-2 as well, and will find them to be the same. This must be so, because the way that the income statement was prepared was to simply take the ending balances from each of the revenue and expense ledger accounts.

EXHIBIT 8-2.
Executive Corporation
Income Statement
For the Year Ending December 31, 2003

Revenue		$56,000
Less Expenses:		
Cost of Goods Sold	$28,000	
Labor	11,000	
Interest	6,000	
Insurance	1,000	
Depreciation	6,000	
Total Expenses		52,000
Net Income		$ 4,000

The Balance Sheet

The retained earnings ledger account in Exhibit 8-1 has the same balance at the end of the year as it had at the beginning of the year. The retained earnings of a firm increase when it has income, and decrease when dividends are declared. In fact, every revenue will increase retained earnings, while expenses and dividends will decrease it. We have had all of these items, but the retained earnings account hasn't changed. The reason for this is that we have simply been keeping track of the specific changes in revenues, expenses, and dividends, instead of showing their impact on the retained earnings account.

By keeping track of revenues and expenses in detail rather than directly indicating their impact on retained earnings, we have generated additional information. This information has been used to derive an income statement. If we simply changed retained earnings directly whenever we had a revenue or expense, we would not have had the information needed to produce an income statement.

Nevertheless, we cannot produce a balance sheet without updating the information in our retained earnings account. Exhibit 8-3 provides a statement that updates both of the stockholders' equity accounts.

EXHIBIT 8-3.
Executive Corporation
Analysis of Changes in Stockholders' Equity
For the Year Ending December 31, 2003

	COMMON STOCK	RETAINED EARNINGS
Beginning Balance 1/1/03	$10,000	$73,000
Capital Contributions during 2003	0	
Net Income for 2003		4,000
Dividends Declared 2003		(3,000)
Ending Balance 12/31/03	$10,000	$74,000

In Exhibit 8-3, we can see that the common stock balance did not change this year. Possible changes would include additional issuance of common stock through a private offering or a general offering to the public, issuance of stock as part of employee incentive plans, or retirement of stock. Retained earnings, as noted above, increase as a result of a positive net income (they decrease as a result of losses), and decrease when dividends are declared. (The parentheses around the $3,000 of dividends indicate that the $3,000 is being subtracted.)

All of the information used in Exhibit 8-3 comes either directly or indirectly from the ledger accounts in Exhibit 8-1. The common stock balance did not change during the year. Had there been changes to the common stock account, we could have determined what they were from the ledger account. Entries into ledger accounts are dated, allowing easy reference to the journal to review any transaction in its entirety. The dividend figure in Exhibit 8-3 is the ending balance in the dividends ledger account from Exhibit 8-1. The net income figure in Exhibit 8-3 does not appear anywhere in Exhibit 8-1. It is, however, merely a summary of the year-end revenue and expense items from the income statement, Exhibit 8-2. All of the Exhibit 8-2 items came directly from Exhibit 8-1. We now have all of the information we need to produce a balance sheet.

The balance sheet for Executive Corporation for 2003 appears in Exhibit 8-4. The asset and liability balances came directly from Exhibit 8-1 and the stockholders' equity balances came from our derivation in Exhibit 8-3. The preparation of this financial statement is really quite simple, given the ledger account balances. The balances are simply transferred to the financial statement, with the main work involved being the determination of which accounts are short-term and which accounts are long-term.

Excel Exercise

Template 8 uses the journal entry information from Template 7 to derive an Income Statement and Balance Sheet. This template is included on the CD that accompanies this book.

EXHIBIT 8-4.
Executive Corporation
Balance Sheet
As of December 31, 2003

ASSETS

Current Assets:		
Cash	$17,000	
Prepaid Insurance	2,000	
Accounts Receivable	60,000	
Inventory	7,000	
Total Current Assets		$ 86,000
Fixed Assets:		
Plant and Equipment, net		54,000
TOTAL ASSETS		$140,000

EQUITIES

LIABILITIES		
Current Liabilities:		
Accounts Payable	$17,000	
Wages Payable	3,000	
Total Current Liabilities		$ 20,000
Long-Term Liabilities:		
Mortgage Payable		36,000
TOTAL LIABILITIES		$ 56,000
STOCKHOLDERS' EQUITY		
Common Stock		$ 10,000
Retained Earnings		74,000
TOTAL STOCKHOLDERS' EQUITY		$ 84,000
TOTAL LIABILITIES & STOCKHOLDERS' EQUITY		$140,000

The Statement of Cash Flows

The one remaining financial statement that is widely used to report the results of operations is the statement of cash flows. As discussed in Chapter 4, this statement focuses on the firm's sources and uses of cash. This statement also provides insight about the firm's liquidity, or its ability to meet its current obligations as they come due for payment.

The statement of cash flows shows where the firm got its cash and how it used it over the entire period covered by the financial statement. This feature is similar to the income statement, which shows revenues and expenses for the entire accounting period, and is different from the balance sheet that shows the firm's financial position at a single point in time. The statement of cash flows is divided into three major sections: cash from operating activities; cash from investing activities; and cash from financing activities.

The operating activities are those that relate to the ordinary revenue- and expense-producing activities of the firm. Firms tend to be particularly interested in how their day-to-day revenues and expenses affect cash balances. These activities include items such as payments to employees and suppliers and collections of cash from customers. A controversial element involves interest and dividends. Many people believe that interest and dividends are more closely associated with investing and financing activities. However, interest and dividends *received* and interest *paid* must be included with operating activities because of their impact on revenues and expenses.

The investing activities of the firm relate to the purchase and sale of fixed assets and securities. It is clear that the purchase of stocks and bonds represents an investing activity. The accounting rule-making body determined that the purchase of property, plant, and equipment also represents an investment, and should be accounted for in this category. Lending money (and receiving repayments) also represents an investing activity.

The financing activities of the firm are concerned with borrowing money (or repaying it), issuance of stock, and the payment of dividends. Note that when a firm lends money, it is investing. However, borrowing money relates to getting the financial resources the firm needs to operate. Thus, borrowing is included in the financing category, along with issuance of stock. Dividends paid are considered to be a financing activity because they are a return of financial resources to the firm's owners. They are not included in operating activities because dividends paid are not classified as an expense, but rather as a distribution to the firm's owners of income earned.

There are two different approaches to calculating and presenting the statement of cash flows. These are the direct and the indirect methods. Exhibit 8-5 presents an example of the Statement of Cash Flows, prepared using the direct method. The direct method lists each individual type of account that resulted in a change in cash.

Looking at Exhibit 8-1, we can see that cash was affected by transactions 1, 2, 5, 8, 9, and 10. Review of each of those journal entries provides the information needed to prepare Exhibit 8-5. For example, transaction 1 consisted of a $3,000 payment for insurance. Therefore, the decrease in cash was for an operating activity, specifically payment for insurance.

This may be a cumbersome task when there are a large number of individual transactions. For example, how much cash was collected from customers during 2003? By looking at transaction 5 from Exhibit 8-1, we know that the answer is $14,000. We can see the increase in cash and the reduction in accounts receivable. Typically, however, there would be an extremely large number of individual journal entries related to receipts from customers.

Rather than review each transaction, accountants usually prepare the cash flows statement by making general inferences from the changes in the balances of various accounts. Note that accounts receivable at the beginning of the year were $18,000, and revenues from sales to customers during the year were $56,000. Combining what was owed to us at the beginning of the year with the amount customers purchased this year indicates that there was a total of $74,000 that we would hope to eventually collect from customers. At the end of the year the accounts receivable balance was $60,000. Therefore we can infer that $14,000 must have been collected (the $74,000 total due us, less the $60,000 still due at the end of the year).

Let's consider another example. The mortgage payable account started with a balance of $40,000 and ended with a balance of $36,000 (Exhibit 8-1). Rather than reviewing all of the journal entries related to

EXHIBIT 8-5.
Executive Corporation
Statement of Cash Flows
For the Year Ending December 31, 2003

Cash Flows from Operating Activities

Collections from Customers	$ 14,000	
Payments to Employees	(18,000)	
Payments to Suppliers	(15,000)	
Payments for Insurance	(3,000)	
Payments for Interest	(6,000)	
Net Cash Used for Operating Activities		$ (28,000)

Cash Flows from Investing Activities

None

Net Cash Used for Investing Activities		0

Cash Flows from Financing Activities

Payment of Mortgage Principal	$ (4,000)	
Payment of Dividends	(3,000)	
Net Used for Financing Activities		(7,000)

NET INCREASE/(DECREASE) IN CASH		$ (35,000)
CASH, DECEMBER 31, 2002		52,000
CASH DECEMBER 31, 2003		$ 17,000

mortgage payments, accountants would infer that $4,000 was spent on the financing activity of repaying debt. However, this inference process requires care. It is possible, for instance that $20,000 was paid on the mortgage principal, but a new mortgage of $16,000 was taken on a new piece of equipment. The statement of cash flows must show both the source of cash from the new mortgage, as well as the payment of cash on the old mortgage. Therefore, preparation of the statement requires at least some in-depth knowledge about changes in the accounts of the firm.

An alternative approach for developing and presenting the statement of cash flows is referred to as the indirect method. The indirect method starts with net income as a measure of cash from operations. It then makes adjustments to the extent that net income is not a true measure of cash flow. Exhibit 8-6 was prepared using the indirect method.

One of the most common adjustments to income is for depreciation. When buildings and equipment are purchased, there is a cash outflow. Each year, a portion of the cost of the buildings or equipment is charged as a depreciation expense. That expense does lower net income, but it does not require a cash outflow. Therefore, the amount of the depreciation expense is added back to net income to make net income more reflective of true cash flows. In Exhibit 8-6 we see that the $6,000 depreciation expense is added to net income.

There are a variety of other items that cause net income to over- or understate the true cash flow. For example, if customers buy our product or service, but don't pay for it before the end of the year, then income will overstate cash inflow. Therefore, in Exhibit 8-6, there is a negative adjustment for the increase in accounts receivable.

Many of the adjustments to net income that are needed to determine cash flow from operating activities are quite confusing. Therefore many people prefer use of the direct method. However, because net income is considered essential to the process of generating cash, the net income reconciliation is required. If the direct method is used, the Cash Flows from Operating Activities portion of the indirect method (Exhibit 8-6) must be included as a supporting schedule.

The information contained in the statement of cash flows is quite dramatic in this example. Although Exhibit 8-2 indicated that there was a positive net income of $4,000, the firm is using substantially more cash than it is receiving. In some cases this might reflect recent spending on buildings and equipment. A decline in cash is not necessarily bad. However, in this case, we note from the statement of cash flows (Exhibit 8-5 or 8-6) that no money was used for investing activities. The largest decline in cash came from operations. What was the single largest cause of the decline? Exhibit 8-5 would seem to indicate that payments to employees were the largest item. They caused the largest cash outflow.

EXHIBIT 8-6.
Executive Corporation
Statement of Cash Flows
For the Year Ending December 31, 2003

Cash Flows from Operating Activities		
Net Income		$ 4,000
Adjustments		
Depreciation Expense	$ 6,000	
Decrease in Inventory	13,000	
Increase in Accounts Receivable	(42,000)	
Increase in Prepaid Insurance	(2,000)	
Decrease in Wages Payable	(7,000)	
Total Adjustments to Net Income		(32,000)
Net Cash Used for Operating Activities		$(28,000)
Cash Flows from Investing Activities		
None		
Net Cash Used for Investing Activities		0
Cash Flows from Financing Activities		
Payment of Mortgage Principal	$ (4,000)	
Payment of Dividends	(3,000)	
Net Cash Used for Financing Activities		(7,000)
NET INCREASE/(DECREASE) IN CASH		$(35,000)
CASH, DECEMBER 31, 2002		52,000
CASH, DECEMBER 31, 2003		$17,000

However, this is an example in which the net income reconciliation provides particularly useful information. Looking at the cash flows from operating activities section of Exhibit 8-6, the most striking number is the $42,000 increase in receivables. A growing company is likely to have growing receivables. In this case, however, the growth in receivables seems to be unusually large. What does this mean? It could mean that the firm needs to make a stronger effort to collect payment from its customers on a timely basis. Or it could mean that sales were made to buyers who can't pay. The statement of cash flows highlights the receivables problem for the user of the statement. If receivables continue to grow at this rate, the firm will run out of cash, probably before the end of the next year. Although there is no crisis yet, there may be unless we take this situation into account in managing the firm and in planning for cash inflows and outflows for the coming year.

LOOKING AHEAD

Part 2 has presented an introduction to accounting, a vital framework for financial management. We have spent a considerable amount of time defining financial statements, their components, how we value items that appear on financial statements, and the mechanics of recording financial information and putting together a firm's set of financial statements. In Part IV we reverse gears and start to tear apart financial statements to learn how to interpret the information they contain. Now that we know where they come from, we will be better able to glean all the information possible out of them, and to use that information to better manage our firm.

However, before we begin the financial statement analysis of Part 4, we will be examining a variety of financial decisions in Part 3. The financial managers of the firm are often faced with decisions that have relatively little impact on the underlying productivity of the firm, but that can have a tremendous impact on its profitability. Nonfinancial managers frequently observe de facto decisions made by financial officers. In Part 3 we examine the reasons why many of these decisions are made.

For example, why accelerate the depreciation on our equipment? Why did we recently shift to a LIFO method of inventory, and what is LIFO anyway? Why do we lease equipment, when you would think it would be cheaper to own it? These are just a few of the questions addressed by Part 3 of this book.

KEY CONCEPTS

Ledger—a book (or computer memory file) in which we keep track of the impact of financial events on each account. The ledger can provide us with the balance in any account at any point in time.

Income statement preparation—The income statement is directly prepared from the year-end ledger balances of the revenue and expense accounts.

Balance sheet preparation—Ledger account balances can be used to provide an analysis of changes in stockholders' equity accounts. This analysis, together with other ledger account balances, is used to prepare the balance sheet.

Statement of cash flows—This statement shows the sources and uses of the firm's cash. It specifically shows cash from operating, investing, and financing activities. It can be prepared under two alternative methods:

a. *the direct method*—Lists the change in cash caused by each account.

b. *the indirect method*—Starts with net income as an estimate of cash flow, and makes a series of adjustments to net income to determine cash flow from operating activities.

Part 3

Financial
Decisions

Nine
Business Plans

One of the ways that organizations prosper is through the introduction of new programs, projects, and other ventures. A business plan is a document that provides the information needed to determine whether the venture is likely to fail or to succeed. A business plan should help you assess whether the proposed venture is sensible, whether it fits the organizational mission, and whether it will be financially viable.

WHY DEVELOP A BUSINESS PLAN?

The more time and effort managers put into a project, the more committed they become to it, and the harder it becomes to recognize the project's limitations. So the first and foremost reason for developing a business plan is to discover weaknesses and eliminate bad proposals at an early stage.

If the plan provides evidence that the proposed venture is a good one, then the plan becomes a vital tool in a number of ways. It provides the details of why the idea is a good one, supporting the idea with evidence instead of merely opinion. It helps to clarify what we do and don't know about the venture. It provides a basis to identify and analyze elements of a proposal that are critical to its success. And finally, it is the primary tool for convincing others (e.g., our boss or investors) that the idea is a good one, worthy of financial support.

A business plan also serves other purposes. First, it communicates the purpose of the project to everyone throughout the organization. The plan also provides a road map for the future, laying out the steps that will be needed to fully implement the new venture. It should include a formal statement of both financial and nonfinancial goals for the project, and forecasts of what resources will be needed and how they will be obtained. These resources are not only financial, but also include elements such as management talent that will be needed to implement and run the new program. Finally, we prepare a plan so that we will have a basis for assessing and controlling organizational performance once the venture is fully operational.

QUESTIONS THAT DRIVE A BUSINESS PLAN

A business plan document represents an effort to provide answers to many questions:

- What is the venture that is being proposed?
- Why would our organization want to do it?
- Who will we provide products or services for?
- How much will potential customers pay?
- How many potential customers are there?
- What will our share of the market be?

We must be as clear as possible in defining the business concept. To make an evaluation of a project, we need to know whether we are responding to an opportunity or a competitive threat, or simply following the next logical step in achieving the organization's mission. We must clearly identify the customer for the products or services that will be provided. Understanding the likely possible pricing and demand for the product or service is critical. Similarly, we must address questions related to marketing approaches.

There are also many questions about specific operating issues that need to be addressed. Where will we do it? Location may be a critical factor in the success of any venture. How will we do it? That is, we need to have some information about the specific operating elements. Who will do it? We need to know both the specific individuals and the organizational elements. Will someone try to stop us from doing it? We cannot consider only our plans without considering the likely response from our competitors.

Four final questions are critical. What resources will we need? If we cannot obtain adequate financing, it is often best not to try to undertake the project. A good idea may waste an incredible amount of time if there is no mechanism that can result in sufficient funding to get the project off the ground. Can it sustain itself? Even if the project fills a tremendous need, we must evaluate whether it can be financially viable. If it can't be, then we need to directly address the question of where a sustaining subsidy might come from. What can go wrong and what will we do if it does? We can never anticipate all problems that may arise. However, the biggest problem with most new plans is that there are risks of failure. To the extent possible we must try to anticipate those risks so that we can evaluate whether the potential payoff justifies taking those risks. Finally, if it's such a good idea, why isn't someone already doing it? This is a tough question, but it is one that is worth thinking about.

THE PLANNING PROCESS

The first step in the process of developing a business plan is to define the business concept. Make it extremely clear what the project will be all about. Next, gather the data we need to answer the questions posed above. As the data is collected, focus and refine the concept. In other words, the project we wind up proposing in a finished business plan is likely to be very different from the one we started with. As we learn more about what might or might not work, the plan should evolve. If, after gathering all the data, things still look positive, put the plan in a "high-impact" format. Remember, you likely will be competing for resources.

THE ELEMENTS OF A BUSINESS PLAN

What does a business plan look like? There is no standard document that fits all projects. Make the plan fit the project, not the reverse. Bear in mind that different projects call for different amounts of detail. Essentially, a plan should be complete enough to make a decision about whether to go forward with the project, and yet as concise and easy to read as possible.

In writing a plan, try to aim its contents at the intended audience, be it a supervisor, board members, bankers, venture capitalists, etc. It may be necessary to have different versions of the plan prepared for different readers. It is quite important that we try to assess their knowledge of our project. The document should meet the reader's information needs. The goal is not to show how much we know, but rather to provide the information the reader needs to know. For example, providing a three-page background on our organization may be useful to a venture capitalist, but is just excess baggage if we are asking our own CEO to review and approve the plan.

Maintain a consistent voice and tense throughout the document. Don't shift between the third person (the organization) and the first person (I or we) and between the present (the clinics see 1,000 clients each year) and the future (the clinics will see 1,000 clients each year).

Although each business plan document will be unique, there are some elements that are typically included. The plan should have a cover memo. Next comes a title page, followed by a table of contents, executive summary, description of the initiative, proposed organizational structure, market analysis and marketing plan, financial/resource requirement plan, financial feasibility analysis, implementation and operating plan, key performance measures, and summary of strengths and weaknesses, including risks. If we need to say more—add a topic!

Cover Memo

This memo, sometimes in the form of a letter, should be a brief explanation of what the business plan document is and the specific action that is requested. That action will vary from a request for funding to simply a request for permission to move forward with implementation. For example, a cover memo might appear as in Exhibit 9-1.

Title Page

The body of the plan should have a title page. This may seem pretty obvious, but it is a simple element that is often forgotten. The title page might appear similar to Exhibit 9-2.

Table of Contents

A table of contents should be provided next. This table should provide page numbers for easy reference. Many readers will choose to skip around, and this table should help keep them from getting frustrated.

EXHIBIT 9-1
Cover Memo

Doc in a Box Clinics (DBC)

Internal Communication

To: C. Eeo

From: Steve Finkler

Date: October 31, 2002

Re: Business Plan for Stress/Anxiety Reduction Clinics

Attached is a copy of the business plan for a proposed chain of Stress/Anxiety Reduction Clinics. The plan describes the clinical, operating, and financial impacts of adding a national chain of clinics focusing on stress reduction.

The new clinics are consistent with the Doc in a Box Clinic mission statement, in that they meet an important health care need, while also being likely to add substantially to the overall profits of the company. The first new clinic in the chain can be operational within six months.

I hope that you will review this plan for our upcoming meeting. It is my recommendation that DBC make a financial and operating commitment to go forward with this clinic.

EXHIBIT 9-2
Title Page

A Proposal

To Establish

A National Chain of

Stress/Anxiety Reduction Clinics

Submitted by

Steven Finkler

Doc in a Box Clinics

Planning Department

October 2002

Executive Summary

Next comes a brief executive summary. Depending on how extensive a project is being proposed, this summary may range anywhere from one to three pages. **It should not be longer.** The summary is written last. Everything else in the plan should be completed before the summary is written. It should give the reader an overview of the entire project.

It is critical to make your points quickly and clearly in this summary. Pique the readers' interest, or they may not go any further. Start quickly, with no more than one or two sentences describing the project, and immediately follow with the financial benefit. If profits are expected, tell the reader right away.

Then summarize all key points and critical numbers from the document. Provide the essence of why the project will succeed. Establish the approach to be taken, the timing, the management and structure of the project, the costs, revenues, and financial viability. Finally, be clear about what you want from the reader. If you grab the readers' attention, they will move into the document to get the details.

Description of the Initiative

The next section should provide a description of the initiative in some detail. The first sentence should define the business concept. The rest of that paragraph should explain the project's importance. The remainder of the section can lay out the proposed venture in somewhat more detail, giving the project's history, current status, and other information. Try to explain why this is different from what others are already doing, and why it isn't already being done by someone else.

Organizational Structure

Management and organizational structure may be critical to a venture's success. The document must clearly explain who will manage both the initial implementation and the ongoing project once it is up and running. Brief bios should be provided for each member of the project management team.

It would be nice to be able to identify each member of the management team, but it is not uncommon for there to be positions listed as "to be announced" in the early stages of planning. Realize, however, that this weakens the plan. You must convince the reader that the management team is capable and can make the plan succeed. If there are too many gaps in the management team, it will erode the reader's confidence.

Market Analysis

The greatest product or service will not be a financial success if no one is interested in buying it. Market analysis must be conducted to assure that there is, in fact, some demand for the product or service. We must also know if the existing or potential competition will make it too difficult to gain adequate market share. The business plan should identify the target market and its scope (local, regional, national, or worldwide).

Will potential customers pay the price we want to charge? How do we know? Is there competition now? If yes, who? What does their company look like—what products or services do they offer? Where? When? What quality? If there isn't any current competition for the product or service, why isn't there? Will competition arise after others see our successful venture? What are our strengths and weaknesses relative to competitors? Can the market bear both companies, or will we have to force them out of the business in order to succeed? How likely are we to be able to do that?

Marketing Plan

Assuming that our market research indicates that there is a potential market for our product at the price we want to charge, how will we gain our desired market share? We will need to inform customers of the availability of our product or service. How do we intend to do that? Will we advertise on the radio, on television, or in newspapers? Will we put flyers on car windshields? Once we let customers know about us, how will we motivate them to buy from us? It is wishful thinking to assume that "if we will build it, they will come." A proactive marketing plan is essential.

Financial/Resource Requirement Plan

The business plan should identify all resources needed for the start-up of the venture, as well as the expected revenues and expenses related to the project. In some cases this may not be very difficult. For example, if the proposal is to replace an existing facility or expand capacity of a successful activity, we may have excellent historical information to use as a guide.

In many cases, however, the project is new, and the financial estimates are more difficult to make. The manager needs to be careful to find out as much as possible about the resources that are likely to be needed and their cost. Any assumptions made should be listed explicitly. As people read the plan, they can add their insights as to the likely accuracy of those assumptions, and help make refinements that will shape a more accurate plan. The plan should include a contingency fund. This represents an extra amount of money that will be raised in advance and will be available to meet unexpected needs during the implementation and early stages of operation.

Financial Feasibility Analysis

A key element of most business plans is the determination of whether the proposed venture is expected to be financially feasible. Usually this requires forecasts of both the future profits and cash flows of the venture.

Forecasting is as much art as science. If possible, before using any method, test its forecasting accuracy over time. Look at past periods, apply the technique retrospectively, and see how well it would have predicted what we now know actually happened. Consider seasonal factors. If possible, look at industry data or comparable ventures. Forecasts used for financial feasibility are largely based on the marketing analyses and implementation plans. The manager must exercise thought and judgment to make the forecast as accurate as possible.

Financial feasibility analysis is often done with a very rough first pass, and then revised over and over as more information is incorporated. Doing all of the analysis on a computer spreadsheet program such as Excel or Lotus 123 is highly recommended.

Anticipating the revenues and expenses will be critical to the financial feasibility analysis. Revenue forecasts require that we anticipate both demand and prices. Discounts that will be offered and a likely rate of bad debts must be considered. Growth rates from month to month must also be factored in as new ventures rarely reach a steady state of sales right from the start. Revenue projections must also consider how long the business will take to get organized before it can begin to see sales. Delays in collecting payments from customers must also be anticipated.

The business plan must document the expected start-up costs, capital equipment needs, and ongoing operating costs. Managers must be careful to include both direct production costs and also indirect costs such as marketing and administration. This information should be fairly detailed. For example, the capital costs should include the amount and cost of equipment and facilities, location, timing of acquisition, and estimated useful life.

Focus on Cash Flow

Profits compare revenues and expenses. Do we sell the product or service for more than it costs us to provide it? If so, then we earn a profit. However, in a world in which we often have to buy and pay for supplies, buildings, and equipment well in advance of when our customers ultimately pay us for the goods and services that they buy from us, cash flow is as critical as profits. Recall from the discussion in the viability section of Chapter 1 that it is possible for a profitable venture to go out of business because it runs out of cash. In fact, the more successful the new venture is, the more likely it is to fail because of the growing needs for cash investment as expansion takes place.

Therefore, the business plan must 1) anticipate how long it will take the organization to achieve profitability, and 2) estimate how long it will take until it achieves a level of positive cash flow.

Pro Forma Financial Statements

Most business plans include a set of *pro forma* income and cash flow statements. Pro forma statements are financial statements that provide projections or forecasts of the future. Generally the business plan will include three years of projections, although five years of pro formas are sometimes provided. Income or cash flow statements that only project each year as a whole don't show the tremendous variability in resource needs and in organizational results within each year. Therefore, pro forma statements often show each month, or at least each quarter, for the first year or two, and sometimes for three to five years. Exhibit 9-3 provides an example of a pro forma cash flow statement for one year.

If a venture is not projected to achieve a positive cash flow position within the first three years, it is unlikely to gain much support from venture capitalists or internal managers who have to make funding decisions.

EXHIBIT 9-3.
Pro Forma Cash Flow Statement for One Year
DBC Stress/Anxiety Clinics
For the Period Beginning January 1, 2003

MONTH	JAN	FEB	MAR	APR	MAY
Beginning Cash Balance	$10,000	$10,000	$10,000	$10,000	$10,000
Cash Receipts					
Product Sales	$ 4,500	$ 4,600	$ 4,800	$ 5,000	$ 5,200
Services	5,000	6,000	7,000	8,000	9,000
Royalties	—	—	—	500	1,000
Total Cash Receipts	$ 9,500	$10,600	$11,800	$13,500	$15,200
Total Cash Available	$19,500	$20,600	$21,800	$23,500	$25,200
Cash Disbursements					
Labor	$24,000	$24,533	$25,600	$26,667	$27,733
Supplies	16,600	16,969	17,707	18,444	19,182
Rent	24,000	24,000	24,000	24,000	24,000
Interest Expense	—	1,891	2,799	3,722	4,455
Marketing	30,000	30,000	30,000	10,000	10,000
Capital Acquisitions	100,000	—	—	—	—
Other	4,000	4,000	4,000	4,000	4,000
Total Disbursements	$198,600	$101,393	$104,106	$86,833	$89,371
Subtotal	-$179,100	-$80,793	-$82,306	-$63,333	-$64,171
+Borrowing/-Loan Payments	189,100	90,793	92,306	73,333	74,171
Ending Cash Balance	$10,000	$10,000	$10,000	$10,000	$10,000
Cumulative Outstanding Loan	$189,100	$279,893	$372,199	$455,532	$519,703

JUN	JUL	AUG	SEP	OCT	NOV	DEC	ANNU
$10,000	$10,000	$10,000	$10,000	$10,000	$10,000	$10,000	$10,0
$ 5,400	$ 5,600	$ 5,800	$ 6,000	$ 6,200	$ 6,400	$ 6,600	$ 66,1
10,000	11,000	12,000	13,000	14,000	15,000	16,000	126,0
1,500	2,000	2,500	3,000	3,500	4,000	4,500	22,5
$16,900	$18,600	$20,300	$22,000	$23,700	$25,400	$27,100	$214,6
$26,900	$28,600	$30,300	$32,000	$33,700	$35,400	$37,100	$224,6
$28,800	$29,867	$30,933	$32,000	$33,067	$34,133	$35,200	$352,5
19,920	20,658	21,396	22,133	22,871	23,609	24,347	243,8
24,000	24,000	24,000	24,000	24,000	24,000	24,000	288,0
5,197	5,947	6,656	7,373	8,098	8,831	9,573	64,5
10,000	5,000	5,000	5,000	5,000	5,000	5,000	150,0
—	—	—	—	—	—	—	100,0
4,000	4,000	4,000	4,000	4,000	4,000	4,000	48,0
$91,917	$89,472	$91,985	$94,506	$97,036	$99,573	$102,120	$1,246,9
$65,017	-$60,872	-$61,685	-$62,506	-$63,336	-$64,173	-$65,020	-$1,022,3
75,017	70,872	71,685	72,506	73,336	74,173	75,020	1,032,3
$10,000	$10,000	$10,000	$10,000	$10,000	$10,000	$10,000	$10,0
594,720	$665,591	$737,276	$809,782	$883,118	$957,291	$1,032,311	

There is a great deal of uncertainty in the world, and it turns out that managers are better at predicting the things that might go right than they are at predicting all of the possible things that might go wrong. Given the unexpected, it is risky to commit to a project that will require cash subsidy far into the future, unless the potential rewards are truly lucrative.

Return on Investment Analysis

The pro forma income statements must also show that the venture will begin to be profitable within a reasonable period of time. But how much profitability is necessary? Suppose that Doc in a Box Clinics (DBC) puts up $10 million for the construction of new stress/anxiety reduction clinics around the country. Assume that the pro formas show that by the second year the clinics start to turn a profit, and by the third year they become self-sufficient from a cash flow basis. Is that enough to warrant going ahead? No.

The two main elements that we have not yet considered are the rate of return on the investment and the element of risk. DBC is contemplating an investment of at least the $10 million to construct the new clinics. That money is spent before the first patient is seen, but the profits earned on providing care will occur in the future. Collection of the revenues earned will occur even farther in the future. The business plan must assure DBC that it will eventually recover its up-front cash investment to build the clinics, as well as the cash subsidy to operate the clinics for the first two years, plus a return on that investment, with an adequate reward for having taken the risk that everything might go wrong and all of the investment might be lost. Chapter 13 discusses investment analysis techniques available for making this type of calculation.

Break-Even Analysis

Another tool often employed to evaluate a new project's potential for profitability is break-even analysis. This technique evaluates the volume necessary for a venture to at least break even. At higher volumes the project will be profitable and at lower volumes losses would be incurred. The reason for this is that virtually all projects have some costs that do not vary as the activity level varies.

For example, once we acquire a machine, we can use it to make a few units each year, or many units. If the annual depreciation on the machine is $10,000 and we use it to make 500 units a year, part of the cost of each unit is a $20 pro rata share for using the equipment ($10,000 ÷ 500 units = $20). If the same equipment is used to make 1,000 units a year, the cost for the equipment is only $10 per unit. The higher the volume (within the capacity of the machine), the lower the cost per unit. Therefore we become more profitable as volume increases. In Chapter 11, the break-even analysis technique is discussed further.

"What-If" Analysis

Finally, a "what-if" sensitivity analysis should be undertaken. This analysis assesses what would happen if the plan's assumptions turn out to be incorrect. For example, what if the volume of sales is 10 percent below expectations? How about 20 percent? What if operating costs are 15 percent higher than planned? If such events mean the project would fail, the reader must know that. The size of the planned contingency fund may be adjusted accordingly.

The financial feasibility analysis can become quite lengthy. It is usually best to summarize all of the financial feasibility information in the body of the business plan, and put most of the detailed calculations, statements, and tables into an appendix.

Implementation/Operating Plan

The implementation plan needs to address the who, what, where, when, and how questions: Who will do the implementation? Exactly what will they do? Where will they do it? When? How? The plan needs to have timetables for hiring various personnel, buying and constructing facilities, and purchasing equipment and supplies, and a complete schedule of the start-up resources that will be needed. In many cases the plan needs to address coordination issues relative to the existing organization.

Clearly the activities that have to take place first can be predicted with a greater degree of accuracy and described in more detail. However, an overall plan is necessary. The plan should include the likely impact of delays. It should distinguish among resources needed right away, those not needed until operations begin, and those not needed until operations are well under way. It is particularly helpful to use a timeline in developing the plan, showing the various activities that will occur at different points in the timeline.

The operations portion of the plan must be as specific as possible about how this organization will operate. It must convince the reader that you have anticipated all of the elements of running the business on an on-going basis.

Key Performance Measures

The financial profitability of the venture, discussed earlier, is one of the most important performance measures. However, for most ventures it is not the only key measure. The plan should consider other outcome measures as well. Targets for sales and market share are often critical. Quality measures of the product or service are essential. Early achievement of customer satisfaction targets may also be a key to long-term success of the venture.

Summary of Strengths and Weaknesses, Including Risks

It is important to itemize not only the positive elements of the venture, but also the business risks and strategies for offsetting them. What might go wrong? What are the implications if those things do go wrong? What can we do to try to avoid those problems? What can we do to minimize the impact if they do occur anyway?

Most implementation plans at some point indicate what will happen "if everything goes according to plan." However, it is rare that at the time operations finally commence, anyone says, "Well, everything went according to plan." Unexpected things always seem to happen. What things? Well, if we could say, then they wouldn't be unexpected! But we must still make our best attempt to say what will happen to the proposed venture if everything does not go according to plan.

How a Business Plan Is Read

Most readers review the executive summary first. After that, the reader will often jump to an area of concern or an area that the reader has the most familiarity with. If the reader has great expertise in marketing, then the marketing plan may be reviewed first. If the reader concludes the plan is naive with respect to market analysis or the marketing plan, that may be as far as he or she goes. Another reader might believe that, ultimately, if the management team is inadequate no idea can succeed. So the first section reviewed might be the organizational structure and management team. Others will jump to the financial statements first.

The writer of a business plan has relatively little control over the way that the reader moves through the document. Therefore the writer should just ensure that, as the readers ask the following questions, there are satisfactory answers in the plan:

- Does the business concept make sense?
- Can and will the market support the business?
- Can the management team do the job?
- Are the financial projections realistic?
- Has management realistically assessed the risk in the venture?
- Do the economics justify the investment?

If the document cannot provide satisfactory answers to these questions, then the person preparing the plan should be the first to argue that it doesn't pay to proceed. If the answers to these questions indicate that the project is a good one, then the document should be designed to convince someone to provide the needed approvals and resources.

A Successful Business Plan

Many business proposals are never implemented. How many times is that because the idea just wasn't any good, and how often because the plan document was not compelling enough? What does a successful business plan do that an unsuccessful one does not do? First, a successful plan gets to the point quickly. Second, it brings together all data needed to make a decision in one document. However, it does not overwhelm the reader with detail. Most of the technical details can be relegated to appendices and supplements. The main document need not be more than twenty to thirty pages long. Third, it clearly defines the reason for the proposal—the business strategy. Fourth, it evaluates the strengths and weaknesses of the proposed venture or project. Fifth, it includes satisfactory consideration of implementation, operations, marketing, and financial issues. Sixth and finally, it makes a strong case that the venture is likely to be successful if implemented.

KEY CONCEPTS

Business plan—a document that provides the information needed to determine whether a proposed new business, program, or project will probably succeed or fail, and the resources needed to implement the project.

Critical questions—What is the venture? Why would we want to do it? How much profit will we make? What are the risks?

Elements of a business plan—cover memo, title page, table of contents, executive summary, description of the initiative, organizational structure, market analysis and plan, financial/resource requirement plan, feasibility analysis, implementation/operating plan, key performance measures, and a summary of strengths and weaknesses, including risks.

Financial feasibility analysis—pro forma income statements, pro forma cash flow statements, return on investment analysis, and break-even analysis.

Ten

Capital Structure—Long-Term Debt and Equity Financing

Organizations need resources to be able to buy land, buildings, equipment, and supplies. The money needed to acquire these assets is referred to as the organization's *capital*. Where does a business get the capital it needs to operate? Once the business is well established, capital can come at least partly from profits. But reinvestment of profits may not provide enough resources for everything the organization wants to do. And during the early life of any business, other sources of capital are essential.

The dominant sources of capital are stock issuance, referred to as *equity financing*, and loans, referred to as *debt financing*. The choices made with respect to obtaining resources determine the *capital structure* of the firm. The capital structure of the organization, therefore, represents the right-hand side of the balance sheet: liabilities and stockholders' equity.

COMMON STOCK

A dominant source of capital in the early life of most corporations is the issuance of *common stock*. Common stockholders own a share of the corporation's assets, have the right to vote to elect the board of directors, are entitled to a proportionate share of distributions (such as dividends), and can freely sell their ownership interest. Common stockholders invest their money, hoping to benefit from dividends and/or increases in the value of the stock.

Once a company is well established, common stock is often issued as a result of mergers (where we pay for the acquired company with stock) or to managers as a result of various compensation arrangements.

However, common stock is generally not used to raise capital at that point because of the potential to dilute the share of the company owned by the current owners.

Dividends are paid to shareholders of common stock if the corporation decides to distribute some of its profits directly to its owners. Alternatively, the corporation may retain some or all of its profits for reinvestment in other potentially profitable opportunities. Hopefully this will result in even greater future profits. If so, the value of each share of stock may rise, and the stockholder will be able to sell the stock for a higher price, resulting in a profit referred to as a *capital gain*.

A significant advantage the corporation gains by issuing common stock is that there are no requirements to make payments to the stockholders. If the corporation has a bad year, at least it doesn't have to worry about getting the cash to make required payments to the common stockholders. A second significant advantage gained by issuing common stock is that it creates an equity base. This provides a safety cushion for lenders and makes it possible for the company to incur debt.

DEBT

Debt is a second major source of financing. Debt represents a loan. The borrower must pay interest and repay the amount borrowed. In order for a company to be stable, a substantial portion of the firm's debt will generally be in the form of long-term debt. This avoids the potential problems created if, for example, a building is financed with a one-year loan that it intends to renew each year. What if the lender decides not to renew the loan when it comes due for payment? Long-term debt also eliminates the risk of interest rates being substantially higher when it is time to renew the loan.

Long-term debt is often issued in the form of a bond. A bond is a debt instrument in which investors (bondholders) lend money to the company in exchange for the right to receive periodic (usually semiannual) interest payments of a set amount on set dates, plus repayment of principal at a maturity date. Bondholders can sell their bonds to other investors in the same way that stock may be sold. Failure to meet these obligations puts the organization at peril of bankruptcy. Interest payments on debt are tax-deductible. This tax treatment lessens the effective cost of debt to the organization.

PREFERRED STOCK

Preferred stock is a hybrid with characteristics of both stock and debt. It is part of stockholders' equity. However, in most respects it is like a bond. The dividends to preferred stockholders are paid at a predetermined rate, much like the interest rate on a bond. Unlike interest on a bond, the dividends are not tax-deductible to the corporation. Why include preferred stock in a corporation's capital structure if the payments are not deductible? The dividend payments may be deferred. When a corporation falls on hard times, it still must pay the interest due on bonds. It does not have to pay the dividends due on the preferred stock. However, dividends on preferred stock must be paid before any dividends may be paid to common shareholders. Some preferred stock is *cumulative* and some is not. With cumulative preferred stock, any dividends that have been skipped in prior years must be paid to the preferred shareholders before dividends may be paid to common shareholders. Preferred stock is often used as part of complex financing arrangements.

COST OF CAPITAL

The choice of the relative mix of stock versus debt is an important one. If the business is very profitable, greater amounts of debt result in higher earnings per share of common stock. (This is the result of something called leverage, which will be discussed in the next chapter.) However, greater amounts of debt substantially increase risk if profits start to decline.

Managers should try to strive for a capital structure that keeps the organization's *cost of capital* low. The cost of capital is a weighted average of the cost of common stock, preferred stock, and debt. The cost of debt is the interest. The cost of preferred stock is the required dividend payment. The cost of common stock is the dividend plus the growth in the value of the stock.

A reasonable level of debt tends to reduce the cost of capital. Not only does it provide the opportunity for increased profits for common shareholders, but also the interest payments, as noted above, are tax-deductible. This tax benefit substantially reduces the cost of debt relative to equity financing. On the other hand, one must always keep in mind the increase in financial risk caused by having debt. Further, if debt levels rise too high, lenders will be reluctant to provide further financing and the cost of debt will rise.

OTHER ELEMENTS OF CAPITAL STRUCTURE

In addition to common stock, preferred stock, and debt, there are several other instruments that have a place in the capital structure of the organization. These include stock options, stock rights, warrants, and convertibles.

Stock Options

Stock options give option holders the right, but not the obligation, to purchase shares of stock at some predetermined price over some specified period of time. Such options are often issued to key employees in an organization to motivate them to help the organization achieve or exceed its goals. For example, suppose that the corporation's common stock is currently selling for $50 a share. The owners of the stock would certainly like that value to increase. Employees may be given options to buy shares of stock at $60 per share. The options might expire in three years.

These options give the employees a vested interest in seeing the price of the stock go up. If the stock price fails to exceed $60, the employees will just let the options expire. However, if the stock price rises to $70, they can then pay just $60 to buy a share of stock that is worth $70.

Stock Rights

At times a corporation will want to raise money through an equity offering, but avoid the high costs of hiring an underwriting firm to sell the stock to the public. They can achieve this through a *rights* offering. A stock right gives the holder the right to buy a share of stock at a stated price. Usually the stated price is somewhat less than the current market price.

Stock rights are usually offered in proportion to a stockholder's current holdings. For example, suppose you owned 1,000 shares of stock in XYZ Corporation, which has 10,000 shares outstanding in total. That means you currently own 10 percent of the corporation. The corporation now plans to use stock rights to issue another 2,000 shares to raise additional capital. You would be entitled to 200 rights, or 10 percent of the total offering. If the corporation's stock is currently selling for $50 a share, and the rights allow you to buy stock at $47 a share, you would either exercise the rights, buying the 200 shares, or you could sell your rights to someone else.

Warrants and Convertibles

Warrants are similar to stock rights, but they generally have an exercise price above the level of the current market. Warrants are often given as an inducement to investors to get them to do something the organization wants. For example, a corporation may have trouble raising debt. As an inducement to lend money to the corporation, warrants may be given to the lender.

Suppose that the corporation's stock currently sells for $5 a share. Warrants may be issued to a lender allowing it to buy a certain number of shares anytime in the next five years for $10 a share. Lenders do not generally share in the extreme successes of the companies they lend to. They just get earned interest and repayment of the loan. However, if this corporation's stock shoots up to $50 a share, the lender could use the warrants to buy shares for $10 and join in the success they helped cause by financing the company.

Similarly, convertible debt or convertible preferred stock is debt or preferred stock that can literally be converted into shares of common stock. This convertible feature generally allows the corporation to borrow at a lower interest rate or issue preferred stock with a lower dividend rate. The lenders or purchasers of the preferred stock will take a lower interest or dividend rate because they have the potential for large profits if the common stock rises in value.

DIVIDENDS

Some companies hold themselves out as growth companies. Growth companies generally retain all or most of their profits to use for additional, hopefully highly profitable ventures. Other companies have a policy of paying dividends to their investors on a regular basis.

Some investors prefer growth companies. By holding stock without receiving dividends, they don't have to pay tax on the dividends. Later they will sell the stock, hopefully at a higher price, and pay tax at a lower, capital gains rate. And in the meantime, the company has invested the entire amount of retained earnings in ventures that are potentially more lucrative than might be available to the investor. If the investor had received dividends, some of them would have been paid in tax, leaving less for reinvestment.

Other investors, however, need dividends to pay for current living expenses. Although they could sell off a little bit of stock from time to time to raise money for such expenses, they like to receive a steady, dependable flow of income. As a result, managers must decide on the dividend policy they wish to adopt. The choice will affect the potential buyers of the firm's stock.

At times, a corporation will issue a stock dividend. For example, there might be a 10 percent dividend, giving the investor one share for every ten shares currently owned. Or there might be a stock split such as a two-for-one split, in which case the investor gets two new shares in exchange for each old share owned. Such dividends and splits are not substantive. If you own 1,000 out of 10,000 shares, you own 10 percent of the company. After a two-for-one split, you own 2,000 out of 20,000 shares. You still own exactly 10 percent of the company.

Stock dividends and splits are generally done for psychological purposes. First, they make you feel like you have more, even if you don't. Second, they may bring the stock price down to a more reasonable trading range. For example, if a growth company keeps growing, its shares will get more and more expensive. Some individuals might be tempted to buy a stock, but might decide that its price is so high, they could only afford to buy a few shares. Instead, they buy a less expensive stock so that they own more shares.

This is illogical. They should purchase the stock of the company with the greatest percentage appreciation potential. Fifty shares of a $100 stock are more valuable than 100 shares of a $50 stock, if the $100 stock has the potential to increase by a greater percentage because of the underlying profit potential of the firm. The key should not be the number of shares, but the likely percent increase in the $5,000 investment.

Nevertheless, some companies believe that if their stock is selling for $120 per share, a three-for-one split will be beneficial. It will bring the price per share down to $40 a share. That is a value that seems substantial, but not prohibitively expensive. These companies believe that this may attract more investors, causing the stock to rise by a greater percentage than it would have without the split.

Reverse splits are also possible. If a stock is selling for a very low price, investors might be skeptical of the value of the company. A reverse split will bring the price back up to a respectable level. For example, a stock selling at $2 a share might have a one-for-ten split that would reduce the number of shares outstanding by 90 percent, but raise the price per share to $20. This latter price might be more likely to attract investor interest.

Some stock exchanges also have minimum dollar prices for the stocks on their exchange. Without a reverse split, a stock might be delisted, substantially reducing the ability of owners of the stock to find a liquid market when they wish to sell their stock.

GETTING CAPITAL

Understanding your desired capital structure is one thing. Getting the money is another. The capital to run a business is obtained by a variety of means. These include venture capital, public stock offerings, private stock placements, debt offerings, and leasing. Each of these is discussed briefly below.

Venture Capital

Start-up businesses must prove that they have a potentially viable business before the general public will be willing to invest in them. However, some investors, called *venture capitalists,* will put up money called *venture capital* or *risk capital* to help a new business get started.

If you can convince these investors that they can make a lot of money by financing your start, they can get money into your firm quickly, without the lengthy and costly process of an initial public offering (IPO) of stock. In return, they generally expect that an IPO will take place within approximately five years.

Businesses often begin with *seed capital* needed to do market research and product development. Seed money is often provided by the entrepreneurs starting the business themselves, or their friends and families. Businesses may raise up to $5 million this way with minimal government registration requirements. After this point, venture capitalists are called upon to provide the *working capital* needed to acquire supplies and hire workers to start producing the product, and in some cases the *acquisition capital* to acquire plant and equipment or a going business.

Venture capitalists rely heavily on the firm's business plan (see Chapter 9) in determining whether to invest in the business. Therefore the business plan may be a critical element in determining if the venture ever gets the initial capital it needs to get off the ground.

Be aware that many liken venture capitalists to the devil. The business may be something that you have conceived of and developed. It is your baby. However, not only will the venture capitalists take a substantial financial share of your business in exchange for their investment, but they will take a major share of the control of the business as well.

Public Stock Offerings

A public stock offering is one in which shares of the company are sold to a broad range of investors to secure capital for the organization. Issuing stock to the public is costly, time-consuming, and complicated. At times, general economic conditions or stock market conditions will have a bigger impact on the success or failure of your offering than the underlying worth of your company will have. On the other hand, to raise significant amounts of capital without incurring an unreasonable level of debt, a public stock offering may be required.

The first time a public stock offering takes place for a company, it is referred to as an Initial Public Offering (IPO). Subsequent offerings of stock to raise additional capital are referred to as *secondary issues*. Whether you are considering an IPO or a secondary offering, stock offerings to the public are expensive. The costs include payments to lawyers, accountants, printers, and *underwriters*.

Underwriters are firms that act as general contractors. They coordinate with all of the accountants, lawyers, and brokerage firms that will initially sell the stock to investors. They help prepare all of the documents that are legally required before stock can be sold, including a prospectus and registration statement.

Once you have "gone public" your organization has an equity base that makes it easier to borrow, broader public recognition, and increased personal net worth for the original owners of the business. On the other hand, there are ongoing reporting expenses, loss of control, and potential liability of officers for failure to comply with a complicated set of rules and regulations.

Private Placements

Given some of the complexities of public offerings, sometimes businesses issue stock through a private placement. The money received from venture capitalists is one type of private placement. Even when the amounts of capital to be raised are substantially higher—perhaps hundreds of millions of dollars or even several billion dollars—a private placement is sometimes possible. Selling stock directly to a few large investors avoids much of the cost of a public offering, and avoids the need to file certain elaborate documents with the government. Large insurance companies often participate in such placements, putting perhaps $50 million or $100 million into a company in exchange for stock.

Private placements can also raise funds much more quickly than a public offering can. However, in most cases the amount of money that can be raised from a private placement may be substantially less than the business might raise from a public offering. It should also be noted that, because of the risks involved to the investor, government regulations tend to prohibit all but sophisticated investors from participating in such placements.

Bond Offerings

Bonds can be issued through private placements or public offerings in the same way as stocks are. As with stocks, private placements are simpler and less expensive, but don't have the ability to raise as much money as a public offering.

Bonds are a particularly good alternative to bank financing because they can be for large amounts of money, they can extend for long periods of time (typically thirty years), providing stability, and they eliminate the intermediary. For example, a bank might pay 4 percent to a depositor and then lend the depositor's money to a corporation for 9 percent. The 5 percent difference represents the bank's costs and profits. If the corporation issues a bond at an interest rate of 6.5 percent, it will pay 2.5 percent less than the bank charges, and the ultimate investors will receive 2.5 percent more than they would have received from the bank. The investors have more risk than they would if they deposited their money in the bank. The corporation has greater costs and legal compliance issues than it would if it borrowed the money from a bank. For a large loan, it is worth paying these higher costs to get a lower interest rate.

Leasing

Another source of financing is leasing. Someone buys an asset, such as a building, and rents it to a business that wants to use that asset. The business using the asset is a lessee and the owner of the asset is a lessor. Leasing is very similar to having borrowed money and purchased the asset directly. Therefore leases are generally considered to be a form of debt financing. Management and tax issues related to leasing are discussed in Chapter 14.

KEY CONCEPTS

Capital—the money needed by the firm in order to acquire resources.

Capital structure—the mix of debt and equity used to finance the firm.

> *Equity financing*—*capital* provided in exchange for an ownership interest, typically through the issuance of stock.
>
> *Debt financing*—*capital* provided in the form of loans.

Stock option—security that gives the holder the right to purchase shares of stock at some predetermined price, usually above market value.

Stock right—security that gives the holder the right to buy a share of stock at a stated price, usually below market value.

Sources of capital—venture capital, public stock offerings, private stock placements, debt offerings, and leasing.

Eleven

Leverage

A fundamental decision made by any business is the degree to which it incurs *fixed costs*. A fixed cost is one that remains the same regardless of the level of operations. As sales increase, fixed costs don't increase. The degree to which a firm locks into fixed costs is referred to as its *leverage position*. The more highly leveraged a firm, the riskier it is because of the obligations related to fixed costs that must be met whether the firm is having a good year or not. At the same time, the more highly leveraged, the greater the profits during good times. This presents a classic problem of making a decision whereby there is a trade-off between risk and return.

There are two major types of leverage, financial and operating. *Financial leverage* is specifically the extent to which a firm gets its cash resources from borrowing (debt) as opposed to issuance of additional shares of capital stock (equity). The greater the debt compared to equity, the more highly leveraged the firm, because debt legally obligates the firm to annual interest payments. These interest payments represent a fixed cost.

Operating leverage is concerned with the extent to which a firm commits itself to high levels of fixed costs other than interest payments. A firm that rents property using cancelable leases has less leverage than a firm that commits itself to a long-term noncancelable lease. A firm that has substantial vertical integration has created a highly leveraged situation. Consider what happens if Executive Corporation vertically integrates by acquiring its raw materials supplier, Embiay, Inc. Raw materials will now cost the company less, because it doesn't have to buy them from an outside firm. But when times are bad, the firm will have to bear the fixed costs associated with the Embiay subsidiary. Had there still been two sep-

135

arate companies, Executive could have simply slowed its purchases of raw materials from Embiay without having to bear Embiay's fixed costs. In the cases of both financial and operating leverage, the crucial question is, how much leverage is appropriate?

FINANCIAL LEVERAGE

Let's start our discussion of financial leverage with an example. Assume you were to buy a small building as a piece of investment property. You buy the building for $100,000 and pay the full amount in cash.

Suppose that a year later you sell the building for $130,000. Your pretax profit is $30,000. This is a 30 percent pretax return on your original investment of $100,000.

As an alternative to paying the full $100,000 cash for the investment, you might put $10,000 cash down and borrow $90,000 from the bank at 15 percent interest. This time when you sell the property for $130,000, you repay the $90,000 loan to the bank, plus $13,500 interest. After deducting your original $10,000 investment, $16,500 is left as a pretax profit. This is a pretax return of 165 percent on your $10,000 investment. Compare the 30 percent we calculated earlier to this rate of return of 165 percent. That's leverage!

Note that we had a net profit of $30,000 without leverage, but only $16,500 in the leveraged case. Although we earned a higher return in the latter case, we had less profits because of the interest we had to pay. In the unleveraged case we had invested $100,000 of our money, but in the leveraged case we had invested only $10,000. If we have additional investment opportunities available to us, we could have invested our full $100,000, borrowed $900,000, and had a pretax profit of $165,000 on the same $100,000 investment that yields $30,000 in the unleveraged situation. Financial leverage can not only increase your yield from investments, but can also allow you to consider projects that are much larger than would be feasible without borrowing.

Suppose, however, that the property was sold after one year for $70,000 rather than $130,000. On a $100,000 unleveraged investment, the loss would be $30,000 before taxes. This would be a 30 percent loss on our original $100,000 investment.

In the leveraged case, the loss will be magnified. We would have to repay the bank the $90,000 loan plus $13,500 of interest. These payments total $103,500, which is $33,500 greater than the $70,000 proceeds from the sale. Further, we've lost our initial $10,000 investment. The total loss is $43,500 before taxes. On our initial investment of $10,000, this constitutes a loss of 435 percent. That's leverage too!

Clearly the firm must decide if the 165 percent possible gain is worth the risk of a 435 percent loss. Whether it is or not depends on the likelihood of the increase in value versus the probability of a decline. If the project really were a sure thing, leverage would certainly make sense. Rarely are projects sure things. Yet, managers should try to decide how confident they are of the success of a project, and weigh that confidence against the implications for the firm if the project does indeed fail.

Some managers and firms tend to be more averse to risk than others. Usually stockholders align themselves with a firm that they feel does things the way they want them done. A person dependent on a steady level of income from stock dividends might prefer to buy the stock of a firm that shuns leverage and prefers a steady, if lesser, income. A person looking for large potential appreciation in stock price might prefer the stock of a firm that is highly leveraged.

The Rule of OPM

In making a decision regarding whether additional funds should be raised by debt or equity, there are several factors to be considered. The first rule of financial leverage is that it only pays to borrow if the interest rate is less than the rate of return on the money borrowed. We can refer to this as the "rule of OPM"—other people's money. If your firm can borrow money and invest it at a high enough rate so that the loan can be repaid with interest and still leave some after-tax profit for your stockholders, then your stockholders have profited on OPM. They have made extra profit with no extra investment. This greatly magnifies the rate of return on the amount they invested.

Stability of Earnings

What factors should you consider in trying to arrive at a reasonable level of leverage? To a great degree, your desired leverage position depends on the degree to which your sales and profits fluctuate. The greater the fluctuation in sales and profits, the less leverage you can afford. If your firm is a stable, noncyclical firm that makes money in good times and bad, then use of OPM will help improve the rate of return earned by your shareholders. If cyclical factors in your industry or the economy at large tend to cause your business to have both good and bad years, then debt entails a greater risk.

For example, the airline industry, with its huge capital requirements for jet purchases, has traditionally been highly leveraged. The results have been very large profits during the good years, but substantial losses during periods when air traffic falls off or competition is particularly intense. As a result, a number of airlines have gone out of business.

Cyclical factors shouldn't scare companies away from having any debt at all. The key is to accumulate no more interest and principal repayment obligations than can reasonably be met in bad times as well as good. Ultimately, considering the variability of your profit stream, a decision must be made regarding the level of extra risk you are willing to take to achieve a higher potential rate of return on stockholder investments.

OPERATING LEVERAGE

While financial leverage is an issue that is almost strictly the domain of the firm's highest levels of management together with its financial officers, operating leverage is an issue that directly affects the line managers of the firm. The level of operating leverage a firm selects should not be decided without input from the managers directly involved in the production process. For example, one of the most significant operating leverage issues is the choice of technology levels. Selection of the highest level of technology available is not always in the best interests of the business.

Suppose that we are opening a chain of copy centers. We are faced with the choice of renting a relatively slow copy machine, or the newest technology machine, which is considerably faster. The faster machine is also considerably more expensive to lease. It will generally be the case that newer technology has a higher fixed cost and lower *variable cost* than the older technology. Variable costs are those that vary directly with volume. If we double the number of copies made, we double the amount of paper, printing ink toner, and labor time needed for making the copies. One of the principle functions of new technology is to reduce the variable costs of production.

It may turn out that a machine that can reduce the variable costs is more expensive to make, and thus has a higher purchase or lease price than the older generation machine. However, even if it doesn't cost more to make, its manufacturer will charge more for the new machine than for the older machine. Intuitively, if the new machine is in some respect better than the old machine and doesn't cost more to buy, then no one will buy the older machine. Thus, anytime we see two technologies being sold side by side, such as slow and fast copy machines, we can expect the faster machine to have a higher rental fee or purchase price, and therefore a higher fixed cost.

Let's assume that we could lease the slower, older technology copy machine for $10,000 per year, or a faster, newer technology copy machine for $25,000 per year. Both produce photocopies of equal quality. Both use the same quantities of paper and ink toner, but the faster machine requires less operator time. Therefore, the labor cost is much lower for the faster machine. As a result, the variable cost of copies on the slow machine is 6 cents each, while the variable cost of copies from the fast machine is only 3 cents each. Is the faster machine the better bet?

That depends. Suppose we sell each copy we make for 10 cents. Then, for each copy we sell we receive 10 cents and spend an extra 6 cents or 3 cents (depending on our choice of machine) for the variable costs. The difference between the price and the variable costs is referred to as the *contribution margin.*

CONTRIBUTION MARGIN = PRICE – VARIABLE COST

This margin represents the amount of money available to be used to pay fixed costs and provide the firm with a profit.

If we use the slower machine, we receive 10 cents and spend 6 cents, leaving 4 cents to be used toward paying the rent on the copy machine. If we sell enough copies, there will be enough individual contributions of 4 cents apiece to pay the full $10,000 rent and leave some receipts for a profit.

Break-Even Analysis

How many copies must we make before we "break even?" Break-even analysis requires dividing the fixed costs by the contribution margin per unit. This is equivalent to saying, "How many times do we have to get a

contribution of 4 cents before we have covered our fixed cost of $10,000?"
The break-even point can be computed using the following formula:

$$\text{Break-Even Quantity} = \frac{\text{Fixed Costs}}{\text{Price} - \text{Variable Cost}}$$

or

$$\text{Break-Even Quantity} = \frac{\text{Fixed Costs}}{\text{Contribution Margin}}$$

For the slower machine, $10,000 divided by 4 cents equals 250,000. We
need to make and sell a quarter of a million copies to break even. For the
faster machine, the contribution margin is 7 cents per unit, because the
price is 10 cents and the variable costs are only 3 cents. The $25,000 rental
fee for the fast machine, divided by a 7-cent contribution margin per unit,
results in a break-even point of 357,143 copies. Apparently, we can make
a profit on the slower machine at a lower output level than we can with the
faster machine.

If we sell more copies than the break-even point for the machine we
have, we make a profit. If we sell fewer copies than the break-even point,
we lose money. Consider sales of 300,000 copies per year. Our revenue
would be $30,000 at 10 cents per copy. For the slow machine, our costs
would be $10,000 fixed rental cost, plus $18,000 of variable cost (300,000
copies at 6 cents). The total cost would be $28,000 and we would have a
pretax profit of $2,000. For the fast machine, the fixed rental cost is
$25,000. The variable cost would be $9,000 (300,000 copies at 3 cents).
The total cost would be $34,000 and we would have a loss of $4,000. We
are above the break-even point for the slow machine, but below the break-
even point for the faster machine.

If we sell 400,000 copies, we might expect the faster machine to
come out better than the slower machine. After all, both are operating at a
level above their break-even point. The faster machine is earning a profit
of 7 cents for every extra copy above the break-even point, while the
slower machine is only earning a profit of 4 cents a copy. While there is
some truth to this reasoning, we must be careful. The slower machine has
been earning profits, albeit not much per copy, ever since the 250,000
copy point was passed. The faster machine has been earning profits, albeit
a larger amount per copy, only since passing 357,143 copies. You can't

assume that the faster machine is better for us as long as our volume exceeds its break-even point. In this case, our revenue is $40,000 (400,000 copies at 10 cents). The slow machine has costs of $10,000 rental plus $24,000 variable (400,000 copies at 6 cents), leaving a pretax profit of $6,000, while the fast machine has a $25,000 rental plus $12,000 of variable cost (400,000 copies at 3 cents). The faster machine is making a profit of $3,000 now, but that's only half as much the slow machine.

At 500,000 copies, the two machines produce an equal pretax profit of $10,000. Above that point, the faster machine generates a higher profit because every extra copy yields a 7-cent profit as compared to the 4 cent profit from the slower machine. On the other hand, for each copy less than 500,000, the slower machine has a higher profit, because its profits go down only 4 cents per copy, while the faster machine's profits fall off at a rate of 7 cents per copy.

Which machine should we lease? That depends on our expected volume and how sure we are of our projections. If we expect to always make more than 500,000 copies, the fast machine is preferred. If we will always make fewer than 500,000 copies, the slow machine is preferred. If we expect to make fewer than 250,000 copies, we should get out of the business.

The problem of operating leverage that faces us is what to do if we expect to make more than 500,000 copies, in general, but sometimes it may be less than that. We can play it safe with the slower machine and be sure of a profit, or at least not a huge loss. We have a lower fixed cost (rent of $10,000) and therefore a lower operating leverage. On the other hand, we can get the faster machine that produces a much higher profit if sales are good. In that case we take a chance. We have a higher fixed cost (rent of $25,000) and therefore a higher operating leverage. If sales fall off, profits will decline much faster, and any loss will be much larger than it would have been.

Again, as in the case of financial leverage, we are trading off risk and return. The less the variability in our production volume, the lower the risk associated with incurring the larger fixed costs in order to achieve a higher profit.

Technology is only one example. Should we buy our buildings and equipment or rent them? If we buy them, we incur fixed charges even if volume falls off. If we rent with relatively short leases, the annual cost is likely to be greater, but it is easier to terminate the fixed costs in the face of business downturns. Another operating leverage decision is whether to acquire plant and facilities and manufacture all components of our product or to subcontract the manufacturing and merely do assembly. With subcontracting, we can terminate contracts when demand declines. If we buy the plant and equipment, the fixed costs remain even when demand falls off.

Ultimately, these decisions fall into management's lap. Once managers consider the likelihood of sales variability, a decision has to be made as to whether the risks associated with the fixed costs of financial and operating leverage are worth the higher potential return. Issues of vertical integration, buying versus renting, and choice of technology can have vital competitive implications.

Both these financial decisions—how much financial leverage and how much operating leverage the firm should have—are fundamental to the firm. We can simply let things develop, handling items on a crisis basis, or we can make such decisions on a rational, planned basis. In Part IV, one of the topics examined is the solvency of the firm. Is the firm able to meet its interest costs and other fixed obligations? More often than not, the firms that have solvency problems are the ones that didn't formally address the leverage issues head on.

KEY CONCEPTS

Leverage—Represents locking in a set level of fixed cost. As revenues rise, these costs don't rise, so profits rise rapidly. As revenues decline, these costs remain, so profits fall rapidly.

Financial leverage—the degree to which the firm chooses to finance its operations by borrowing money, thus locking in fixed interest charges.

The rule of OPM—If the return from invested capital exceeds the current interest rate on borrowed funds, then the firm's owners benefit if the firm borrows, thus allowing the owners to profit from the use of other people's money.

Operating leverage—the degree to which the firm chooses to lock in fixed costs other than interest in order to leverage profits during good times. Examples of high operating leverage are vertical integration and the use of high technology.

Stability of earnings—The less variable the firm's earnings, the lower the risks and the greater the advantages of being highly leveraged.

Twelve
Strategic Planning and Budgeting

Management needs vision. Great managers are those individuals under whose stewardship organizations make great strides forward. In some cases, vision may come from inspiration that only a few people ever have. In many cases, however, vision is a result of hard work and careful planning. It takes careful thought and planning to excel. What is the organization trying to achieve? Why does it want to achieve that goal? How does it intend to translate that goal into results? Successful managers and organizations specifically address these questions, rather than simply letting things happen. This is accomplished through a process of strategic planning and budgeting.

STRATEGIC PLAN

A *strategic plan* is a document that defines a broad set of goals for the organization and selects the primary approaches that the organization will take to achieve those goals. Generally, strategic plans do not have specific financial targets. However, they set the stage for specific, detailed budgets that will be established to achieve the goals.

For example, suppose that the mission of a soup kitchen was to ensure an adequate supply of nutritious food for the homeless. It could attempt to achieve that mission by any of a number of different approaches. It could be a lobbying organization, raising money and using it to lobby for legislation requiring the government to provide nutritious food for the homeless. That would be one strategy. Another strategy would be to solicit donations of food and money, and to use those resources to prepare and serve meals directly to the homeless. Suppose that the soup kitchen chose the latter strategy.

In addition to a strategy, the strategic plan should have goals. For example, given its strategy to directly provide meals, the soup kitchen might adopt the following two goals (among others):

- Increase the percentage of the target population served from 20 percent to 60 percent within five years.
- Expand funding sources to cover the increase in services.

Once you have a strategic plan that identifies your strategies and goals, the next step is to translate the goals of the strategic plan into attainable objectives.

LONG-RANGE PLAN

While the strategic plan establishes goals and broad strategies, the *long-range plan* (sometimes referred to as the *operating plan*) considers how to achieve those goals. Long-range plans establish the major activities that will have to be carried out in the coming three to five years. This process provides a link between the strategic plan and the day-to-day activities of the organization.

For example, one element of the strategic plan for the soup kitchen is expansion of meals provided from 20 percent to 60 percent of the target population. This cannot be achieved by simply carrying out the existing daily routine, day after day, year after year. The managers will have to determine what must happen to attain the goals. A variety of approaches or tactics might be considered and developed into a long-range plan.

The managers decide that the most efficient way to expand from 20 percent to 60 percent coverage (the goal) would be to add three new locations and four more vehicles (specific tactics to achieve the goal). Money will be needed to buy equipment and vehicles, and to pay rent, buy food, and hire staff. The long-range plan will also have to consider how to raise the money and when to spend it (more tactics). A reasonable long-range plan for the soup kitchen might include the following objectives:

Year 1:   Establish fund-raising campaign, and begin fund-raising. Raise enough money to open one new site.

Year 2:   Add a food distribution/soup kitchen location. Raise additional money to acquire and operate a vehicle and open another location. Solicit more restaurants for leftover food donations.

Year 3:   Add another food distribution/soup kitchen location and a new vehicle. Raise additional money to acquire and operate a vehicle and open another location. Solicit more restaurants for leftover food donations.

Year 4:   Add another food distribution/soup kitchen location and a new vehicle. Raise additional money to acquire and operate two vehicles. Solicit more restaurants for leftover food donations.

Year 5:   Add two new vehicles. Raise additional money to begin replacement of old kitchen equipment and old vehicles. Get enough contributions to at least reach a steady state where replacements take place as needed.

As can be seen from the above objectives, unless planning is done in year one to raise money, the organization will never be able to undertake the acquisition and expansion in years two through five. The organization cannot be satisfied with raising enough to get through the coming year. For it to thrive, rather than merely survive, it must think ahead. The long-range plan provides the opportunity to think ahead prior to making budgets for the coming year.

The objectives included in the long-range plan can be thought of as quantified targets. These targets can relate to both inputs and outputs. For example, we can think in terms of specific fund-raising objectives, specifying the total dollar amount of donations we plan to receive each year over the coming five years. We can also think in terms of the specific number of delivery vans to be purchased. These targets or objectives make it possible to create specific detailed budgets for the organization in financial terms.

DEFINITION AND ROLE OF BUDGETS

A budget is simply a plan. Despite any unpleasant connotations the term has picked up over time, a budget is simply a plan. In business, budgets are formalized (that is, written down) and quantitative (expressed in dollars).

One reason for having a budget is to take the strategic and long-range plans and fill in the specific details to achieve their targets. A second reason for having a budget is to allow for effective evaluation. A third reason for having budgets is to force managers to think ahead. When plans are made well in advance, more choices are generally available than when decisions are made on a fire-fighting or crisis basis. Advance planning provides the necessary lead time for effective decisions. Once decisions are made, they must be acted upon by the organization. The fourth key use for a budget is as a tool of communication and coordination. Even if the chief executive officer has great plans for the organization, they can only be put into operation if they are communicated to the appropriate individuals in the firm. The budget serves this purpose.

THE MASTER BUDGET

The master budget contains a projection of each of the key financial statements, as well as a variety of supporting schedules giving the assumptions and calculations used as a basis for the components of each statement. The master budget is generally broken down into an operating budget and a financial budget. The operating budget provides all the information necessary to prepare a budgeted income statement. It includes revenue projections; cost-of-goods-sold projections, which include the projected costs of materials, labor, and overhead for a manufacturing firm, or cost of purchases for a merchandising firm; selling expenses; administrative expenses; and finally financing (interest cost) expenses. These separate elements are combined into a projected income statement. Exhibit 12-1 provides an example of an operating budget. The financial budget includes the cash budget and financial statement projections other than the income statement.

Excel Exercise

Template 9 may be used to prepare an operating budget for your organization. The template is included on the CD that accompanies this book.

EXHIBIT 12-1.
Executive Corporation
Operating Budget
Projected Revenues and Expenditures

Revenues	
Product Sales	$14,000,000
Other	500,000
Total Revenues	$14,500,000
Expenses	
Cost of Goods Sold	
Labor	$ 5,000,000
Materials	4,800,000
Overhead	1,700,000
Selling Expenses	1,500,000
Administration	500,000
Interest	600,000
Total Expenses	$14,100,000
Profit	$ 400,000

In addition to the operating and financial budgets, there are often special capital budgets that review all of the capital projects the firm is considering. These projects are evaluated according to the methods discussed in Chapter 13. Furthermore, the master budget includes performance reports. The area of budgeting is primarily thought of in terms of planning because the definition of a budget is a plan. However, budgeting encompasses both planning and control. Frequent comparison of actual and budgeted results, with investigation and correction of problems when we stray from our budget, helps managers control operations.

Budgets are generally prepared annually. Within the annual budget, we usually prepare monthly projections. This allows us to make evaluations after each month and to make necessary adjustments throughout the year.

BUDGET PREPARATION

Preliminaries

The first step in budget preparation is the completion of an environmental statement. The firm cannot effectively plan for the coming year without a clearly stated idea of what its position is vis-à-vis its suppliers, competitors, and customers. An annual evaluation of industry trends, changes in customer base, technological changes, and so on can help the firm to better determine where it should be going.

The next step is for top management to develop a set of general objectives and policies. This statement should be a broad-based look at what the firm hopes to achieve. Is the coming year one of holding the line against competitors, or is it to be a year of rapid growth? Is the firm looking for domestic expansion, or establishment of foreign markets? Does the firm expect to increase the market share in existing products, or to be aggressive in the introduction of new products? If top management communicates the desired direction of the firm, middle management can set out to move in that direction.

Before the actual budget can be developed, a set of assumptions must be adopted. What will inflation be in the coming year? What actions do we expect competition to take that might affect our sales or the price of our product? Will suppliers be raising their prices? Will new sources of raw materials become available? Are there going to be more significant shifts in consumer demand? All of these and many more questions must be answered; but there is no way to know the answer, so assumptions must be made and communicated to those directly involved in the budget preparation process.

Finally, specific, measurable goals should be established. Here we are not dealing simply with the general direction of the firm, but with the actual operating objectives. For example, sales should increase by 10 percent and profits by 15 percent. These are two ambitious objectives—more often than not, a firm that doesn't budget, or that doesn't control the budget, will not have much success in achieving such goals.

Forecasting

A critical step in the budget process is the preparation of forecasts of what would happen under a variety of alternatives. What if we raise our price? What if we import partially assembled parts? What if we automate? In all of these cases, how much will we sell, at what price, and at what cost?

Forecasts can be quite simple, such as a projection that indicates that what happened this year would happen again next year. Or they can be based on extremely complex mathematical formulas. Most forecasting is based, to a major extent, on historical patterns. An accurate forecast must also consider any changes that may make the future different from the past. These changes can be due to various decisions we've made, improved technology, initiatives by competitors, changes in laws, world events, etc.

Computers make sophisticated forecasting techniques accessible to managers. Some software programs allow the user to select from a range of statistical forecasting methods, or to simply have the computer automatically select the best forecasting method for your data.

Some software programs can take seasonal patterns into account. If a firm has times of the year that are generally very busy or unusually slow for production, sales, or both, a forecast for the year as a whole is not fully satisfactory. A manager gains a significant advantage by knowing which months are likely to be unusually busy or slow, and how busy or slow. Such information may be used to minimize the cost of staffing and inventory throughout the year, while still allowing for adequate staff and inventory during peak periods of demand.

Data Needs for Forecasting

The forecasting process should begin with some basic assumptions about the likely future of the industry. Too often managers are myopic, looking within their own firms and missing industrywide cycles or trends. If the future sales outlook for the industry is turning negative, managers cannot ignore that information just because their own sales have historically been strong.

Working from a base of the outlook for the industry, managers can then turn their attention to a forecast of the company's sales. Sales in the future are often largely a reflection of sales in the past. Information on how many units of each product or service have been sold in the last five to ten years provides a basis for the forecast of the future. Techniques to use this historical data for the forecast are discussed below. Once the historical data for sales is used to predict future sales, that information can be used to forecast the necessary materials, labor, and other expenses.

What to Do When Historical Data Are Not Available

At times historical data may not be available. This is generally the case when a new service or program is suggested. How can forecasts be made in the absence of such data? To some extent, one can rely on engineering calculations. A determination can be made of exactly what resources should be required for each unit of the service provided. Another useful approach is to base such forecasts on the collective opinion of groups of individuals. Industrial experience has shown that when a team of experts arrives at a consensus, subjective forecasts can be reasonably accurate. There are two techniques for achieving consensus: Nominal Group and Delphi. Both approaches select a team of individuals who are likely to have reasoned insights with respect to the item being forecast.

The Nominal Group technique brings individuals together in a structured meeting. Each member writes down a forecast. The forecasts are then presented to the entire group without discussion. Once all of the forecasts have been revealed, the reasoning behind each one is discussed. Through a repetitive process, a group decision is eventually made.

There are weaknesses to this approach. In some cases it may be impossible to get the group to reach consensus. A more common problem concerns politics and personalities. As members of the group defend their forecasts, extraneous issues having to do with whose idea it is may bias the group decision. Some individuals may be reluctant to share their ideas in public for a variety of reasons.

The Delphi technique overcomes those weaknesses. In the Delphi approach, the group never meets. All forecasts are presented in writing to a group leader who provides summaries to all group members. After several rounds, a decision is made based on the collective responses. The weakness of the Delphi method is that it takes more time and is more cumbersome than the Nominal Group method. But, by avoiding a face-to-face meeting, the Delphi technique avoids confrontation. Decisions are based more on logic than on politics or personality.

Forecasts Based on Historical Data

In cases for which historical data do exist, forecasting is somewhat easier. Knowledge about the past is often an excellent starting point for predicting the future.

The simplest approach to forecasting using a series of historical data points is simply to take an average. The data for five years can be aggregated and divided by five to get an estimate for the coming year. Such an averaging approach, however, assumes that there is no underlying pattern, and that results are essentially random.

A somewhat superior approach is the linear regression statistical technique. This method plots historical points and uses the information to develop a trend line. That trend is projected into the future to make a forecast. This is generally more accurate than a simple average. The limitation of regression is that it is based on a straight line. Straight lines do a poor job of forecasting seasonal patterns.

However, a number of forecasting software programs, such as SmartForecasts for Windows,* can produce curved-line forecasts. Such forecasts can more closely match a seasonal historical pattern. This results in a much more accurate forecast. These programs may be used to forecast overall sales or expenses, sales of a given product, expenses of a given type, and virtually anything else for which the organization has historical data.

Consider Table 12-1. This table, for simplicity, provides quarterly data. Managers can further improve the usefulness of their forecasts by using monthly data. Figure 12-1 provides a time-series forecast graph from the SmartForecasts program. Time is shown on the horizontal axis, beginning with the first quarter of Year 1 and ending with the last quarter of the Year 4. Data from the first three years are used to forecast the fourth year. Sales in units are shown on the vertical axis.

*SmartForecasts for Windows. Belmont, MA: SmartSoftware, Inc. (800) 762-7899.

TABLE 12-1.
Historical Data

QUARTER	SALES VOLUME
Year 1	
July–September	20,000
October–December	23,000
January–March	27,000
April–June	20,000
Year 2	
July–September	21,000
October–December	25,000
January–March	29,000
April–June	20,000
Year 3	
July–September	19,000
October–December	24,000
January–March	26,000
April–June	21,000

Figure 12-1. Forecast for Table 12-1 Data, Using Curvilinear Forecasting

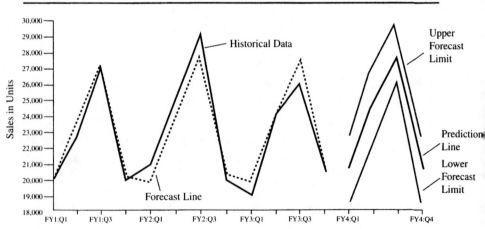

The solid line from FY1:Q1 to FY3:Q4 in the graph in Figure 12-1 represents the actual historical data points connected from quarter to quarter. The dashed line is the forecast line. For the future year being forecast, the prediction line is bracketed above and below by gray lines that indicate a *forecast interval*. It is expected that 90 percent of the time, the actual results for the coming year will remain within that range. The forecast interval can be set at a different level if desired. For example, the range could be set at 99 percent, so that the actual result would fall outside of the predicted range in only one out of 100 predictions.

Table 12-2, generated by the computer program, provides the forecast for each of the next four quarters, along with lower and upper limits. This is extremely valuable managerial data. Not only do we have a forecast, but we also have detailed information that can be used for planning. For example, the third quarter will likely have a high rate of activity, but substantial reductions are likely in the fourth quarter. Based on the upper limit column in Table 12-2, we know that we need to plan on only enough labor and materials to make 22,252 units in the fourth quarter, at most.

TABLE 12-2.
Forecast and Forecast Interval Limits for Figure 12-1

| | APPROXIMATE 90 PERCENT FORECAST INTERVAL | | |
TIME PERIOD	LOWER LIMIT	FORECAST	UPPER LIMIT
FY4:Q1	18,228	19,998	21,768
FY4:Q2	22,240	24,010	25,780
FY4:Q3	25,432	27,330	29,228
FY4:Q4	18,433	20,343	22,252

Given that software programs such as this one are extremely easy to use, one cannot help but be impressed by the potential for improvements in a wide variety of forecasts throughout the organization. Nevertheless, managers should always bear in mind that forecasts are merely educated guesses about the future. As a manager you know more about your business than any formula or mathematical technique. Managers should rely on their judgment to modify forecasts to take into account factors the computer software may not have considered. Once forecasts have been made, the budgets can be prepared.

Departmental Budgets

Having completed the preliminary budget activities, and having prepared forecasts for the key elements of the budget, the next step is the actual preparation of the budget. The organizational budget consists of a compilation of the operating and capital budgets for the various departments. Based on the total requirements for each department, cash flow projections can also be made.

Each department must compile its budget based on the specific costs that it expects to encounter and, if it is a revenue center, the revenues that it projects as well. Budgets should be as detailed as possible, to ensure that all relevant items have been included. The budgeting task sometimes seems very complicated because of the specific forms that any given organization requires to be completed. However, the essential process is not complicated. Each organization strives to get an itemization of the various costs that it will encounter for the coming year, and the associated revenues.

Once these itemizations are completed, there is a process of evaluation. Are the requests reasonable? Do the departments need all of the resources they are requesting, or are they building fat into the budget? If the budget is carried out as specified, will it result in a satisfactory outcome for the organization? Will sales be high enough? Will costs be low enough?

Even if a department's budget is reasonable, there may still be limitations on what the organization can, or will, approve. It is possible that a series of capital expenditures, even if profitable in the long term, will require more cash than the organization believes will be available. Thus, there is an interplay between the operating and capital budgets prepared by departments, and the resulting projections of cash flows prepared by the financial office. All of the elements of the master budget must come together to result in a satisfactory outcome for the organization before the individual components can be approved.

THE CASH BUDGET

The *cash budget* is a plan for expected cash receipts and payments. For organizations using an accrual basis of accounting, the cash budget provides vital information. The operating budget focuses on revenues and expenses, regardless of when revenue is collected in cash or expenses are paid. However, organizations cannot afford to run out of cash, even if they are making profits! The cash budget provides the information needed to know if there will be adequate cash on hand at all times.

The cash budget allows the organization either to arrange for sources of cash to alleviate an expected shortage (such as a loan from the bank) or to change the organization's planned revenues and expenses to avoid the shortage.

Monthly cash budgets are typically prepared for the coming year. Cash flow forecasting is complicated by the fact that collections and payments are not constant throughout the year. Monthly cash budgets assist in planning for short-term investments and loans during the year.

Cash budgets start with the cash balance expected to be on hand at the beginning of the month. The expected cash receipts for the month are added to this beginning balance to find the expected available cash for the month. Expected payments are subtracted to find the anticipated balance at the end of each month. Surpluses can be invested and are subtracted from the balance. Deficits require borrowing. The amount to be borrowed is added to the balance. The final projected balance for each month becomes the beginning balance for the next month. The general format for cash budgets is as follows:

Beginning Cash
+ Cash Receipts
Subtotal: Available Cash
– Less Cash Payments
Subtotal
+ Borrowing or – Investments
Ending Cash Balance

It is important to bear in mind that depreciation expense is not a cash payment. When a long-term asset is acquired, the payment for that asset is a cash outflow. However, as the asset is used over time, the depreciation expense charged each year does not require a cash payment. Therefore depreciation does not appear in a cash budget.

Conversely, operating budgets include interest expense, but not loan repayments. Cash budgets include payments for both interest and repayments of loans.

Excel Exercise

See Template 10 for a worksheet you may use to develop a detailed, monthly cash budget for your organization. The template is on the CD that accompanies this book.

ZERO-BASED BUDGETING

Zero-based budgeting (ZBB) is an approach that requires evaluation of all proposed spending. It gets its name from the fact that each department or program starts with a zero base of justified costs. All spending from zero on up must be explained and justified. ZBB helps to keep budgets from developing "fat." No expenditure is automatically accepted without some explanation of why the organization is better off with that expenditure.

This contrasts with the more typical *incremental budgeting* that focuses on just the increase in a budget. With incremental budgeting, there is negotiation over how large an increase will be authorized. While incremental budgeting implicitly assumes that every department can spend what they spent the prior year and then some, ZBB requires justification of all spending, not just the increase from one year to the next.

ZBB argues that some departments might have a need for a 10 percent budget increase, while another might not need any increase at all. Some departments should even be cut, because they no longer have needs that justify the budget level of the previous year. As a result of this philosophy, ZBB is better at allocating an organization's resources to the areas that have the greatest needs.

However, the evaluation of each and every item in each budget is a very time-consuming process. Some organizations use a rotating approach, with each department receiving a thorough ZBB review every three (or four or five) years, and incremental budgets in the intervening years.

ZBB not only requires justification of all costs in the budget, but it also focuses on alternatives. Information is collected into a decision package. This package provides the analysis of the program or department being evaluated. It contains broad information about why something is being done, the negative effects of not doing it, and the costs and benefits. One of the key elements of a decision package is a statement of alternatives.

ZBB requires evaluation of alternatives in a variety of ways. Different programs aimed at the same goal should be compared. Different ways of performing each given program should be compared. Different quality and quantities of each program should be compared. For example, if we could buy a top-model machine to make our product, or a middle-of-the-road model, ZBB requires explicit evaluation of the extra costs and extra benefits related to the top-model machine. By examining alternative approaches and the costs and benefits of each approach, managers are placed in a better position to make informed choices when allocating limited resources. Each alternative is ranked, with the manager giving consideration to the costs and benefits of the differing approaches. As a result, ZBB is a valuable budget technique.

VARIANCE ANALYSIS: USING BUDGETS FOR CONTROL

Static Budgets

The usual master budget is a "static" budget. The static budget is used to compare expected results with actual results. Any difference is called a variance. If the amount actually spent on an expense item is greater than the budgeted amount, it is considered to be an unfavorable variance. On the other hand, if less was spent than anticipated, it is a favorable variance.

Within this framework, the more detailed the budget is, the greater the amount of control we can exercise. For example, if we know only the total budget, we have very little information. Consider the case of hypothetical Bud Jet Corporation. In Exhibit 12-2 we see that Bud Jet had total manufacturing costs of $200,000 more than expected for a particular month. Why? From the information in this exhibit it is hard to tell. If we had information by department, we would have a better idea of what has occurred.

EXHIBIT 12-2.
Total Manufacturing Variance
Bud Jet Corporation

BUDGETED TOTAL COSTS	ACTUAL TOTAL COSTS	VARIANCE FAVORABLE/ (UNFAVORABLE)
$2,000,000	$2,200,000	$(200,000)

From Exhibit 12-3, we can see that although the Polishing department had a good year, the Processing, Assembly, and Packing departments were substantially over budget. This is the first step toward discovering what has happened. Now we can begin to investigate why cost overruns occurred so that we can hopefully avoid them in future months. Specifically, we can focus our attention on the departments where the largest variances occurred.

EXHIBIT 12-3.
Manufacturing Variances by Department
Bud Jet Corporation

DEPARTMENT	BUDGETED COSTS	ACTUAL COSTS	VARIANCE
Purchasing	$1,000,000	$1,010,000	$ (10,000)
Processing	200,000	280,000	(80,000)
Assembly	400,000	460,000	(60,000)
Polishing	100,000	90,000	10,000
Packing	300,000	360,000	(60,000)
TOTALS	$2,000,000	$2,200,000	$(200,000)

Yet, we still don't really have adequate information. Consider the large Processing Department variance. We do know whom to ask about the variance. We want the manager of the Processing Department to explain what happened. But the financial officers haven't given the manager of that department much to go on. He simply knows he was $80,000 over budget. If the static budget is broken down even further by line item for each department, such as personnel cost, materials, and overhead, it becomes easier to determine why excess costs occurred. Exhibit 12-4 presents such an analysis for the Processing Department at Bud Jet.

EXHIBIT 12-4.
Processing Department Line-Item Variances
Bud Jet Corporation

	BUDGETED COSTS	ACTUAL COSTS	VARIANCE
Processing Dept.			
Personnel	$ 80,000	$ 80,000	$ 0
Materials	100,000	180,000	(80,000)
Overhead	20,000	20,000	0
TOTALS	$200,000	$280,000	$(80,000)

Note that the entire variance occurred in the area of materials. Investigation might show that this was unavoidable due to a significant unexpected rise in the price of raw materials used. On the other hand, we might find that employees had been quite careless in the use of materials, resulting in significant waste. This latter possibility makes clear the fact that budget variances should be calculated and investigated frequently. Although there may be little that can be done about rises in the prices of raw materials, we should catch waste and correct it long before year-end.

Line-item analysis of variances can, of course, be quite detailed. We can calculate the variance with respect to each type of labor or raw material input. However, even that still does not help us to isolate the cause of the variance as much as we would like. Did the processing department go over on its materials budget because it wasted materials or because the price of materials had risen? We have gone as far as we can with the static budget. In order to gain additional information about the cause of variances, we now have to turn our attention to flexible budgeting.

Flexible Budgeting

The key problem with static budgets is that they provide an expected cost for one particular volume, hence the name *static*. At the end of a reporting period such as a month or a year, it is highly unlikely that we will have attained exactly the expected output level. If we produce more units than we had planned because sales are up substantially over our expectations, then it is logical to assume that we will have to go over our budget. On the other hand, if volume is down, then costs should be under budget. Flexible budgets provide an after-the-fact device to tell what it should have cost for the volume level actually attained. Adjusting the static budget for the actual production volume achieved results in the flexible budget.

Flexible Budget Variance and Volume Variance

Suppose we expect the variable cost per unit to be $10. If we expect to produce 100,000 units, then we expect a total variable cost of $1,000,000. What if we only produced 85,000 units, and we had a total variable cost of $900,000? The static budget comparison would be that we had a budgeted variable cost of $1,000,000, and we only spent $900,000, so we had a favorable variance of $100,000. But it should have cost only $850,000 to produce 85,000 units. We actually spent more than we should have, given the level of actual production. We should have noted an unfavorable variance! In this example, the actual cost was $900,000, the static budget was $1,000,000, and the flexible budget was $850,000.

The total variance between the actual cost of $900,000 and the static budget of $1,000,000 is a favorable variance of $100,000, as noted earlier. Exhibit 12-5 shows that we can decompose this total variance into two parts. The first part, on the right side of the exhibit, is the difference between the static budget and the flexible budget. This is a $150,000 favorable variance. However, by favorable we simply mean we spent less than expected. This variance is called a volume variance: it is caused because our volume varied from what was expected. It is likely that, because volume was below that expected, this was an unfavorable event, even though the accountant called it a favorable variance.

On the left side of Exhibit 12-5 is the difference between the actual cost and the flexible budget, which gives rise to an unfavorable flexible budget variance of $50,000. That is, we actually spent $50,000 more than we would have budgeted for the level of production attained. The flexible budget variance and the volume variance in total are equal to the total variance.

EXHIBIT 12-5.
Flexible Budget Variance and Volume

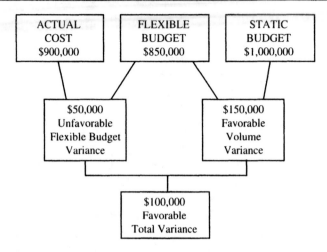

Price and Quantity Variances

We can get still more information from variance analysis. For each variable cost item, we can calculate not only the volume and flexible budget variances, but also a price and a quantity variance.

The difference between the flexible budget and the actual costs incurred makes up the flexible budget variance. The accountant may then break down this flexible budget variance into two components: 1) the part of the total variance caused because we paid a different price for our inputs, and 2) the part of the difference caused because we used more or less of an input than expected for the actual volume of production. See Exhibit 12-6. The total of the price, quantity, and volume variances makes up the total variance between actual costs and the original static budget.

Excel Exercise

Template 11 may be used to calculate price, quantity, volume, and total variances. The template is on the CD that accompanies this book.

EXHIBIT 12-6.
Price, Quantity, and Volume Variances

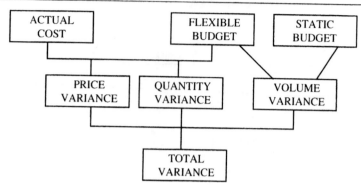

When we consider materials, we refer to the price variance simply as a price variance, and we refer to the quantity variance as a use variance. While the term *price* is adequately clear, the word *use* allows us to visualize that the variance refers to how much material we used to make the amount of product. With respect to variances in the cost of labor, we generally refer to these variances as rate and efficiency variances. The term *rate* is based on the rate we pay labor. The term *efficiency* is based on the fact that frequently, when we consume more labor than expected to produce a given level of output, inefficiency exists. However, this may not always be the case.

We should be especially careful in interpreting variances. The accountant uses the word *favorable* to imply that less money was spent than was expected. The term *unfavorable* is used to mean that more money was spent than was expected. There is no sense of good, bad, efficient, or inefficient implied by the terms *favorable* and *unfavorable* in an accounting context. If we have an unfavorable labor efficiency variance, this doesn't necessarily imply that labor worked inefficiently. There may have been a machine breakdown or a stockout of a key material. It is possible the purchasing department bought inferior materials that required more labor input.

The benefit of using price and quantity variances is that it can help to very narrowly pinpoint the specific areas where we went over or under budget. However, the variances themselves should not be considered causes for punishment or congratulations. All that variances can do is point the direction for investigations to take to determine the underlying causes for variances. But by undertaking such investigations on a timely basis, we can better control results, so that we come as near to achieving or surpassing the plan as possible.

KEY CONCEPTS

Budget—a formalized (written), quantitative (in dollars) plan.

Uses of budgets—Set goals; evaluate results; improve the effectiveness of decision making by planning ahead; improve communication and coordination.

Master budget—a projection of the key financial statements, cash flow, and capital projects. The master budget also describes performance reports to be used.

Budget Preparation

Preliminaries—An environmental statement should be developed to determine the position of the firm relative to customers, suppliers, and creditors. General objectives should be set, specific assumptions made, and measurable goals established.

Forecasts—The essential ingredient for compilation of budgets is a set of forecast information. Generally, forecasts use such mechanical means as statistics and computers to project the past into the future. Managers must be aware that judgment should be used to modify forecast results.

Departmental budgets—The organization budget consists of the aggregation of budgets from each department. The departmental budgets itemize revenues and expenses in detail.

Static budget—a budget prepared before the year begins, establishing what it should cost for the anticipated output level.

Flexible budget—an after-the-fact budget establishing what it should have cost for the actual attained output level.

Variance—the difference between an actual result and a budgeted amount.

Volume variance—the difference between the static budget and the flexible budget.

Price variance—the portion of the difference between the flexible budget and actual costs caused by paying a different price for each unit of raw material or hour of labor than had been anticipated.

Quantity variance—the portion of the difference between the flexible budget and the actual costs caused by using more raw materials or labor for each unit produced than had been anticipated.

Total variance—The volume variance, plus the price variance, plus the quantity variance make up the total variance for the variable inputs. This is equal to the difference between the static budget and the actual costs.

Thirteen

Investment Analysis

Analysis of investments in long-term projects is referred to as *capital budgeting*. Long-term projects are worthy of special attention because of the fact that they frequently require large initial investments, and because the cash outlay to start such projects often precedes the receipt of cash inflows by a significant period of time. In such cases, we are interested in being able to predict the profitability of the project. We want to be sure that the profits from the project are greater than what we could have received from alternative investments or uses of our money.

This chapter focuses on how managers can evaluate long-term projects and determine whether the expected return from the projects is great enough to justify taking the risks that are inherent in long-term investments. Several different approaches to capital budgeting are discussed: the payback method, the net present value method, and the internal rate of return method. The latter two of these methods require us to acknowledge the implications of the "time value of money."

The time value of money refers to the fact that money received at different points in time is not equally valuable. To give a rather elementary example, suppose that someone offered to buy your product for $250, and that they are willing to pay you either today or one year from today. You will certainly prefer to receive the $250 today. At the very least, you could put the $250 in a bank and earn interest in the intervening year.

Suppose, however, that the buyer offered you $250 today or $330 in twenty-two months. Now your decision is much more difficult. How sure are you that the individual will pay you twenty-two months from now? Perhaps he or she will be bankrupt by then. What could we do with the money if we received it today? Would we put the $250 in some investment that would yield us more than $330 twenty-two months from today? These are questions that we have to be able to answer in order to evaluate long-term investment opportunities. But first let's discuss some basic issues of investment analysis.

INVESTMENT OPPORTUNITIES

The first step that must be taken in investment analysis is to identify the investment opportunity. Such opportunities fall into two major classes: new project investments, and replacement or reinvestment in existing projects. New project ideas can come from a variety of sources. They may be the result of research and development activity or exploration. Your firm may have a department solely devoted to new product development. Ideas may come from outside of the firm. Reinvestment is often the result of production managers pointing out that certain equipment needs to be replaced. Such replacement should not be automatic. If a substantial outlay is required, it may be an appropriate time to reevaluate the product or project to determine if the profits being generated are adequate to justify continued additional investment.

DATA GENERATION

The data needed to evaluate an investment opportunity are the expected cash flows related to the investment. Many projects have a large initial cash outflow as we acquire plant and equipment and incur start-up costs prior to actual production and sale of our new product. In the years that follow, there will be receipt of cash from the sale of our product (or service) and there will be cash expenditures related to the expenses of production and sales. We refer to the difference between each year's cash receipts and cash expenditures as the net cash flow for that year.

You're probably wondering why we have started this discussion with cash flow instead of net income for each year. There are several important reasons. First, net income, even if it were a perfect measure of profitability, doesn't consider the time value of money. For instance, suppose that we have two alternative projects. The first project requires that we purchase a machine for $10,000 in cash. The machine has a ten-year useful life. Depreciation expense is $1,000 per year.

A totally different project requires that we lease a machine for $1,000 a year for ten years, with lease payments at the start of each year. Are the two alternative projects equal? No, they aren't. Even though they both have an expense of $1,000 per year for ten years, one project requires us to spend $10,000 at the beginning. The other project requires an outlay of only $1,000 in the first year. In this second project, we could hold on to $9,000 that had been spent right away in the first project. That $9,000 can be invested and can earn additional profits for the firm before the next lease payment is due.

The data needed for investment or project analysis includes cash flow information for each of the years of the investment's life. Naturally we cannot be 100 percent certain about how much the project will cost and how much we will eventually receive. There is no perfect solution for the fact that we have to make estimates. However, we must be aware at all times that, because our estimates may not be fully correct, there is an element of risk. Project analysis must be able to assess whether the expected return can compensate for the risks we are taking. It should also include consideration of any taxes that will have to be paid.

THE PAYBACK METHOD

The payback method of analysis evaluates projects based on how long it takes to recover the amount of money put into the project. The shorter the payback period, the better. Certainly there is some intuitive appeal to this method. The sooner we get our money out of the project, the lower the risk. If we have to wait a number of years for a project to "pay off," all kinds of things can go wrong. Furthermore, given high interest rates, the longer we have our initial investment tied up, the more costly it is for us.

Exhibit 13-1 presents an example of the payback method. In the exhibit, four alternative projects are being compared. In each project, the initial outlay is $400. By the end of 2005, projects one and two have recovered the initial $400 investment. Therefore, they have a payback period of three years. Projects three and four do not recover the initial investment until the end of 2006. Their payback period is four years, and they are therefore considered to be inferior to the other two projects.

EXHIBIT 13-1.
Payback Method—Alternative Projects

| | PROJECT CASH FLOWS | | | |
	ONE	TWO	THREE	FOUR
January 2003	$(400)	$(400)	$(400)	$ (400)
2003	0	0	399	300
2004	1	399	0	99
2005	399	1	0	0
2006	500	500	500	5,000
TOTAL	$ 500	$ 500	$ 499	$4,999

It is not difficult at this point to see one of the principal weaknesses of the payback method. It ignores what happens after the payback period. The total cash flow for project four is much greater than the cash received from any of the other projects, yet it is considered to be one of the worst of the projects. In a situation in which cash flows extend for twenty or thirty years, this problem might not be as obvious, but it could cause us to choose incorrectly.

Is that the only problem with this method? No. Another obvious problem stems from the fact that according to this method, projects one and two are equally attractive because they both have a three-year payback period. Although their total cash flows are the same, the timing is different. Project one provides $1 in 2004, and then $399 during 2005. Project two generates $399 in 2004 and only $1 in 2005. Are these two projects equally as good because their total cash flows are the same? *No.* The extra $398 received in 2004 from project two is available for investment in other profitable opportunities for one extra year, as compared to project one. Therefore, it is clearly superior to project one. The problem is that the payback method doesn't formally take into account the time value of money.

This deficiency is obvious when looking at project three as well. Project three appears to be less valuable than projects one or two on two counts. First, its payback is four years rather than three, and second, its total cash flow is less than either project one or two. But if we consider the time value of money, then project three is better than either project one or two. With project three, we get the $399 right away. The earnings on that $399 during 2004 and 2005 will more than offset the shorter payback and larger cash flow of projects one and two.

Although payback is commonly used for a quick and dirty project evaluation, problems associated with the payback method are quite serious. There are several methods commonly referred to as discounted cash flow models that overcome these problems. Later in this chapter, we will discuss the most commonly used of these methods, net present value and internal rate of return. However, before we discuss them, we need to specifically consider the issues and mechanics surrounding time value of money calculations.

THE TIME VALUE OF MONEY

It is very easy to think of projects in terms of total dollars of cash received. Unfortunately, this tends to be misleading. Consider a project in which we invest $400 and in return we receive $520 after three years. We have made a cash profit of $120. Because the profit was earned over a three-year period, it is a profit of $40 per year. Because $40 is 10 percent of the initial $400 investment, we have apparently earned a 10 percent return on our money. While this is true, that 10 percent is calculated based on simple interest.

Consider putting money into a bank that pays a 10 percent return "compounded annually." The term *compounded annually* means that the bank calculates interest at the end of each year and adds the interest onto the initial amount deposited. In future years, interest is earned not only on the initial deposit, but also on interest earned in prior years. If we put $400 in the bank at 10 percent compounded annually, we would earn $40 of interest in the first year. At the beginning of the second year we would have $440. The interest on the $440 would be $44. At the beginning of the third year, we would have $484 (the $400 initial deposit plus the $40 interest from the first year, plus the $44 interest from the second year). The interest for the third year would be $48.40. We would have a total of $532.40 at the end of three years.

The 10 percent compounded annually gives a different result from the 10 percent simple interest. We have $532.40 instead of $520 from the project. The reason for this difference is that in the case of the project, we did not get any cash flow until the end of the project. In the case of the bank, we were given a cash flow at the end of each year. We reinvested that cash to earn additional interest.

Consider a cash amount of $100 today. We refer to it as a present value (PV or P). How much could this cash amount accumulate to if we invested it at an interest rate (i) or rate of return (r) of 10 percent for a period of time (N) equal to two years? Assuming that we compound annually, the $100 would earn $10 in the first year (10 percent of $100). This $10 would be added to the $100. In the second year our $110 would earn $11 (that is, 10 percent of $110). The future value (FV or F) is $121. That is, two years into the future we would have $121.

Mechanically this is a simple process—multiply the interest rate times the initial investment to find the interest for the first period. Add the interest to the initial investment. Then multiply the interest rate times the initial investment plus all interest already accumulated to find the interest for the second year.

While this is not complicated, it can be rather tedious. To simplify this process, mathematical formulas have been developed to solve a variety of "time value of money" problems. The most basic of these formulas states that:

$$FV = PV(1 + i)^N$$

This formula and the others that follow have been built into both business calculators and computer spreadsheet programs. If we supply the appropriate raw data, the calculator or spreadsheet software performs all of the necessary interest computations.

For instance, if we wanted to know what $100 would grow to in two years at 10 percent, we would simply tell our calculator that the present value, P or PV (depending on the brand of calculator you use), equals $100; the interest rate, %i or r, equals 10 percent; and the number of periods, N, equals 2. Then we would ask the calculator to compute F or FV, the future value.

Can we use this method if compounding occurs more frequently than once a year? Bonds often pay interest twice a year. Banks often compound monthly to calculate mortgage payments. Using our example of $100 invested for two years at 10 percent, we could easily adjust the calculation for semiannual, quarterly, or monthly compounding. For example, for semiannual compounding, N becomes 4 because there are two semiannual periods per year for two years. The rate of return, or interest rate, becomes 5 percent. If the rate earned is 10 percent for a full year, then it is half of that, or 5 percent, for each half year.

For quarterly compounding, N equals 8 (four quarters per year for two years) and i equals $2^{1}/_{2}$ percent (10 percent per year divided by four quarters per year). For monthly compounding, N equals 24 and i equals 10 percent/12. Thus, for monthly compounding, we would tell the calculator that PV = $100, i = 10%/12, and N = 24. Then we would tell the calculator to compute FV. We need a calculator designed to perform present value functions in order to do this.

If we expect to receive $121 in two years, can we calculate how much that is worth today? This question calls for a reversal of the compounding process. Suppose we would normally expect to earn a return on our money of 10 percent. What we are really asking here is, "How much would we have to invest today at 10 percent, to get $121 in two years?" The answer requires unraveling compound interest. If we calculate how much of the $121 to be received in two years is simply interest earned on our original investment, then we know the present value of that $121. This process of removing or unraveling the interest is called *discounting*. The 10 percent rate is referred to as a discount rate. Using the calculator, this is a simple process. We again supply the i and the N, but instead of telling the calculator the PV and asking for the FV, we tell it the FV and ask it to calculate the PV.

Earlier in this chapter, we posed a problem of whether to accept $250 today or $330 in twenty-two months. Assume that we can invest money in a project with a 10 percent return and monthly compounding. Which choice is better? We can tell our calculator (by the way, if you have access to a business-oriented calculator, you can work out these calculations as we go) that FV = $330, N = 22, and i = 10%/12. If we then ask it to compute PV, we find that the present value is $275. This means that if we invest $275 today at 10 percent compounded monthly for twenty-two months, it accumulates to $330. That is, receiving $330 in twenty-two months is equivalent to having $275 today. Because this amount is greater than $250, our preference is to wait for the money, assuming there is no risk of default. Looking at this problem another way, how much would our $250 grow to if we invested it for twenty-two months at 10 percent? Here we have PV = $250, N = 22, and i = 10%/12. Our calculation indicates that the FV = $300. If we wait, we have $330 twenty-two months from now. If we take $250 today and invest it at 10 percent, we only have $300 twenty-two months from now. We find that we are better off waiting for the $330, assuming we are sure that we will receive it.

Are we limited to solving for only the present or future value? No, this methodology is quite flexible. Assume, for example, that we wish to put $100,000 aside today to pay off a $1,000,000 loan in fifteen years. What rate of return must be earned, compounded annually, for our $100,000 to grow to $1,000,000? Here we have the present value, or $100,000; the number of periods, fifteen years; and the future value, or $1,000,000. It is a simple process to determine the required rate of return. If we simply supply our calculator with the PV, FV, and N, the calculator readily supplies the i, which is 16.6 percent in this case.

Or, for that matter, if we had $100,000 today and knew that we could earn a 13 percent return, we would calculate how long it would take to accumulate $1,000,000. Here we know PV, FV, and i, and we wish to find N. In this case, N = 18.8 years. Given any three of our four basic components, PV, FV, N, and i, we can solve for the fourth. This is because the calculator is simply using our basic formula stated earlier and solving for the missing variable.

So, far, however, we have considered only one single payment. Suppose that we don't have $100,000 today, but we are willing to put $10,000 aside every year for fifteen years. If we earn 12 percent, will we have enough to repay $1,000,000 at the end of the fifteen years? There are two ways to solve this problem. We can determine the future value, fifteen years from now, of each of the individual payments. We would have to do fifteen separate calculations because each succeeding payment earns interest for one year less. We would then have to sum the future value of each of the payments. This is rather tedious. A second way to solve this problem is by using a formula that accumulates the payments for us. The formula is:

$$FV = PMT \left[\frac{(1 + i)^N - 1}{i} \right]$$

In this formula, PMT represents the payment made each period, or annuity payment. Although you may think of annuities as payments made once a year, an annuity simply means payments that are exactly the same in amount, and are made at equally spaced intervals of time, such as monthly, quarterly, or annually. For example, mortgage payments of $321.48 per month represent an annuity.

To solve problems with a series of identical payments, we have five variables instead of the previous four. We now have FV, PV, N, i, and PMT. However, PV doesn't appear in our formula. There is a separate formula that relates present value to a series of payments. This formula is:

$$PV = PMT \left[\frac{1 - \left[\frac{1}{(1 + i)^N} \right]}{i} \right]$$

Annuity formulas are built into business calculators and computer spreadsheet programs such as Excel or Lotus 123. With the spreadsheet program or calculator, you can easily solve for PV, or i, or N, or PMT, if you have the other three variables. Similarly, you can solve for FV, or i, or N, or PMT given the other three. For instance, how much would we pay monthly on a twenty-year mortgage at 12 percent if we borrowed $50,000? The present value (PV) is $50,000, the interest rate (%i) is 1 percent per month, and the number of months (N) is 240. Given these three factors, we can solve for the annuity payment (PMT). It is $551 per month.

Annuity formulas provide you with a basic framework for solving many problems concerning receipt or payment of cash in different time periods. Keep in mind that the annuity method can be used only if the amount of the payment is the same each period. If that isn't the case, each payment must be evaluated separately.

THE NET PRESENT VALUE (NPV) METHOD

The net present value (NPV) method of analysis determines whether a project earns more or less than a stated desired rate of return. The starting point of the analysis is determination of this rate.

The Hurdle Rate

The rate of return required in order for a project to be acceptable is called
the *required rate of return* or the *hurdle rate*. An acceptable project should
be able to hurdle over, that is, be higher than this rate.

The rate must take into account two key factors. First, we require a
base profit to compensate for investing money in the project. We have a
variety of opportunities for which we could use our money. We need to be
paid a profit for foregoing the use of our money in some alternative venture. The second element concerns risk. Any time we enter a new investment, there is an element of risk. Perhaps the project won't work out
exactly as expected. The project may turn out to be a failure. We have to
be paid for being willing to undertake these risks. The two elements taken
together determine our hurdle rate.

There is no one unique, standard required rate of return that is used
by all companies. Different industries tend to have different base rates of
return. Further, within an industry one firm may have some advantage
over other firms (for example, economies of scale) that allow it to have a
higher base return. On top of that, different firms, and even different projects for one firm, have different types and degrees of risk. Buying a
machine to use for putting Coca-Cola in bottles involves much less risk
than developing new soft drink products.

One of the most prevalent risks that investors take is loss of purchasing power. That is, price-level inflation makes our money less valuable over time. Suppose we could buy a TV for $100, but instead we invest
that money in a business. If the firm uses that money to generate a pretax
profit of $4 in a year when the inflation rate is 4 percent, did we have a
good year, bad year, or neutral year? Because we have to pay some taxes
to the government on our $4 pretax profit, we had a bad year. After pay-
ing taxes we have less than $104 at the end of the year. But, due to infla-
tion, it costs $104 to buy a TV set. This means that in deciding if a project
is worthwhile, we have to consider whether the rate of return is high
enough to cover our after-tax loss of purchasing power due to inflation.

We must also consider a variety of business risks. What if no one
buys the product, or he or she buys it, but fails to pay us? If the product is
made or sold internationally, we incur foreign exchange risk and foreign
political risk. The specific types of risks faced by a company depend on
its industry. The company's past experience with projects like the one
being evaluated should be a guide in determining the risk portion of the
hurdle rate.

When we add the desired return to all of the risk factors, the total is the firm's hurdle rate. In most firms, the top financial officers determine an appropriate hurdle rate or rates and inform nonfinancial managers that this hurdle rate must be anticipated for a project to receive approval. Therefore, you will not usually have to go through a calculation of the hurdle rate yourself.

NPV Calculations

Once we know our hurdle rate, we can use the NPV method to assess whether a project is acceptable. The NPV method compares the present value of a project's cash inflows to the present value of its cash outflows. If the present value of the inflows is greater than the outflows, then the project is profitable because it is earning a rate of return that is greater than the hurdle rate. For example, suppose that a potential project for our firm requires an initial cash outlay of $10,000. We expect the project to produce a net after-tax cash flow (cash inflows less cash outflows) of $6,500 in each of the two years of the project's life. Suppose our after-tax hurdle rate is 18 percent. Is this project worthwhile?

The cash receipts total $13,000, which is a profit of $3,000 overall, or $1,500 per year on our $10,000 investment. Is that a compounded return of at least 18 percent? At first glance it would appear that the answer is "no" because $1,500 is only 15 percent of $10,000. However, we haven't left our full $10,000 invested for the full two years. Our positive cash flow at the end of the first year is $6,500. We are not only making $1,500 profit, but we are also getting back half ($5,000) of our original investment. During the second year, we earn $1,500 profit on a remaining investment of only $5,000. It is not simply how much money you get from the project, but when you get it that is important.

The present value of an annuity of $6,500 per year for two years at 18 percent is $10,177 (PV = ?; PMT = $6,500; N = 2; i = 18%). The present value of the initial $10,000 outflow is simply $10,000 because it is paid at the start of the project. The NPV is the present value of the inflows, $10,177, less the present value of the outflows, $10,000, which is $177. This number is greater than zero, so the project does indeed yield a return greater than 18 percent, on an annually compounded basis.

It may not be intuitively clear why this method works, or indeed, that it works at all. However, consider making a deal with your friend who is a banker. You agree that you will put a sum of money into the bank. At the end of the first year, the banker adds 18 percent interest to your account and you then withdraw $6,500. At the end of year two, the banker credits interest to the balance in your account at an 18 percent rate. You then withdraw $6,500, which is exactly the total in the account at that time. The account will then have a zero balance. You ask your friend how much you must deposit today in order to be able to make the two future withdrawals. He replies, "$10,177."

If we deposit $10,177, at an 18 percent rate, it will earn $1,832 during the first year. This leaves a balance of $12,009 in the account. We then withdraw $6,500, leaving a balance of $5,509 for the start of the second year. During the second year, $5,509 earns interest of $991 at a rate of 18 percent. This means that the balance in the account is $6,500 at the end of the second year. We then withdraw that amount.

The point of this bank deposit example is that when we earlier solved for the present value of the two $6,500 inflows using a hurdle rate of 18 percent, we found PV to be $10,177. We were finding exactly the amount of money we would have to pay today to get two payments of $6,500 if we were to earn exactly 18 percent. If we can invest a smaller amount than $10,177, but still get $6,500 per year for each of the two years, we must be earning more than 18 percent because we are putting in less than would be needed to earn 18 percent, but are getting just as much out. Here, we invest $10,000, which is less than $10,177, so we are earning a rate of return greater than 18 percent.

Conversely, if the banker had told us to invest less than $10,000 (that is, if the present value of the two payments of $6,500 each at 18 percent was less than $10,000), then it means that by paying $10,000 we were putting in more money than we would have to in order to earn 18 percent; therefore we must be earning less than 18 percent.

The NPV method gets around the problems of the payback method. It considers the full project life, and considers the time value of money. Clearly, however, you can see that it is more difficult than the payback method. Another problem with it is that you must determine the hurdle rate before you can do any project analysis. The next method we will look at eliminates the need to have a hurdle rate before performing the analysis.

THE INTERNAL RATE OF RETURN METHOD (IRR)

One of the objections to the NPV method is that it never indicates what rate of return a project is earning. We simply find out whether it is earning more or less than a specified hurdle rate. This creates problems when comparing projects, all of which have positive net present values.

One conclusion that can be drawn from our net present value (NPV) discussion is that when the NPV is greater than zero, we are earning more than our required rate of return. If the NPV is less than zero, then we are earning less than our required rate of return. If the NPV is zero, we must be earning exactly the hurdle rate. Therefore, if we want to determine the exact rate that a project earns, all we need to do is to set the NPV equal to zero. Because the NPV is the present value (PV) of the inflows less the present value of the outflows, or:

$$NPV = PV \text{ Inflows} - PV \text{ Outflows}$$

then when we set the NPV equal to zero,

$$0 = PV \text{ Inflows} - PV \text{ Outflows}$$

that is equivalent to:

$$PV \text{ Inflows} = PV \text{ Outflows.}$$

All we have to do to find the rate of return that the project actually earns, or the "internal rate of return" (IRR), is to find the interest rate at which this equation is true.

For example, consider our NPV project discussed earlier that requires a cash outlay of $10,000 and produces a net cash inflow of $6,500 per year for two years. The present value of the outflow is simply the $10,000 (PV = $10,000) we pay today. The inflows represent a two-year (N = 2) annuity of $6,500 (PMT = $6,500) per year. By supplying our calculator with the PV, N, and PMT, we can simply find the i or r (IRR). In this case, we find that the IRR is 19.4 percent.

Variable Cash Flow

This calculation is simple for any business calculator that can handle time value of money, frequently called discounted cash flow (DCF) analysis. However, this problem was somewhat simplistic because it assumed that we would receive exactly the same cash inflow each year. In most capital budgeting problems, it is much more likely that the cash inflows from a project will change each year. Many business calculators are not sophisticated enough to determine the IRR if the cash flows are not the same each year. However, computer spreadsheet programs are able to do the calculation.

PROJECT RANKING

Often, we may be faced with a situation in which there are more acceptable projects than the number that we can afford to finance. In this case, we wish to choose the best projects. A simple way to do this is to determine the internal rate of return on each project and then to rank the projects from the project with the highest IRR to the one with the lowest. We then simply start by accepting projects with the highest IRR and go down the list until we either run out of money or reach our minimum acceptable rate of return.

In general, this approach allows the firm to optimize its overall rate of return. However, it is possible for this approach to have an undesired result. Suppose that one of our very highest-yielding projects is a parking lot. For a total investment of $50,000, we expect to earn a return of $20,000 a year for the next forty years. The internal rate of return on that project is 40 percent. Alternatively, we can build an office building on the same site. For an investment of $10,000,000 we expect to earn $3,000,000 a year for forty years, or an IRR of 30 percent. We can either use the site for the parking lot or the building, but not both. Our other projects have an IRR of 20 percent.

If we build the parking lot because of its high IRR, and therefore bypass the building, we will wind up investing $50,000 at 40 percent and $9,950,000 at 20 percent instead of $10,000,000 at 30 percent. This is not an optimal result. We would be better off to bypass the high-yielding parking lot and invest the entire $10,000,000 at 30 percent. Our decision should be based on calculating our weighted average IRR for all projects that we accept.

```
┌─────────────────────────────────────────────────────────────┐
│                      Excel Exercises                          │
│                                                               │
│   Templates 12–15 may be used to calculate present values,    │
│   future values, net present values, and internal rates of    │
│   return, respectively, using your data. These templates are  │
│   on the CD that accompanies this book.                       │
└─────────────────────────────────────────────────────────────┘
```

SUMMARY

Capital budgeting represents one of the most important areas of financial management. In essence, the entire future of the company is on the line. If projects are undertaken that don't yield adequate rates of return, they will have serious long-term consequences for the firm's profitability—and even for its viability.

To adequately evaluate projects, discounted cash flow techniques should be employed. The two most common of these methods are NPV and IRR. The essential ingredient of both of these methods is that they consider the time value of money. A nonfinancial manager doesn't necessarily have to be able to compute present values. It is vital, however, that all managers understand that *when* money is received or paid can have just as dramatic an impact on the firm as the amount received or paid.

KEY CONCEPTS

Capital budgeting—analysis of long-term projects with respect to risk and profitability.

Net cash flow—the difference between cash receipts and cash disbursements. Cash flow is more useful than net income for project evaluation because net income fails to consider the time value of money.

Time value of money—Other things being equal, we would always prefer to receive cash sooner, or pay cash later. This is because cash can be invested and earn a return in exchange for its use.

Compounding—calculation of the return on a project, including the return earned on cash flows generated during the life of the project.

Discounting—a reversal of the compounding process. Discounting allows us to determine what a future cash flow is worth today.

Annuities—cash flows of equal amounts, paid or received at evenly spaced periods of time, such as weekly, monthly, or annually.

Project Evaluation

Payback—a method that assesses how long it will take to receive enough cash from a project to recover the cash invested in that project.

Discounted cash flow (DCF) analysis—methods that consider the time value of money in evaluating projects.

a. *Net present value*—method determining whether a project earns more than a particular desired rate of return, also called the hurdle or required rate of return. The hurdle rate is based on a return for the use of money over time, plus a return for risks inherent in the project.

b. *Internal rate of return*—method that finds the specific rate of return a project is expected to earn.

Fourteen

Lease or Buy? A Taxing Question

While taxes are a pervasive element in all business decisions, in few areas are their impacts as significant as in leasing. A large number of leasing arrangements are made in which the key or even the sole purpose of the lease is tax avoidance. Bear in mind that while tax *evasion* is illegal, tax *avoidance* is not only legal, but it is considered to be an inalienable right guaranteed by the Constitution.

This chapter is divided into three major sections. The first examines the accounting issues and mechanics of leasing. The second section considers some of the pros and cons of leasing from a strictly managerial perspective, ignoring tax issues. Finally, the chapter focuses on the tax aspects of leasing.

ACCOUNTING ISSUES

Operating vs. Capital Leases

Leases are classified as either *operating leases* or *capital leases*. Operating leases are treated by the lessee (the party leasing the asset from the lessor) on a strictly rental basis. Rental payments are expenses. The asset is not considered to be owned by the lessee and it doesn't show up on the balance sheet. In contrast, a lessee treats a capital lease as if the property was bought and financed with a mortgage. The leased property appears as an asset on the balance sheet. There is also a liability on the balance sheet to account for future payments to be made on the lease.

Short-term leases are always treated as operating leases. This stems from the fact that there is no strong ownership displayed by someone who leases the property for only a short period of time. In contrast, if there

183

appears to be a significant ownership interest in the property on the part of the lessee, it is usually treated as a capital lease.

Many firms make covenants, or agreements, with lenders that restrict management from taking certain risky actions. A common type of covenant is to agree to maintain a certain amount of assets relative to the amount of liabilities. For instance, a firm may agree that it will always have two dollars of assets on the balance sheet for every dollar of liabilities. This reduces risk because if the firm does get into financial difficulty, creditors will be fully protected if the firm can get at least 50 cents for every dollar of assets it owns.

Suppose a firm had made such an agreement, and that it currently has $20,000,000 in assets and $10,000,000 in liabilities. At this point, the president of the company sees a building that is the perfect building for the firm. The firm has been looking for a building like this one for years. The price is $5,000,000, which it plans to pay by borrowing $4,000,000 from a bank on a twenty-year mortgage, and paying $1,000,000 in cash. Unfortunately, that would result in assets of $24 million (the original $20 million + $5 million building – $1 million cash down payment), and liabilities of $14 million (the original $10 million + $4 million mortgage). But to sustain $14 million of liabilities, the firm would need $28 million in assets. The firm cannot buy the building without defaulting on the loan agreement.

However, what if the firm merely rents the building? What if the firm takes out a twenty-year lease, with a provision that the property automatically becomes the firm's at the end of the twenty years? In that case, if the lease were an operating lease, the firm wouldn't be in violation of the letter of its agreement with the bondholders! It would, however, certainly be violating the spirit of the agreement. Leasing property rather than buying it, with the main purpose being to avoid showing the asset and liability on the balance sheet, is referred to as "off-balance-sheet financing." It gets that name because you have effectively financed a purchase without explicitly showing the long-term commitment the firm has made.

Criteria for Capital Leases

As one might suspect, lenders weren't too pleased with this type of behavior. Ultimately, the accountants modified their generally accepted accounting principles (GAAP) to handle this type of situation. Current GAAP specify that long-term, noncancelable leases must be treated as capital leases if they were entered into with the lessee intending to have an ownership interest in the property. A technical set of rules is used by the CPA to assess whether a lease must be treated as a capital lease. If it is a capital lease, then an asset and a liability appear on the balance sheet. This eliminates most opportunities for off-balance-sheet financing.

MANAGEMENT CONSIDERATIONS FOR LEASING

Many financial managers are strong supporters of leasing due to the added flexibility it provides. If you know you'll need a piece of equipment for only half of its useful life, a lease can eliminate the effort required to dispose of the asset after you no longer need it. If you're afraid that technology will make the item obsolete, a cancelable lease can protect you.

A lease also provides a greater degree of financing. Purchases financed by a mortgage typically require a down payment of perhaps 20 percent or more. Banks are quite reluctant to lend 100 percent of the cost for any item they use as collateral. Therefore, the firm with a great idea but no cash may not be able to get started. A lease provides an alternative way to start production with less equity financing.

Leases, however, tend to cost more than mortgages. We would expect that, considering the risk and return issues. Certainly the leasing company bears more risk than a mortgagor does, if only because it bears all of the normal risks of ownership, such as assuring that fire insurance is maintained. Further, while the lessee has more flexibility to avoid technological obsolescence, the lessor charges a higher rent because of added risk. The same thing is true with respect to 100 percent financing. The potential loss due to lessee default is greater to the lessor than to the mortgagor because there is no sizable down payment to absorb losses on foreclosure sales.

In some cases, leasing may be more efficient. Consider the firm that needs two autos. If it leases the autos, it may pay more for the autos than if it bought them outright, but it might get a wholesale service contract with the lease. The leasing company is willing to give a discount on service to get the lease. On the other hand, if the firm needs 2,000 autos, all in one geographic area, it might pay to buy them and open its own auto repair shop, thus maintaining the autos at cost, rather than wholesale or retail rates.

One final consideration: Who owns the property at the end of the lease? Well, unless it is specified one way or the other in the lease contract, the property belongs to the lessor. The lessor stands to gain from any increase in the value of the property. Frequently, the right of ownership upon termination of the lease is given to the lessee for "free." In such leases, the monthly or annual lease payments are higher than they would have to be if the lessor retained ownership of the property.

None of these managerial considerations provide absolute weight in favor of or against leasing. There are some benefits for the lessee, but they tend to raise the risk to the lessor, who therefore charges a higher price. Clearly, by adding a lessor instead of buying direct, we have brought in a participant who will want to earn a profit. This profit must come from the lease payments. As we turn to our next section, however, it will become apparent that tax considerations can provide a situation in which the lessor and the lessee may both clearly benefit from a lease arrangement.

TAX CONSIDERATIONS FOR LEASING

Tax Bracket Shifting

Suppose that a taxpayer in a low tax bracket—perhaps 15 percent—was anticipating buying a machine directly versus leasing it from a taxpayer in the 35 percent tax bracket. Every dollar of depreciation taken as a deduction by the taxpayer in a 15 percent tax bracket would reduce taxes paid by him or her to the government by 15 cents. If the taxpayer in the 35 percent bracket takes that same dollar of depreciation as a tax deduction, it will reduce his or her taxes by 35 cents. Therefore, there is a tax savings if a high tax bracket taxpayer buys property and leases it to a lower tax bracket taxpayer. The high tax bracket taxpayer gets the depreciation deduction, and can share the benefit with the low tax bracket payer through lower lease rental charges. (Note that the value of this approach has been lessened substantially by IRS Passive Activity Loss rules, which limit allowable deductions.)

Sale and Leaseback

Developed real estate is commonly sold and then leased back by the seller. This "sale and leaseback" technique allows for effective depreciation of land for tax purposes. If we simply own an office building, we can depreciate the building, but not the land it sits on. If we sell the building and lease it back, all of the lease payments are deductible. In areas where land is expensive, this can result in substantial tax savings.

Care must be exercised, however. First, if the real estate is sold at a profit, taxes are paid on the gain. Second, once sold, any increases in value belong to the new owner.

Alternative Minimum Tax

The Alternative Minimum Tax (AMT) also has interesting implications for leasing. The AMT is designed to ensure that taxpayers pay at least some minimum tax on their income. Depreciation deductions or net operating losses, both of which may be generated by leases, can trigger the AMT. However, it is an extremely complicated area, and is beyond the scope of this book. In general, tax issues with respect to leasing are extremely complex. There are a number of potential pitfalls. The discussion here should alert you to the fact that even if a lease doesn't have strong managerial rationale, the tax consequences may make it attractive. However, you must seek out the advice of a tax expert to review the specifics of any potential lease. The tax law in this area is extremely volatile. Congress closes loopholes as fast as it opens them. You cannot be advised strongly enough that a lease should not be undertaken without a tax expert specifically reviewing the tax consequences of the lease.

KEY CONCEPTS

Accounting Issues

Operating leases—leases treated as rental arrangements in which no asset or liability appears on the balance sheet of the lessee.

Capital lease—leases treated as if the lessee had acquired the property. An asset and liability appear on the lessee's balance sheet.

Managerial Issues

Advantages of leasing—flexibility, ease of disposal, protection against technological change, 100 percent financing, lower risk.

Disadvantages of leasing—higher cost (you pay for risk shifted to lessor and for lessor's profit). The lessor gets the residual value unless the contract specifies otherwise.

Tax Issues

Shifting deductions—to taxpayers in higher tax brackets; effective depreciation of land; salvaging investment tax credits that might otherwise be lost.

Consultation of experts—Whenever managerial decisions are made on the basis of generating tax savings, a tax expert should be consulted regarding the current tax law and the specific situation involved.

Fifteen

Depreciation: Having Your Cake and Eating It Too!

The matching principle of accounting requires that firms use depreciation. Suppose we buy a machine with a ten-year useful life. This machine will produce products over its entire ten-year lifetime. Therefore, it will be generating revenues in each of those ten years. The matching principle holds that we would be distorting the results of operations in all ten years if we considered the entire cost of the machine to be an expense in the year in which it was acquired. We would be understating income in the first year and overstating it in subsequent years.

Instead of expensing the equipment, we consider it to be a long-term asset when it is acquired. As time passes and the equipment becomes used up, we allocate a portion of the original cost as an expense in each year. Thus, the revenue received each year from the sale of the machine's output is matched with some of the machine's cost.

Okay, if we have to do it that way, there is some intuitive rationale. But where is the financial decision? It seems as if there is little choice left for the financial manager. In fact, that is not true. There are several complicating factors. First we must determine the valuation to be used as a basis for determining each year's depreciation. Next we must consider whether the asset really does get used up proportionately throughout its life. Perhaps it gets used up to a greater extent in some years than in others. Finally, what are some of the tax implications of the depreciation methods we decide to use? These issues make up the topic of this chapter.

AMORTIZATION

Amortization means the spreading out of a cost over a period of time. It is a generic term used for any type of item that is being prorated over time. The term *depreciation* is a specialized subset of amortization. Depreciation refers to the wearing out of a tangible asset such as a building or piece of equipment.

Some items don't wear out per se, and we don't refer to them as depreciating over time. For example, natural resources such as oil, gas, and coal are said to deplete. Deplete means to empty out and this is essentially what happens to a coal mine or oil well. Finally, some items neither deplete nor depreciate. For example, a patent loses its value over time. It doesn't break down, wear out, or empty out—it simply expires with the passage of time. When neither of the terms *depreciation* or *depletion* is applicable, we refer to the item as amortizing. Therefore, for a patent, the annual reduction in value is referred to as amortization expense. This chapter speaks exclusively of depreciation, even though the principles generally apply in a similar fashion for assets to be depleted or amortized.

ASSET VALUATION FOR DEPRECIATION

Asset valuation for depreciation basically follows the rules of historical cost. Chapter 6 stated that the historical or acquisition cost of an asset is simply what we paid for the item when we acquired it. However, for depreciation purposes, determination of asset cost is somewhat more complex.

The first problem that arises is the issue of what to do with the costs of putting an asset into productive service. For example, suppose that we purchase a machine for $20,000, and the machine cannot be used by us without modification of our electrical system. If we pay an electrician $1,000 to run a heavy-duty power line to the spot where the machine will be located, is that a current period expense? No; according to GAAP, the cost of the electrical work provides us with benefits over the entire useful life of the machine. Therefore, matching requires that we spread the cost of the electrical work over the same period as the life of the machine. The way that is handled is by adding the cost of the electrical work to the cost of the equipment. Instead of our equipment showing a cost of $20,000, it will have a cost of $21,000 and we will depreciate that amount over its lifetime.

In fact, all costs to put an item into service will be added to the cost of that item so that they can be matched with the revenues over the useful life of the asset. This would include freight on the purchase, insurance while in transit to our factory, new fixtures, plant modifications, etc.

Further, while repairs and maintenance are current period expenses, replacements and improvements to an asset must be added to the cost and depreciated over the life remaining at the time of the replacement or improvement. Replacements and improvements are simply expenditures that extend the useful life of the asset, improve its speed or quality, or reduce its operating costs.

If a motor burns out, is its replacement a routine repair or a *capitalizable* (capitalize means to add to the cost of a long-term item shown on the balance sheet) event? That depends on the circumstances. Do motors burn out quite regularly, or is it a rare event? Regular replacement may well be a repair, but infrequent major overhauls lead to treatment as a replacement. However, there is no clear right or wrong answer in many instances.

The Depreciable Base

Our problems are not yet over. How much of the asset's cost do we depreciate? Your first reaction may well be to say the entire cost, including the various additions to the purchase price that we have just discussed. This is basically true, except that there is still a matching problem. We wish to depreciate property that wears out in the productive process in order to get a portion of its cost assigned to each period in which it helped generate revenues. However, we only want to match against revenues those resources that actually have been used up. We don't necessarily consume 100 percent of most assets.

Suppose if we bought a machine with a ten-year expected life at a cost of $20,000, including all of the costs to put it into service. Suppose further that after ten years we expect to be able to sell the machine for $2,000. Then we really have not used up $20,000 of resources over the ten years. We have used up only $18,000 and we still have a $2,000 asset left over. This $2,000 value is referred to as the machine's *salvage value*.

Therefore, from an accounting perspective, we depreciate a machine by an amount equal to its cost less its anticipated salvage value. That difference is referred to as its *depreciable base*.

The salvage value will have to be estimated—at best, it will be an educated guess. Your accountant reviews the reasonableness of your salvage value estimates for financial statement preparation.

Accumulated Depreciation

In Chapter 8, the balance sheet had a line for *Plant and Equipment, Net*. This means the cost of the plant and equipment, less any depreciation that has been charged to that plant and equipment while we have owned it. The full amount of depreciation that has been taken on a piece of depreciable property over all the years you have owned it is called *accumulated depreciation*. It is important to distinguish between each year's depreciation expense and the accumulated depreciation.

Suppose that we have a piece of equipment that cost $20,000, has a $2,000 salvage value, and has an $18,000 depreciable base. Assume that we plan to depreciate it at a rate of $1,800 a year for ten years. The first year that we own it, $1,800 of depreciation expense is shown on the income statement. The same is true each year for ten years.

How does the equipment appear on the balance sheet? At the end of the first year, it will appear as $18,200, net. This is the $20,000 cost, less the first year's depreciation expense. By the end of the second year, we will have taken a total of $3,600 of depreciation expense (i.e., $1,800 per year × 2 years). That $3,600 is referred to as the accumulated depreciation for that piece of equipment. The net value of the equipment is now shown on the balance sheet as $16,400 (i.e., the $20,000 cost, less the $3,600 of accumulated depreciation).

Asset Life

How long will a machine last? We attempt to depreciate an asset over its useful life. If we depreciate it over a period longer or shorter than its useful life, we won't obtain an accurate matching between revenues and the expenses incurred in order to generate those revenues. However, we can only guess an asset's true useful life. Often we see equipment that lasts well after the estimated useful life. This is not surprising considering the

GAAP of conservatism. Better to write off an asset too quickly and under-state its true value, than to write it off too slowly (anticipating a longer life than ultimately results) and overstate its value.

What happens if we are still using the asset after its estimated useful life is over? We stop taking further depreciation. The role of depreciation is to allocate some of the cost of the asset into each of a number of peri-ods. Once we have allocated all of the cost (less the salvage value), we simply continue to use the asset with no further depreciation. That means we will have revenues without depreciation expense matched against them. That is simply a result of a matching based on estimates instead of perfect foreknowledge.

What if we sell the asset for more than its salvage value? That pres-ents no problem—we can record a gain for the difference between the sell-ing price and the asset's *book value*. The book value of an asset is the amount paid for it, less the amount of depreciation already taken. Thus, if we bought our machine for $20,000, and sold it after ten years during which we had taken $18,000 of depreciation, the book value would be $2,000. According to our financial records, or books, its value is $2,000. If we sold it for $5,000, there would be a gain of $3,000.

What if the asset becomes obsolete after three years due to techno-logical change and it is sold at that time for $500? Assuming we were depreciating it at a rate of $1,800 a year (to arrive at $18,000 of depreci-ation over ten years), then we would have taken $5,400 of depreciation (3 years at $1,800 per year) during those first three years. The book value ($20,000 cost less $5,400 of accumulated depreciation) is $14,600, and at a sale price of $500, we would record a loss of $14,100.

STRAIGHT-LINE VS. ACCELERATED DEPRECIATION

In the previous example we noted that $5,400 of depreciation had been taken over three years, if we assumed depreciation of $1,800 per year. The $1,800 figure is based on *straight-line* depreciation. It assumes that we take an equal share of the total depreciation each year during the asset's life.

In fact, we have choices for how we calculate the depreciation. The straight-line approach is just one of several methods available to us. Not all equipment declines in productive value equally in each year of its useful life. Consider a machine that has a capacity of one million units of output over its lifetime. If it is run three shifts a day, it will be used up substantially quicker than if it is run only one shift a day. The *units of production* or *units of activity* method of depreciation bases each year's depreciation on the proportion of the machine's total productive capacity that has been used in that year. For instance, if the machine produces 130,000 units in a year, and its estimated total lifetime capacity is one million, we would take 13 percent (130,000 divided by 1,000,000) of the cost less salvage value as the depreciation for that year. Of course, this method entails substantial extra bookkeeping to keep track of annual production.

Two other methods exist that are commonly used—the *declining balance method* (really this is a group of similar methods as discussed below) and the *sum-of-the-years digits* method. These are called *accelerated* methods. The basic philosophy behind these methods is that some assets are likely to decline in value more rapidly in the early years of their life than in the later years. A car is an excellent example. If we consider the decline in value for a car, it is largest in its first year, not quite as large in the following year, and eventually tails off to a point where there is relatively little decline per year in the latter part of its life.

COMPARISON OF THE DEPRECIATION METHODS

We will use an example to demonstrate the principal depreciation methods and to allow us to compare the results using each method. Assume that we buy a machine for $20,000 and we have $4,000 of costs to put the machine into service. We expect the machine to have a useful life of six years and a salvage value of $3,000.

The straight-line method (STL) first calculates the depreciable base, which is the cost less salvage. In this case, the cost is the $20,000 price plus the $4,000 to put the machine into service. The salvage value is $3,000, so the depreciable base is $21,000 ($20,000 + $4,000 – $3,000). The base is then allocated equally among the years of the asset's life. For a six-year life, the depreciation would be ⅙ of the $21,000 each year, or $3,500 per year. The straight-line method is rather straightforward.

The declining balance method accelerates the amount of depreciation taken in the early years and reduces the amount taken in the later years. When someone refers to accelerated depreciation, he or she is not referring to a shortening of the asset life for depreciation purposes. The life remains six years under the accelerated methods. Declining balance represents a group of methods. We will start with double declining balance (DDB), also referred to as 200 percent declining balance. We will discuss the other declining balance methods later.

The DDB approach starts out with a depreciable base equal to the asset cost ignoring salvage value. The cost is multiplied, not by $\frac{1}{6}$ as in the STL method, but by a rate that is double the STL rate. In this case we would multiply the depreciable base by 2 times $\frac{1}{6}$, or by $\frac{2}{6}$. Hence the word double in the name of this method. If we take $\frac{2}{6}$ of $24,000 (remember that cost includes the various costs to get the machine into service, and that this method ignores salvage value), we get $8,000 of depreciation for the first year. At that rate, the asset will be fully depreciated in just three years, and we've said that accelerated methods generally do not shorten the asset life!

Therefore, we need some device to prevent the depreciation from remaining at that high level of $8,000 per year. This device is the *declining balance*. Each year we subtract the previous year's depreciation from the existing depreciable base to get a new depreciable base. In this example, we start with a base of $24,000 and take $8,000 of depreciation in the first year. This means that in the second year there will be a new depreciable base of $16,000 ($24,000 − $8,000). In the second year, our depreciation would be $\frac{2}{6}$ of $16,000 or $5,333. For year three, we will determine a new base equal to $16,000 less year two's depreciation of $5,333. Thus we have a new base of $10,667, and so on.

However, there is one caveat to this process. We cannot take more depreciation during the asset's life than the asset's cost less its salvage value. In this problem, we can take no more than $21,000 of depreciation, regardless of the method chosen. We have achieved our goal of having higher depreciation in the early years and less in each succeeding year. The method, which simply doubles the STL rate, does have some intuitive appeal as an approach for getting the desired accelerated effect.

The declining balance family also includes 150 percent declining balance and 175 percent declining balance. In each of these methods, the only difference from the 200 percent, or DDB, is that the STL rate is multiplied by 150 percent or 175 percent instead of 200 percent to find the annual rate.

Sum-of-the-years-digits (SYD) is a similar accelerated method. SYD takes the cost less salvage, that is, $21,000, the same as STL, and multiplies it by a fraction that consists of the life of the asset divided by the sum of the digits in the years of the life of the asset. That sum simply consists of adding from one to the last year of the asset's life, inclusive. In our example, we would add 1 + 2 + 3 + 4 + 5 + 6, because the asset has a six-year life. The sum of these digits is 21. Therefore, we would multiply $21,000 by $^6/_{21}$ (the life of the asset divided by the sum). This gives us first-year depreciation of $6,000.

In each succeeding year, we would lower the numerator of the fraction by one. That is, for year two the fraction becomes $^5/_{21}$ and the depreciation would be $5,000 ($21,000 × $^5/_{21}$). For year three the fraction becomes $^4/_{21}$ and the depreciation $4,000, and so on. It is hard to find any intuitive appeal to this manipulation. All we can say is that it does achieve the desired result of greater depreciation in the early years, and it does account for the proper amount of total depreciation.

Exhibit 15-1 compares the three methods for this piece of equipment for its entire six-year life. It is especially important to note that all three methods produce exactly the same total depreciation over the life of the asset.

EXHIBIT 15-1.
Comparison of Depreciation Methods

YEAR	STRAIGHT-LINE (STL)	DOUBLE DECLINING BALANCE (DDB)	SUM-OF-THE-YEARS-DIGITS (SYD)
1	$ 3,500	$ 8,000	$ 6,000
2	3,500	5,333	5,000
3	3,500	3,556	4,000
4	3,500	2,370	3,000
5	3,500	1,607	2,000
6	3,500	134	1,000
Total	$21,000	$21,000	$21,000

Ideally, in choosing a depreciation method for your firm, you would select from among STL, declining balance, and SYD based on the method that most closely approximates the manner in which your particular resources are used up and become less productive. You need not use the same method for all of your depreciable property.

Many firms simply choose the STL approach for reporting depreciation on their financial statements to be issued to their stockholders. The apparent reason for this is that it tends to cause net income to be higher in the early years than it would be using the accelerated methods and their high charges to depreciation expense.

Excel Exercise

Template 16 may be used to calculate straight-line and accelerated depreciation using your firm's data. The template is included on the CD that accompanies this book.

Up until now, we have been speaking strictly in terms of recording information for financial statements. It is now time to consider the special tax treatment of depreciation.

MODIFIED ACCELERATED COST RECOVERY SYSTEM (MACRS)

The first and most important point that the reader should be aware of is that this is one place where you can actually have your cake and eat it too! It is not required that firms use the same method of depreciation for reporting to the Internal Revenue Service (IRS) as they use for reporting to their stockholders. The implications of that are enormous. We can use straight-line depreciation on our financial statements, thus keeping our depreciation expense relatively low, and be able to tell our stockholders that we had a very fine year. Then we can use the IRS accelerated depreciation system, called the Modified Accelerated Cost Recovery System (MACRS), which accelerates depreciation, lowering income and taxes in the early years of an asset's life.

We will highlight many of the important issues here. However, we can't stress strongly enough the benefits of consulting a tax expert. Tax law is an area that requires up-to-date expertise. The tax law changes constantly not only because of congressional action, but also as a result of IRS rulings and interpretations and the results of court cases. No tax decisions should be made based solely on the information contained in this book.

The most important aspect of the IRS depreciation system is that it assigns shorter lives to assets. Generally these shorter lives are not used in preparation of financial statements for reports to stockholders. The law does give some leeway in extending the life of the asset or choosing a less accelerated approach, but most firms find that the basic MACRS approach provides the quickest allowable deductions and therefore is beneficial in most cases. By accelerating a deduction, a profitable firm can push its tax payments off to the future, thus effectively getting an interest-free loan from the government.

Under MACRS, asset lives are substantially shorter than their useful life estimates, and salvage value is ignored until we actually dispose of the asset. The government-imposed lifetimes for depreciation under MACRS for different types of assets are three, five, seven, ten, fifteen, twenty, twenty-seven and a half, and thirty-nine years.

The three-, five-, seven-, and ten-year classes are depreciated under the 200 percent or DDB system that substantially accelerates depreciation. The fifteen- and twenty-year classes are depreciated using a 150 percent declining balance method. The twenty-seven and one-half- and thirty-nine-year classes are depreciated on an STL basis.

The MACRS three-year category includes items such as tractors, some machine tools, and racehorses over twelve years old. Leave it to Congress!

The MACRS five-year category includes property with a useful life of more than four but less than ten years. This class specifically includes computers, cars, trucks, and research and experimental equipment.

The MACRS seven-year class includes property that has a life of ten to fifteen years. This generally includes office furniture and fixtures and property that does not explicitly fall into another category.

The MACRS ten-year class is for property with a life of sixteen to nineteen years. Included are vessels, barges, and tugs.

The MACRS fifteen-year class includes property with a life of twenty to twenty-four years. This category includes billboards, service station buildings, and land improvements.

The MACRS twenty-year class is for property with a useful life of twenty-five years or more, such as utilities and sewers.

Residential rental property falls into the twenty-seven and one-half-year class, and most nonresidential real property has a class period of thirty-nine years.

Although all of this may make your head swim, the government has kindly provided tables giving the percentage of the asset's cost to be taken as depreciation for tax purposes in each year of the asset's life. For example, Exhibit 15-2 provides a table showing the portion of the asset to be depreciated each year under MACRS, for the three- through twenty-year classes. Note that the table contains twenty-one years because it is generally assumed that each asset (except real property) is put into service halfway into the year. The first and last years each contain only a half-year of depreciation. (It should be noted as an aside that there is a less favorable mid-quarter convention that applies if substantial portions of a year's assets are placed into service in the last three months of the tax year.)

Excel Exercise

Template 17 may be used to calculate MACRS depreciation for your organization. The template is included on the CD that accompanies this book. Tax law is complex and changes frequently. Do not file tax returns based on information from the use of this template without first consulting a tax expert.

In some instances, it is possible to deduct in one tax year up to $24,000 of assets, rather than depreciating them under MACRS. The amount will rise from $24,000 to $25,000 in 2003. This is an option available to the taxpayer for some types of property used in a trade or business. It is referred to as a *Section 179 expense.* The available deduction is phased out if more than $200,000 worth of qualified property is placed into service during the tax year. To the extent that you can avail yourself of this rule, it can provide an even faster tax write-off of the asset than MACRS would generate.

Another tax issue concerns "Section 197 Intangibles." This refers to goodwill and other purchased intangibles. Firms may deduct the cost of such intangibles as an expense for tax purposes on an STL basis over a fifteen-year period.

EXHIBIT 15-2.
MACRS Schedule for Property
Placed in Service after 1986

APPROPRIATE PERCENTAGE

YEAR	3-YEAR CLASS	5-YEAR CLASS	7-YEAR CLASS	10-YEAR CLASS	15-YEAR CLASS	20-YEAR CLASS
1	33.33	20.00	14.29	10.00	5.00	3.750
2	44.45	32.00	24.49	18.00	9.50	7.219
3	14.81	19.20	17.49	14.40	8.55	6.677
4	7.41	11.52	12.49	11.52	7.70	6.177
5		11.52	8.93	9.22	6.93	5.713
6		5.76	8.92	7.37	6.23	5.285
7			8.93	6.55	5.90	4.888
8			4.46	6.55	5.90	4.522
9				6.56	5.91	4.462
10				6.55	5.90	4.461
11				3.28	5.91	4.462
12					5.90	4.461
13					5.91	4.462
14					5.90	4.461
15					5.91	4.462
16					2.95	4.461
17						4.462
18						4.461
19						4.462
20						4.461
21						2.231

What's the bottom line to all this? Essentially, you can base the income you report to your stockholders on STL depreciation extended over the asset's useful life and using a salvage value, and at the same time, use the MACRS method for reporting to the IRS. Thus, you will tell your stockholders a net income that is higher than you tell the IRS. You therefore report relatively high income to the owners (your bosses), and yet pay relatively low taxes because of the higher depreciation reported to the government. Have you actually reduced your tax payments, or just shifted them off to the future? That is a very interesting question and one that is the basis for the discussion of deferred taxes.

DEPRECIATION AND DEFERRED TAXES: ACCOUNTING MAGIC

Above we discussed the use of straight-line depreciation for financial statements and MACRS for the tax return. The fact that we can tell different depreciation stories to our stockholders and the IRS has interesting ramifications for the firm and its financial statements. It creates something called a *temporary difference*. Our financial records record taxes in a different year than our tax return does.

If we tell our stockholders that we had a good year, then they expect the firm to pay a lot of taxes on the profits we are currently making. Even if we don't pay those taxes now, but instead defer payment to the future, the matching principle would seem to require that we record the tax expense based on our depreciation in our financial records, rather than when the IRS calculates the depreciation and taxes. In fact, that is exactly the case. Taxes are recorded on the firm's financial statements as tax expense and a liability, called a *deferred tax* liability. However, the implications of this deferred tax are quite unusual—almost magical.

Generally, if we can postpone payment of taxes, with no other change in the operation of our business in any respect, we should do so, For any one asset, the deferred tax liability represents an interest-free loan that will eventually be repaid to the government. However, what is true for one asset is not necessarily true for the entire firm. For many companies the balances in the deferred tax account will not become zero, but rather will grow continuously into the future.

This rather amazing result is simply explained. If we had one depreciable asset, over its lifetime we would first defer some tax and later repay it. But if we are constantly replacing equipment—buying new equipment as old equipment wears out—the deferral increase on the new assets will offset the deferral reduction on the old assets, often causing the deferral to effectively become a permanent interest-free loan. However, the magic of deferred taxes is not yet fully apparent.

Consider what happens for a firm that is growing. Such a firm is not only offsetting higher taxes on older equipment with deferred taxes on an equal amount of new equipment. The expansion in fixed assets will cause the deferred liability to grow each year. For growing companies, the startling result is that deferred taxes represent both a growing and permanent interest-free loan. A bit of accounting magic.

KEY CONCEPTS

Matching—Depreciation is an attempt to match the cost of resources used up over a period longer than one year with the revenues those resources generate over their useful lifetime.

Amortization—a generic term for the spreading out of costs over a period of time. Depreciation is a special case of amortization.

Amounts to be depreciated—The cost of an asset, less its salvage value, is depreciated over the asset's useful life. The cost is the fair market value at the time of acquisition, plus costs to put the asset into service, plus the costs of improvements made to the asset.

Depreciation methods—The asset may be depreciated on a straight-line basis, taking equal amounts in each year, or by an accelerated method, which results in greater depreciation in the earlier years of the asset's life. Two common accelerated depreciation methods are double declining balance and sum-of-the-years-digits.

Modified Accelerated Cost Recovery System (MACRS)—the depreciation method used for tax reporting.

Deferred taxes—If the pretax income reported to stockholders is more than that reported to the IRS, then a tax deferral will arise; that is, some of our current tax expense becomes a liability to be paid at some unstated time in the future, rather than being paid currently.

Sixteen
Working Capital Management and Banking Relationships

WORKING CAPITAL MANAGEMENT

An organization's *net working capital*, or simply working capital, is its current assets less its current liabilities. This chapter focuses on *working capital management*: techniques and approaches designed to maximize the benefit of short-term resources and minimize the cost of short-term obligations.

Working capital is based on a cycle of outflows and inflows. For example, Coffin Corporation might use cash to buy raw materials inventory. The inventory is used to construct coffins. The employees making the coffins must also be paid. The coffins can then be sold to funeral homes, resulting in receivables. Once those receivables are collected, the cycle starts over, as that money can be used to buy more inventory and pay workers to construct more coffins.

The cycle may be delicately balanced. At the beginning of the cycle, Coffin Corporation may have just enough to pay for inventory and wages if it receives payments promptly from its customers. If Coffin issues bills once a month instead of weekly or daily, it may be more convenient for the bookkeeper, but it postpones collection of cash from customers. That cash is needed as soon as possible so that Coffin can cover its expenses.

In performing working capital management, it is the role of the manager to ensure that there is adequate cash on hand to meet the organization's needs and also to minimize the cost of that cash. To do this, the manager must carefully monitor and control cash inflows and outflows. Cash not immediately needed should be invested, earning a return for the organization. Excess inventory should not be kept by the organization.

The money spent to pay for inventory that is not yet needed could be better used by the organization for some other purpose. At a minimum, the money could be earning interest. Similarly, if the organization pays its bills before they are due, it will also lose interest it could have earned if it had left the cash in its savings account for a little longer.

SHORT-TERM RESOURCES

The most essential element of working capital is cash. When accountants refer to cash they mean both currency on hand and also amounts that can be withdrawn from bank accounts. A second type of short-term resource is *marketable securities*. These are investments such as stock and debt that can be bought and sold in financial markets, such as the New York Stock Exchange. In most organizations, accounts receivables and inventory are also important parts of working capital. These short-term resources are discussed in this section.

Cash

There are three principal reasons that organizations want to keep some cash on hand or in their bank accounts. First, cash is needed for the normal daily transactions of any activity. For example, cash is needed to pay employees and suppliers. Second, although many activities can be anticipated, managers can never foresee everything that might happen. Experience has shown that it makes sense for organizations to have a safety cushion available for emergencies. A third reason for holding cash is to have it available if an attractive investment opportunity arises.

Given these three reasons to hold cash, one might think that the more cash we have, the better. That is not the case. Cash earns a very low rate of return (e.g., bank savings account interest) at best. If we use our cash to buy buildings and equipment we can probably earn higher profits. But then we wouldn't have cash for transactions and emergencies. At the other extreme, we can keep all our resources in cash, but then we wouldn't earn much of a profit. In practice, managers must find a middle role, trying to keep enough cash available, but not too much.

Short-Term Cash Investments and Marketable Securities

Cash should be earning a return whenever possible. Organizations should have specific policies that result in cash and checks received being deposited promptly into interest-bearing accounts. In fact, even after a check is written to make a payment, it is possible to continue to earn interest on the money. The period from when you write a check until it clears your bank account is called the *float*. Many banks have arrangements that allow money to be automatically transferred from an interest-bearing account to a checking account as checks are received for payment.

Although interest-bearing accounts are better than noninterest accounts, they pay relatively low rates of interest. There are a variety of alternative short-term investments that have the potential to earn a higher rate of return. In a world of no free lunches, however, there is generally a trade-off when one obtains a higher rate of return. The two most common trade-offs are decreased liquidity and increased risk. Decreased liquidity means that the money is not immediately accessible. For example, *certificates of deposit* (*CDs*) pay higher interest rates than savings accounts, but there is often a penalty for early withdrawal.

Although CDs may tie up money for a period of time, they are generally quite safe. Other investments hold promise of even higher rates of return, but entail greater risks. Marketable securities can be sold almost immediately and cash from the sale can be received within a few days. However, such investments are subject to market fluctuations. The prices of stocks and bonds may go up and down significantly, even on a daily basis.

Other Short-Term Investment Options

Other options exist for short-term investments of cash. A *Treasury bill* (often called "T-bill") is a debt security issued by the U.S. government. Maturities range from four weeks to one year. If the bill is held until it matures, the federal government guarantees to pay the maturity value. Treasury bills can be purchased directly from the federal government without a fee through the Treasury Direct system on-line at www.publicdebt.treas.gov/. It is possible to sell a T-bill prior to its maturity date. Most stock brokerage firms will buy or sell Treasury bills for a fee of about $50.

Another alternative is money market funds. These investments tend to pay a rate below that of CDs, but competitive with Treasury bills and higher than the rate paid on a bank savings account. Interest is earned daily and money can be deposited or withdrawn at any time. Although the investment has no guarantee, money market funds are generally considered to be reasonably safe investments and they are very convenient to use.

The next type of money market instrument is a *negotiable certificate of deposit* issued by a U.S. bank. A negotiable CD can be sold to someone else, just as a bond can be sold. Sales commissions will be incurred and the value of the CD at the time of sale will depend on what has happened to market interest rates and the creditworthiness of the lender during the time since the investment was made.

Another type of money market instrument is *commercial paper*. Commercial paper generally represents a note payable issued by a corporation. Typical maturities are less than one year, and the interest rate is higher than a Treasury bill. The buyer of the paper is lending money to a corporation. There is a risk, albeit small, that the corporation will not repay the loan.

Repurchase agreements, or *repos*, are types of short-term investments that are collateralized by securities. Repos may be for as short a period of time as overnight. The organization with idle cash provides it to the borrower at an agreed-upon interest rate, which may fluctuate daily. Although repos are quite liquid, they do have a variety of risks. For example, if the borrower defaults, the collateral may turn out to be insufficient to cover the full investment.

Another option is *derivatives*. Derivatives are securities whose value is derived from the value of something else. For example, we could establish a security that will have as its value the average value of the stock price of five large corporations. Derivatives can be designed to reduce risk by allowing an investor to have the average gain or loss from a large number of securities, without having the expense of investing in all of those securities.

However, derivative securities often allow investors to enter into an investment without paying the full cost of that investment. This concept, called leverage, was discussed in Chapter 11. Leverage offers the potential for much higher returns if the investment performs the way that the investor would like it to, or much greater losses if it does not.

Commercial paper, negotiable CDs, repos, and derivatives would generally be suitable only for organizations that have substantial amounts of cash (perhaps over a million dollars) available for short-term investment. These investments can be quite complicated and should be used only by organizations that employ competent advisors knowledgeable in their intricacies and potential risks.

Accounts Receivable

One should always attempt to collect accounts receivable as quickly as possible. The sooner we collect all of our receivables, the sooner the organization has the cash available for its use, at least for investment in an interest-bearing bank account. Also, the longer we allow an account receivable to be outstanding, the lower the chances that it will ever be collected.

Accounts receivable are collected as a result of a cycle of activities, as follows:

Invoice Issued in Person or by Mail		Invoice Received by Customer		Invoice Is Paid by Customer		Payment Is Received		Payment Is Deposited		Payment Check Clears Bank
	$\Rightarrow$		$\Rightarrow$		$\Rightarrow$		$\Rightarrow$		$\Rightarrow$	

The faster and more accurately we compile the information needed to issue an invoice, and the sooner we actually issue the invoice, the faster payment can be expected.

However, management of accounts receivable does not stop when we issue an invoice. We need to establish credit policies that reduce the amount of money lost because customers fail to pay the amounts they owe us. We also need to monitor unpaid receivables to minimize such losses. An aging schedule, showing how long our receivables have been outstanding, is a very helpful device. When receivables are collected, there should be specific procedures to safeguard the cash until its ultimate deposit in the bank.

Credit Policies

Credit policies relate to deciding which customers will be allowed to make purchases on account. Organizations require some (or all) customers to pay cash at the time of purchase if there is a high risk that payment would not be received later. However, by excluding individuals or organizations from buying our goods or services on account, we may lose their business. You want to give credit terms that are as good as the competition, but don't want to give credit to customers who wind up never paying their bills. This requires a skillful credit manager to weigh the risks versus the benefits of extending credit to specific customers.

The Billing Process

The activities concentrated around issuing bills are critical. They must be done quickly, but also correctly. Something as minor as a missing zip code in the billing address could lead to a payment delay of several months or more. When we have gathered all necessary information and reviewed the information for both completeness and accuracy, a bill should be issued promptly . Even speeding up collections by two or three days can have a significant impact. For any one bill, it does not seem to matter if there are a few delays. However, when all bills are considered, the impact of prompt billing is significant.

Electronic Billing and Collections

One method to speed collections is electronic billing. In addition to allowing faster collection, electronic billing may prove to be less expensive to process than paper billing because it uses less labor. Electronic billing also allows for quicker communication of problems. The sooner we know that a customer has a problem with an invoice, the greater the likelihood that the organization can still gather any data needed to correct the invoice, and the more likely it is that it will ultimately be paid.

Many businesses now use electronic transfers to collect payment from their customers. Clearly, if your organization can draw money directly from its customers' bank accounts, it can increase the speed of collections and reduce the amount of bad debts.

Aging of Receivables

Once bills have been issued, it is important for the organization to monitor receivables and to follow up on unpaid bills. A useful tool for this process is an accounts receivable *aging schedule*. An aging schedule shows how long it has been between the current date and the date when uncollected bills were issued. For example, at the end of July, a summary aging schedule for the Coffin Corporation might appear as the example in Exhibit 16-1.

EXHIBIT 16-1.
Coffin Corporation
Receivables Aging Schedule
As of July 31, 2002

PAYER	1–30 DAYS	31–60 DAYS	61–90 DAYS	>90 DAYS	TOTAL
By Total Dollars					
Independent Homes	$8,052,342	$995,028	$702,556	$93,050	$9,842,976
Mortuaries, Inc.	3,250,000	475,000	56,000	22,000	3,803,000
In Your Time of Need	861,232	223,637	27,333	2,222	1,114,424
Undertakers of America	583,474	389,640	4,500	2,760	980,374
Total	$12,747,048	$2,083,305	$790,389	$120,032	$15,740,774
By Percentage					
Independent Homes	81.8%	10.1%	7.1%	1.0%	100.0%
Mortuaries, Inc.	85.5	12.5	1.5	.5	100.0
In Your Time of Need	77.3	20.1	2.5	.1	100.0
Undertakers of America	59.5	39.7	0.5	.3	100.0
Total	81.0%	13.2%	5.0%	.8%	100.0%

In Exhibit 16-1, we notice that the largest share of Coffin's receivables is from independent funeral homes. Coffin also has several large funeral home chains as customers: Mortuaries, Inc., In Your Time of Need, and Undertakers of America. Because those three chains are much larger than Coffin's other customers, they are listed individually. We can see from the bottom half of the aging schedule that 81 percent of Coffin's receivables have been outstanding for less than one month. Less than 1 percent of its receivables are outstanding for more than ninety days. In the period shortly after invoices are issued, Undertakers of America is the slowest customer to pay, with only 60 percent collected in the first month. In the longer period, the independent homes lag with 7 percent being collected in the 61–90 day period and 1 percent still outstanding after ninety days.

> ### Excel Exercise
>
> **You may use Template 18 to prepare an aging schedule for your organization. The template is on the CD that accompanies this book.**

The aging schedule is a valuable tool because problem areas can be quickly identified. Efforts to collect payment should begin as soon as the invoice is issued. If anything goes beyond the current column (i.e., 1–30 days), there should be a formal procedure, such as the issuance of a reminder statement. If an account exceeds sixty days, there should be procedures such as mailing another statement, often colored pink to get greater attention. The "over-ninety-day" category in an aging schedule is a particular concern, even though it may be a small part of the total. Amounts in that category probably reflect problems encountered in processing the bills or else an inability or unwillingness to pay. All organizations should have specific follow-up procedures for accounts that fall into this category. These procedures should include not only monthly statements, but also late charges and telephone calls to determine why payment has not been made. The longer an invoice goes unpaid, the less likely it will ever be paid.

In some cases, it is necessary to use a collection agency if other efforts have failed. This is a costly approach, since collection agencies retain as much as half of all amounts that they are successful in collecting.

Lockboxes

Some organizations have payments sent directly to a *lockbox* rather than to the organization itself. Lockboxes are usually post office boxes that are emptied by the bank rather than the organization. The bank opens the envelopes with the payments and deposits them directly into the organization's account.

One advantage of this approach is that the bank will empty the box and deposit the money at least once a day. This gets the money into interest-bearing accounts faster than if it had to go through the organization. Secondly, use of a lockbox tends to substantially decrease the risk that receipts will be lost or stolen.

Inventory Management

Careful management of inventory can also save money for the organization. The lower the level of inventory kept on hand, the less you have paid out to suppliers, and the greater the amount of money kept in your own interest-bearing savings accounts. On the other hand, for many organizations, there are uncertainties that require inventory both for current use and as a safety measure. Management must develop systems to ensure adequate availability of inventory when needed while keeping overall levels as low as possible.

Centralized storing of inventory should be used if possible. If separate locations for inventory are created, convenience rises but so do costs. The more separate storage sites, the greater the amount of each inventory item the organization is likely to have. The ordering process should also be as centralized as possible to minimize employee time spent processing orders, and maximize the possibility of volume discounts.

Economic Order Quantity (EOQ)

There are a variety of costs related to inventory in addition to the purchase price. We must have physical space to store it, we may need to pay to insure it, and there are costs related to placing an order and having it shipped. A method called the *economic order quantity* (EOQ) considers all of these factors in calculating the optimum amount of inventory to order at one time.

The more inventory ordered at one time, the sooner we pay for inventory (taking money out of our investments or interest-bearing accounts) and the greater the costs for things such as inventory storage. These are called *carrying* or *holding* costs. On the other hand, if we keep relatively little inventory on hand to keep carrying costs low, we will have to order inventory more often. That drives *ordering* costs up. EOQ balances these two factors to find the optimal amount to order.

There are two categories of carrying costs. These are *capital cost* and *out-of-pocket costs*. The capital cost is the cost related to having paid for inventory, as opposed to using those resources for other alternative uses. At a minimum this is the foregone interest that could have been earned on the money paid for inventory. Out-of-pocket costs are other costs related to holding inventory, including rent on space where inventory is kept, insurance and taxes on the value of inventory, the cost of annual inventory counts, the losses due to obsolescence and date-related expirations, and the costs of damage, loss, and theft.

Ordering costs include the cost of having an employee spend time placing orders, the shipping and handling charges for the orders, and the cost of correcting errors when orders are placed. The more orders, the more errors.

There is an offsetting dynamic in inventory management. The more orders per year, the less inventory that needs to be on hand at any given time, and therefore the lower the carrying cost. However, the more orders per year, the greater the amount the organization spends on placing orders, on shipping and handling costs, and on error correction. The total costs of inventory are the sum of the amount paid for inventory, plus the carrying costs, plus the ordering costs.

Total Inventory Cost = Purchase Cost + Carrying Cost + Ordering Cost

The goal of inventory management is to minimize this total without reducing the quality of services the organization provides.

We will use N for the total number of units of inventory ordered per year, C for the annual cost to carry one unit of inventory, and O for the costs related to placing one order. The EOQ represents the optimal number of units to order at one time.

Suppose that Coffin pays $10 per gold-plated coffin handle. They buy 2,000 handles per year. Each time they place an order, it takes a paid clerk $5 worth of time to process the order. The delivery cost is $10 per order. The $15 is the total of ordering costs. Coffin earns an average of 6 percent interest on invested money. Therefore, the capital part of the carrying cost is 60 cents per handle per year (6% × $10 price = $.60). Other carrying costs (such as storage and insurance) are estimated to be $2.40 per handle per year. Therefore the total carrying costs are $3 per handle per year.

The formula to determine the optimal number to order at one time is:

$$EOQ = \sqrt{\frac{2\,ON}{C}}$$

where EOQ is the optimal amount to order each time.

$$EOQ = \sqrt{\frac{2 \times \$15 \times 2,000}{\$3}}$$

$$= 141$$

This result indicates that we should order 141 handles at a time, to minimize costs related to acquiring and holding inventory.

Excel Exercise

Template 19 may be used to calculate the Economic Order Quantity for your organization. The template is on the CD that accompanies this book.

The basic EOQ model, as presented here, makes a number of assumptions that are often not true. For example, it assumes that any number of units can be purchased. In some cases an item might only be sold in certain quantities, such as hundreds or dozens. Another assumption is that the price per unit does not change if we order differing numbers of units with each order. It is possible that we might get a quantity discount for large orders. Such a discount could offset some of the higher carrying cost related to large orders. Managers should adjust the EOQ based on the impact of these issues.

Another assumption is that we use up our last unit of an item just when the next shipment arrives. A delay in processing, however, could cause inventory to arrive late, and we might run out of certain items. To avoid negative consequences of such *stock outs*, we might want to keep a safety stock on hand. How large should that safety stock be? That will depend on how long it takes to get more inventory if we start to run out, and on how critical the consequences of running out are.

Just-in-Time Inventory

One aggressive approach to inventory management is called *just-in-time (JIT)* inventory. This method argues that carrying costs should be driven to an absolute minimum. This is accomplished by having inventory arrive just as it is needed for production. The advantages are obvious: no storage costs, reduced handling costs, minimum breakage, and no need to pay for inventory before you need it. However, there are clear disadvantages as well: increased ordering and shipping costs, and the risk that it will be necessary to stop production lines if inventory doesn't arrive as it is needed.

The application of JIT really centers on how close one can come to the ideal. There will invariably be problems when implementing a JIT system. For any organization, workflow will not necessarily proceed in an orderly manner. There will be peaks and valleys in demand. Such variability creates major challenges for the implementation of a JIT system.

SHORT-TERM OBLIGATIONS

To this point, this chapter has focused on short-term resources. We now turn our attention to management of short-term obligations, or current liabilities. Careful management of such obligations can save a substantial amount of money. Some short-term obligations that need management attention are *accounts payable*, *payroll payable*, *notes payable*, and *taxes payable*.

Accounts payable represents amounts that the organization owes to its suppliers. Payroll payable is an amount owed to employees. Notes payable represents an obligation to repay money that has been borrowed. Taxes payable includes income, sales, real estate, payroll, and other taxes.

As a general rule, managers should try to delay payment of short-term obligations in order to keep resources in the organization available to earn interest, or to avoid unnecessary short-term borrowing and related interest expenses. However, this must be balanced against any negative consequences related to delayed payments.

Accounts Payable

Accounts payable is often called *trade credit*. In most cases, there is no interest charge for trade credit, assuming that payment is made when due. For example, Coffin might order and receive a shipment of mahogany lumber. Shortly afterward, it receives an invoice from the supplier. The invoice will generally have a due date.

Some suppliers charge interest for payments received after the due date. Others do not. A common practice in many industries is to offer a discount for prompt payment. On an invoice, under a heading called *terms*, there may be an indication such as: 2/10 N/30. This would be read as "two ten, net thirty." A discount of 2/10 N/30 means that if payment is received within ten days of the invoice date, the payer can take a 2 percent discount off the total. If payment is not made within ten days, then the full amount of the bill is due thirty days from the invoice date. Some companies state their terms in relation to the end of the month. Terms of 2/10 EOM (two ten, end of month) mean that the buyer can take a 2 percent discount for payments received by the company no later than ten days after the end of the month in which the invoice is issued.

One confusing element is that if you don't take the early payment discount, you pay the "net" amount, which is the full amount on the invoice. Usually net refers to a number after a subtraction has been made. The reason for this strange terminology is that many times organizations negotiate a discount from the full price at the time an order is placed. For example, suppose that the regular wholesale price for silver-plated coffin handles is $2.50 each. However, Coffin successfully negotiated a 20 percent discount off the official or "list" price. Perhaps this is a volume discount. Alternatively, it may be a discount that the handle manufacturer offers to meet a competitor's price. From the seller's viewpoint, $2.50 is the list or gross price, $2.00 is the invoice or *net price*, and $1.96 is the net price less a discount for prompt payment (the $2.00 negotiated price less the 2 percent discount = $1.96).

Does it make sense to take advantage of discounts for prompt payment? A formula can be used to determine the annual interest rate implicit in trade credit discounts:

$$\text{Implicit Interest Rate} = \frac{\text{Discount}}{\text{Discounted Price}} \times \frac{\text{365 Days}}{\text{Days Sooner}} \times 100\%$$

For example, suppose that Coffin purchased $5,000 of casket liners with payment terms of 2/10 N/30. A 2 percent discount on a $5,000 purchase would be $100. This means that if the discount is taken, only $4,900 would have to be paid. By taking the discount, Coffin must make payment by the tenth day rather than the thirtieth day. This means that payment is made twenty days sooner than would otherwise be the case.

$$\text{Implicit Interest Rate} = \frac{\$100}{\$4,900} \times \frac{365 \text{ Days}}{20 \text{ Days}} \times 100\% = 37.2\%$$

While the stated discount rate of 2 percent seems to be rather small, it is actually quite large on an annualized basis. Gaining a 2 percent discount in exchange for paying just twenty days sooner represents a high annual rate of return. Suppose that the organization has $4,900 of cash available to pay the bill on the tenth day. In order for it to make sense not to pay the bill promptly and take the discount, it would have to invest the money for the next twenty days in an investment that would earn at least $100 over that period. Any investment that could give us that return would be earning profits at a rate of at least 37.2 percent per year. Since most organizations do not have access to short-term investments that are assured of earning such a high rate, it pays to take the discount and pay promptly. Even if you have to borrow money to take the discount you should, as long as you can borrow at an interest rate of less than 37.2 percent per year.

This assumes, of course, that the invoice will be paid on time if the discount is not taken. Suppose, however, that Coffin often pays its bills late. Sometimes, it pays after three months. Would it make sense to take the discount and pay in ten days, or to wait and pay the bill after ninety days? Paying after ten days is eighty days earlier than if we normally wait for ninety days before making our payment.

$$\text{Implicit Interest Rate} = \frac{\text{Discount}}{\substack{\text{Discounted} \\ \text{Price}}} \times \frac{365 \text{ Days}}{\substack{\text{Days} \\ \text{Sooner}}} \times 100\%$$

$$\text{Implicit Interest Rate} = \frac{\$100}{\$4,900} \times \frac{365 \text{ Days}}{80 \text{ Days}} \times 100\% = 9.3\%$$

If Coffin can earn more than 9.3 percent on its investments, or if Coffin does not have enough money to pay the bill and a bank would charge more than 9.3 percent to lend the money, then Coffin is better off waiting. However, that assumes its suppliers are willing to wait and will not charge interest for late payments. Otherwise, Coffin should pay promptly and take the discount.

Excel Exercise

Use Template 20 to calculate the implicit interest rate for any discount for prompt payment. The template is on the CD that accompanies this book.

Payroll Payable

Each organization must decide upon a number of general policies, such as how many holidays, vacation days, and sick days employees get. Most new organizations are well advised to be fairly conservative to start. It is much easier to later decide that you can afford to give employees more vacation than it is to reduce the vacation allowance. The benefits of employee morale from a more liberal policy must be weighed against the cost of paying for days not worked.

Another policy decision relates to whether employees will receive pay for sick days in cash if they do not use them. If employees are allowed to accumulate sick days and know they will get paid eventually whether they take them or not, then they are more likely to accumulate a substantial bank of sick leave for a serious illness. When sick leave is lost each year if it is not used, employees are more likely to take sick days when they are not sick. This encourages a culture whereby employees lie to the organization.

Although it is costly to pay employees for accumulated sick leave, it is important to bear in mind that for many employees it will be years or decades before that payment is made. In the intervening time the employer has had the benefit of earning interest on that money. If sick leave can't be accumulated, most of it will be used and paid for currently. So it may actually turn out to be less costly to allow accumulation than to enforce a "use it or lose it" policy.

Each organization must also decide on the length of the payroll period, and how soon payment is made to employees once the payroll period ends. Employees could be paid daily, weekly, biweekly, or monthly. They could be paid on the last day of the payroll period, or a few days or a week later. The less frequently you pay, the fewer checks that must be written, reducing bookkeeping costs. Further, paying less frequently and later means that the employer holds onto the cash for a longer period, earning more interest. On the other hand, employees obviously prefer to be paid more often and sooner. Poor morale can turn out to be more costly than the benefits that the organization may have accrued in the form of extra interest.

Payroll policy must also focus on other *fringe benefits*. The organization must decide what fringes to offer, and how much will be paid by the employer versus the portion paid by the employee. Other fringes (in addition to vacation, holidays, and sick leave) include items such as health and dental insurance, life insurance, child care, car allowances, parking, and pensions.

Accounting and Compliance Issues

Payroll accounting is complicated by the various deductions that must be made from wages. The most prominent reason for payroll deductions relates to tax compliance issues. It is necessary to withhold income taxes, Social Security (FICA) taxes, unemployment insurance, and disability insurance. Most states also have state income taxes that must be withheld, and some localities have payroll or income taxes.

Calculating taxes can be complicated. At times the government changes the tax rates or the amount of income subject to tax. It is also critical to submit payments to the various governments on a timely basis. We don't want to pay early, because we are better off holding the money in our interest-bearing account for as long as possible. On the other hand, there are costly penalties for late payment that should be avoided.

In addition to taxes and other government-required deductions, there are a number of other types of deductions from payroll. These include amounts for health and dental insurance, pensions, life insurance, and other similar items. Often the employer pays for part or most of these benefits, and the employee makes a lesser contribution. Payroll can be further complicated if your organization pays bonuses, overtime, or piecework pay, or if your employees receive tips.

It is probably inadvisable for nonfinancial managers to attempt to take on too much of the payroll process themselves. Either the organization needs to have a payroll department that can specialize in this process, or an outside payroll vendor should be used. Each organization must determine whether it is best to prepare the payroll in-house or to use a service. At least part of this analysis must rest on:

- the relative cost of preparing the payroll internally versus using a service;
- a determination of whether the company has the expertise to be able to prepare payroll internally; and
- whether the organization's employees have the time to prepare the payroll internally.

Suppose that you decide to use an outside service. That doesn't mean that your company will have nothing left to do. First, all payroll changes, such as newly hired employees or raises, must be carefully recorded. Second, employees need to be clearly classified between professional staff, hourly employees, commission-based, and piecework employees. Finally, your company must accurately record hours worked, sales, or other key information needed to calculate wages earned.

Notes Payable

Notes payable are short-term loans evidenced by a written document signed by all parties that specifies the amount borrowed, the interest rate, and the due date for repayment. Often such notes are *demand notes*. This means that the lender has the right to call for immediate payment of the full amount borrowed, plus accrued interest, at any time.

The interest on a note or loan is equal to the amount of the loan, multiplied by the annual interest rate, multiplied by the fraction of the year that the loan is outstanding:

Interest = Loan Amount × Interest Rate per Year × Fraction of Year

For example, the interest on an 8 percent, six-month note for $10,000 would be:

$$\text{Interest} = \$10,000 \times 8\% \times \tfrac{1}{2} = \$400$$

Typically, organizations obtain short-term debt by borrowing money from banks using *unsecured* notes. An unsecured note has no specific asset that will be delivered to the lender if the borrower fails to make required payments. Such an asset would be referred to as *collateral*. A secured note is one that has collateral. If the borrower fails to repay an unsecured loan, the lender joins with all other creditors in making a general claim on the resources of the organization. This is riskier than having collateral; unsecured loans, therefore, often have higher interest rates to offset the lender's higher risk.

For organizations that have limited financial resources, another approach for obtaining short-term financing is to borrow money from an organization that specializes in financing and factoring receivables. A *factoring* arrangement is one in which we sell our receivables. The buyer is called a factor. The right to collect those receivables then belongs to the factor. In most cases, if receivables are factored, the organization receives less than it would have received but it gets the cash sooner. Alternatively, a financing arrangement is one whereby money is borrowed with the receivables being used as collateral in case we cannot repay the loan.

Taxes Payable

Taxes payable represents a short-term obligation. As with other short-term obligations, these should not be paid before they are due. However, since there are often penalties in addition to interest for late payment, managers must have a system in place to ensure that taxes are paid on time.

BANKING RELATIONSHIPS

Working capital management often requires a good working relationship with one or more banks. A system of checking and savings accounts will be required by most organizations. Many short-term investments are made with one of the organization's banks. And, of course, money is often borrowed from banks.

Many people think of banks as a place to go when you need a loan. However, you are much more likely to get a loan if you establish a long-term relationship with a bank. Let the bank get to know your organization. Use the bank for some of your investment needs. Teach the bank about the cyclical patterns in your business that are likely to generate cash surpluses at some times of the year, and cash deficits at other times.

It is important to be able to show banks that your organization has thought through its working capital situation. How much money do you expect to borrow over the next year? When? What for? How long will you need the money? Banks are more likely to lend to organizations that can anticipate temporary cash needs long before the cash is needed, especially if you can show when you expect to be able to repay the loan. In Chapter 12 we discussed the cash budget. Such a budget is very important when the time comes to approach a bank about a loan.

Some organizations borrow specific amounts on short-term *commercial* loans. Such loans, often called commercial paper, were discussed earlier in the short-term investment section of this chapter. If your needs are intermediate-term, then a *term* loan, typically from one to five years, can be arranged. Such commercial loans and term loans can be arranged at the time the money is needed. However, many organizations arrange for a line of bank credit at a time when they currently have more than adequate cash.

For example, Coffin Corporation might arrange for a $10 million line of credit at the bank where it handles most of its routine financial transactions. The arrangement would typically include repayment terms and interest rates tied to some benchmark rate that may vary over time. The *prime rate* is the interest rate banks charge their most creditworthy clients. Coffin Corporation might negotiate for a loan at 2 percent over prime (referred to as "2 OP") at a time when the prime rate is 7 percent. Suppose that Coffin doesn't need to borrow any of its $10 million credit line for six months. At that time the prime has fallen to 5.5 percent. The interest rate on money borrowed against the line of credit would be 7.5 percent, which is 2 percent over the then-current prime. If the prime rate changes again, the interest rate on the outstanding portion of the loan will change as well. A common alternative to the prime rate, especially for companies with international operations, is the London Interbank Offered Rate (LIBOR). The LIBOR rate represents the rate that banks charge each other in the London Eurocurrency market. Having a credit line allows the organization to hold lower cash reserves than it might otherwise need.

In exchange for credit arrangements, many times banks require the organization to keep *compensating balances* in the bank. That is, the organization must always keep a certain amount of money in the bank. Why agree to a compensating balance arrangement? Because the line of credit greatly exceeds the compensating balance and provides a level of cash safety that the organization might not otherwise have.Will the bank make a loan to your organization, or offer it a line of credit? The bank will look for things such as positive cash flow from your operations, a strong management team, and adequate collateral. The weaker your position in these areas, the higher the rate of interest you will be charged. If you are too weak, the bank will not make the loan.

However, this is a two-way street. You don't want to borrow from just any bank. You need to pick the right bank for you. You need a big enough bank to meet all your needs, but not such a big bank that you are irrelevant to them. You need a bank that has experience serving businesses in your industry. Such a bank will better understand your problems and needs. Does your business have international operations? If so, you may want to chose a bank that has an international department. You need a bank with a range of services to meet your needs now, and as you grow. Banks can be useful in many ways, sometimes offering advice on how to run your business better, or even linking you with potential customers.

Concentration Banking

Although many companies deal with more than one bank, they often maintain a significant presence at one or more banks, which are referred to as *concentration banks*. Arrangements can be made with the concentration bank to *sweep* or transfer money into and out of accounts automatically.

For example, suppose that a nationwide company has many individual locations around the country that collect cash from customers, and deposit that cash in local banks. The company wants to have access to those deposits to make disbursements for various purposes. An arrangement may be made in which the concentration bank transfers balances from these other feeder accounts to a master account at the concentration bank. There could be daily, weekly, or monthly transfers, depending on the expected balances in the accounts.

The process can also be reversed with *zero-balance accounts*. An organization can write checks on an account that has a zero balance. When the checks are presented for payment, the bank keeps a tally of the total amount disbursed. That amount is then automatically transferred from one central account at the concentration bank into the zero-balance account.

This type of automatic transferring of funds back and forth allows the organization to have quicker access to its cash resources for payment needs. It also allows it to maintain less cash in total than it would if it had cash balances in many different accounts. The excess cash can be invested and may enable the organization to earn a higher yield on investments by purchasing securities in larger denominations.

KEY CONCEPTS

Working capital management—management of short-term resources and short-term obligations to maximize financial results.

Short-term resource management:

Cash is kept for transactions, safety, and investment opportunities.

Short-term investments—bank deposits, certificates of deposit, money market funds, T-bills, unsecured notes, commercial paper, repurchase agreements (repos), derivatives, and similar securities.

Accounts receivable aging schedule—management report that shows how long receivables have been outstanding.

Inventory management—Inventory levels should be kept as low as possible, while allowing for adequate inventory for current use and as a safety measure.

a. *Economic order quantity (EOQ)*—technique used to calculate the optimal amount of inventory to purchase at one time.

b. *Just-in-time (JIT)*—inventory management approach that calls for the arrival of inventory just as it is needed, resulting in zero inventory levels.

Short-term obligation management:

Trade credit and terms—payables to suppliers. Terms represent the payment agreement, sometimes including a discount for prompt payment.

Payroll payable—amount owed to employees. Payroll policy must consider payroll benefits, and also when and how often payroll is paid.

Notes payable—short-term loans that may be unsecured or secured by collateral.

Banking relationships—needed for transactions (e.g., checking), short-term investments, and borrowing.

Concentration bank—bank where an organization keeps a significant presence.

Short-term loans—*commercial* loans, *term* loans, and *lines of credit*. The interest rate may be a specific set rate, or may vary with a benchmark such as the prime rate.

Compensating balances—balances that must be maintained on deposit at all times in exchange for a line of credit (prearranged loan to be made when and if needed in an amount up to an agreed-upon limit.)

Seventeen

Inventory Costing:
The Accountant's World
of Make-Believe

THE INVENTORY EQUATION

Inventories are merely a stock of goods held for use in production or for sale or resale. Retailers and wholesalers have merchandise inventory. They buy a product basically in the same form as that in which it is sold. Manufacturers have several classes of inventory—raw materials that are used in the manufacturing process to make a final product; work in process that consists of goods on which production has begun that has not yet been finished; and finished goods that are complete and awaiting sale.

Just as there is a basic equation of accounting, there is a basic equation for keeping track of inventory and its cost.

$$\text{Beginning Inventory (BI)} + \text{Units Purchased (P)} - \text{Units Sold (S)} = \text{Ending Inventory (EI)}$$

This equation can be understood from a reasonably intuitive point of view. Consider a firm selling clay statuettes. At the start of the year, it has 1,000 statuettes. During the year, it buys 4,000 statuettes. If it sells 3,000 statuettes, how many will be left at the end of the year?

$$\text{BI} + \text{P} - \text{S} = \text{EI}$$
$$1,000 + 4,000 - 3,000 = 2,000$$

We can readily see that there should be 2,000 statuettes on hand at year-end.

PERIODIC VS. PERPETUAL INVENTORY METHODS

Firms must make a major decision about the fashion in which they intend to keep track of the four items in the inventory equation. This year's beginning inventory is always last year's ending inventory. All accounting systems are designed so as to keep track of purchases. A problem centers on the cost of goods sold and ending inventory.

If we wish, we can keep track of specifically how much of each of our products is sold. However, this requires a fair amount of bookkeeping. Certainly we keep track of the total dollars of sales from each transaction, but that in itself does not tell which goods (if our firm has more than one product) or how many are sold. Consider a hardware store that stocks thousands of small items. To record which items and how many of each are being sold could more than double the time it takes to ring up each sale. This could mean paying for at least twice as many cash register clerks.

A far simpler approach is to simply wait until year-end and then count what is left. Once we know the ending inventory, we can use our inventory equation to determine how many units of each product were sold. For example, if we started with 1,000 statuettes and purchased 4,000, then a year-end count of 2,000 on hand would indicate that we had sold 3,000 during the year.

$$BI \quad + \quad P \quad - \quad S \quad = \quad EI$$

If:

$$1,000 \ + \ 4,000 \ - \ S \quad = 2,000$$
then $\qquad\qquad\qquad\qquad\quad S \quad = 3,000$

This method is called the *periodic method of inventory*. It requires us to take a physical count to find out what we have on hand at any point in time. It gets this name because we keep track of inventory from time to time, or periodically.

A major weakness of the periodic system is that, at any point in time, we don't know how much inventory we've sold and how much we have left. Therefore, our control over our inventory is rather limited. If running out of an item creates a serious problem, this method is inadequate.

There are several easy solutions to that problem in some situations. If parts are kept in a bin or a barrel, we can paint a stripe two-thirds of the way down the bin or barrel. When we see the stripe, we know it's time to reorder. Bookstores often solve this problem by placing a reorder card in a book near the bottom of the pile. When that book is sold an order is made to replenish the stock.

The periodic method has other weaknesses as well. Although we calculate a figure for units sold based on the three other elements of the inventory equation, we don't know for sure that just because a unit of inventory isn't on hand, it was sold. It may have broken, spoiled, evaporated, or been stolen.

An alternative to periodic inventory accounting is the *perpetual method* for keeping track of units of inventory. Just as the name implies, you always, or perpetually, know how much inventory you have, because you specifically record each item. This method has been considered appropriate for companies selling relatively few high-priced items. In such cases, it is relatively inexpensive to keep track of each sale relative to the dollar value of the sale. Furthermore, control of inventory tends to be a more important issue with high-priced items.

Which of the two methods is considered more useful? Clearly the perpetual method gives more information and better control. However, it also adds substantial bookkeeping cost. Most firms would choose perpetual if they could get it for the same money as periodic, but typically they can't. The result is a management decision as to whether the extra benefits of perpetual are worth the extra cost.

Computers have made significant inroads in allowing firms to switch to perpetual inventory without incurring prohibitively high costs. For example, supermarkets were a classic example of the type of firm that couldn't afford perpetual inventory. Imagine a checkout clerk in the supermarket manually writing down each item as it's sold. The clerk rings up one can of peas, and then turns and writes down "one 6-ounce can of Green Midget peas." Then the clerk rings up one can of corn, and turns and writes down, "one 4-ounce can of House Brand corn," and so on. At the end of the day, another clerk would tally up the manual logs of each checkout clerk. The cost of this would be enormous. In such a situation, a firm would just keep track of total dollars of sales, and would take periodic inventories to see what is still on hand. Yet supermarkets run on extremely tight margins, so they can ill afford to run out of goods, nor can they afford the carrying cost of excess inventory.

Supermarkets were among the leaders in adopting use of bar codes. These computer-sensitive markings allow the store to save the cost of stamping the price on goods. The computer that reads the bar code knows how much the price of each item is, so the clerk no longer needs to see a stamped price. It also allows the clerk to ring up the goods at a much faster pace. Finally, it automatically updates the inventory. In many of the supermarkets using this system, the cash register tape gives you more information than just the price. Not only does it tell you that you bought a 4-ounce container of yogurt, but also that it was blueberry yogurt. That detailed information tells the purchasing department specifically the size, brand, and flavor of yogurt to be restocked. The potential time saved in stamping prices on goods and in the checkout process can offset much of the cost of the computerized system.

It should be noted that even on a perpetual system there is a need to physically count inventory from time to time (typically at least once a year). The perpetual method keeps track of what was sold. If there is pilferage or breakage, our inventory records will not be correct. However, when we use a perpetual system, we know what we should have. When we count our inventory, we can determine the extent to which goods that have not been sold are missing.

THE PROBLEM OF INFLATION

The periodic and perpetual methods of inventory tracking help us to determine the quantity of goods on hand and the quantity sold. We must also determine which units were sold and which units are on hand. Consider the following situation:

	QUANTITY	COST
Beginning Inventory	10,000	$ 100 each
Purchase March 1	10,000	110 each
Purchase June 1	10,000	120 each
Purchase September 1	10,000	130 each
Sales during Year	30,000	

How many units are left in stock? Clearly from our basic inventory equation the answer to that is 10,000. Beginning inventory of 10,000, plus the purchases of 30,000, less the sales of 30,000 leaves ending inventory of 10,000. What is the value of those 10,000 units? Here a problem arises. Which 10,000 units are left? Does it matter? From an accounting point of view it definitely does matter. In Chapter 5 we noted that generally accepted accounting principles require us to value items on the balance sheet at their cost. In order to know the cost of our remaining units, we must know which units we sold and which are still on hand. This requires the manager to make some assumptions, referred to as *cost-flow assumptions*.

This is particularly important during periods of high inflation. Recently inflation has been modest, but at some point in the near future the rate of inflation may accelerate. Therefore managers need an understanding of the impact of the cost-flow assumptions that they make.

COST-FLOW ASSUMPTIONS

The methods for determining which units were sold and which are on hand are referred to as cost-flow assumptions. There are four major alternative cost-flow assumptions.

Specific Identification

This is the accountant's ideal. It entails physically tagging each unit in some way so that we can specifically identify the units on hand with their cost. Then, when a periodic inventory is taken, we can determine the cost of all the units on hand and therefore deduce the cost of the units sold.

As you might expect, for most businesses such tagging would create a substantial additional bookkeeping cost. Think of the supermarket not just trying to keep track of how many cans of peas are sold, but also the specific cans. Can any type of business go to this effort? Certainly some can—typically those firms that keep close track of serial numbers for the items sold. For example, a car dealership buys only a few units at a time. The invoice the dealership receives for each car indicates a serial number. When the dealership sells a car it also records the serial number. At the end of the accounting period, it is not overly burdensome for the dealership to determine specifically which units are on hand and which were sold.

First-In, First-Out (FIFO)

The second cost-flow approach is called first-in, first-out, and is almost always referred to by the shorthand acronym FIFO. This method allows you to keep track of the flow of inventory without tagging each item. It is based on the fact that, in most industries, inventory moves in an orderly fashion. We can think of a factory or a warehouse as a building with a front door and a back door. Raw materials or new deliveries of merchandise are received at the back door and put on a conveyor belt. They move along the conveyor belt and right out the front door. We would never have occasion to skip one unit ahead of the other items already on the conveyor belt ahead of it.

A good example of FIFO is a dairy. It is clear that the dairy would always prefer to sell the milk that comes out of the cow today, before they sell the milk that the cow produces tomorrow. We've all seen in the supermarket that the fresh milk is put on the back of the shelf so that we will purchase the older milk from the front of the shelf first. Of course, we know the fresh milk is in the back so we sometimes reach back to get it. But then, they know we know so they sometimes. . . . Nevertheless, the point is clear—the supermarket's desire is for us to buy the oldest milk first; they want to sell the milk in a FIFO fashion.

In most industries there is a desire to avoid winding up with old, shopworn, obsolete, dirty goods. Therefore, FIFO makes reasonable sense as an approach for processing inventory.

Weighted Average (WA)

The weighted average approach to inventory cost-flows assumes that our entire inventory gets commingled and there is no way to determine which units we are selling. For example, consider a gas station that fills up its underground tanks with gasoline costing $1.20 per gallon. A week later when the tanks are half full, they are refilled with additional gasoline costing $1.40 per gallon. When we now sell gasoline to a customer, are we selling gallons that cost the gas station $1.20 or $1.40? Because there is really no way to know, the WA method assumes that all of the gasoline has been thoroughly mixed, and therefore the gas being sold cost $1.30 per gallon. This method would be appropriate whenever the inventory gets stirred or mixed together and it is physically impossible to determine what has been sold.

Last-In, First-Out (LIFO)

The last of the four methods of cost-flow for inventory is last-in, first-out, which has received much attention in the last decade. The LIFO method is just the reverse of the FIFO method. It assumes that the last goods we receive are the first goods we ship. In the case of the dairy it would mean that we always would try to sell the freshest milk first and keep the older, souring milk in our warehouse.

Does the LIFO method make sense for any industries at all? Yes. In fact it is the logical approach to use for any industry that piles their goods up as they arrive, and then sells from the top of the pile. For example, a company mining coal or making chemicals frequently piles them up and then simply sells from the top of the pile. However, for most firms it doesn't provide a very logical inventory movement. Nevertheless, a large number of firms have shifted from the FIFO method to the LIFO method. Why?

COMPARISON OF THE LIFO AND FIFO COST-FLOW ASSUMPTIONS

Financial statements are not ideally suited for inflationary environments. During inflation we have problems trying to report inventory without creating distortions in at least one key financial statement.

Consider an example in which we buy one unit of inventory on January 2 for $10 and another unit of inventory on December 30 for $20. On December 31, we sell a unit for $30. What happens to the financial statements if we are using the FIFO method of inventory tracking? The FIFO method means that the inventory that is first-in is the inventory that is the first-out. The January 2 purchase was the first one in, so the cost of the unit sold is $10 and the cost of the unit remaining on hand is $20 (the December purchase). Is the balance sheet a fair representation of current value? It says that we have one unit of inventory that cost $20. What would it cost to buy a unit of inventory near year-end? Well, we bought one on December 30 for $20, so the balance sheet seems pretty accurate.

However, consider the income statement under FIFO. We presumably sold the first-in, which cost $10, for a selling price of $30, leaving us with a $20 profit. Is that a good indication of the profit we could currently earn from the purchase and sale of a unit of inventory? Not really. At year-end we could have bought a unit for $20 and sold it for $30, leaving a profit of only $10. Thus, during periods of rising prices, the FIFO method does not give users of financial statements a current picture of the profit opportunities facing the firm.

We do not have that problem with LIFO. Under LIFO, the last-in is the first-out, which means that we sold the unit that was purchased on December 30. That unit had cost us $20, and by selling it for $30 we realize a profit of $10. When we tell our stockholders that our profit was $10, we are giving them a reasonably current picture of the profit we can currently make by buying and selling a unit.

Unfortunately this gives rise to another problem. Under LIFO, we have sold the unit that cost $20, so we must have held onto the unit that cost $10. Therefore, the inventory number to be shown on the balance sheet is $10. Is it true that we could currently go out and buy more inventory for $10 a unit? No, by year-end the price we paid was already up to $20. So, under LIFO, the value of inventory on the balance sheet is understated.

There is no readily available solution to this problem. The weighted average method simply leaves both the balance sheet and income statements somewhat out of whack, instead of causing a somewhat bigger problem with respect to one or the other, as results under LIFO and FIFO. In the face of this problem, firms have shifted to LIFO for a very simple reason: to save taxes.

Let's take a second to consider the implications of our example. If we use a FIFO system during inflationary periods, we report a pretax profit of $20 because we have sold a unit that cost $10 for $30. Under LIFO, we report a pretax profit of only $10 because we have sold a unit that cost $20 for $30. Therefore, by being on the LIFO system, we can reduce our tax payments. Are the tax savings worth the fact that we will be reporting lowered profits on our financial statements? Absolutely. If we can lower our taxes by using allowable GAAP, we should take advantage of that opportunity.

However, it gets even better. Suppose we purchased a unit on January 2 for $10. On July 1 we sold that unit. On December 30 we buy a unit for $20. Which unit did we sell? You probably think we sold the unit we paid $10 for. However, you are now entering the accountant's world of make-believe.

Inventory accounting make-believe is played this way. Under FIFO we record $10 of expense and $20 of inventory as an asset. But under LIFO we record $20 of expense on the income statement and $10 as an asset on the balance sheet! That implies that we sold the unit we acquired on December 30, even though the sale took place six months earlier.

The accountant knows that obviously this can't physically be so. But that's okay. We'll just make believe that that's what happened. Under LIFO there is no need for us to actually move our inventories on a LIFO basis. We don't have to throw our conveyor belt into reverse, or keep milk on hand until it turns sour. If our product is dated, there is no need to feel we can't be on a LIFO system because we can't afford to keep stock on hand past the expiration date.

The firm on LIFO can continue to behave all year long as if it were on FIFO. Your managers should continue to make their product decisions based on the current cost of inventory items—and that usually requires a FIFO-type approach. However, your accountant at year-end will make adjustments to your financial records to calculate your income as if you were shipping on a LIFO basis.

Assume the following:

Beginning Inventory	$ 0
January 3, Purchase 1 Unit @	$10
July 1, Sell 1 Unit @	$30
December 1, Purchase 1 Unit @	$20

Under either method, the first unit purchased was physically shipped and the second unit purchased was physically on hand at the end of the year. From a standpoint of physical movement of goods, the FIFO income statement tells the truth. However, by making believe that we shipped a unit that we hadn't even received by the shipping date, we can report a higher cost of goods sold expense, and therefore report a lower profit and pay the government less tax.

The LIFO Conformity Rule

When we talked about depreciation in Chapter 15, we noted that we could have our cake and eat it too. We could tell our stockholders what a good year we had, but we could also tell the government how miserable things had really been. This is not true with LIFO. The government requires that the firm use the same method of inventory reporting to stockholders as it uses to report to the government.

Who Shouldn't Use LIFO

Many, many firms could benefit from LIFO, but there are some that would not. LIFO is not necessarily advantageous if the cost of your inventory is highly uncertain, and veers downward as often as upward. For many firms dealing in commodities, WA remains a better bet. Firms whose inventory costs are actually falling (computer chips, for example) will have lower taxes by staying on FIFO.

What if your inventory contains some items with rising cost and some items with falling cost? If you segment the inventory adequately, it is possible to report some of your inventory using one method and some of it based on another method.

LIFO Liquidations

The lower tax paid by a firm on LIFO is caused by reporting to the government that the most recent, high-priced purchases were sold while the old, low-cost items were kept. If we ever liquidate our inventory and sell everything we have, we incur a high profit on the sale of those low-cost items and have to pay back the taxes we would have paid had we been on FIFO all along. However, in the meantime we have had an interest-free loan from the government. If our year-end inventory is always at least as big as the beginning inventory, we will never have that problem and we will never have to repay those extra taxes to the government.

KEY CONCEPTS

The Inventory Equation

$$\text{Beginning Inventory (BI)} + \text{Units Purchased (P)} - \text{Units Sold (S)} = \text{Ending Inventory (EI)}$$

Periodic vs. perpetual inventory—different methods for keeping track of how many units have been sold, and how many units are on hand.

Periodic—Goods are counted periodically to determine the ending inventory. The number of units sold is calculated using the inventory equation.

Perpetual—The inventory balance is adjusted as each unit is sold so that a perpetual record of how many units have been sold and how many are on hand is maintained at all times.

Cost-flow assumptions—Inventory is valued at its cost. Therefore, it is necessary to know not only how many units were sold and how many are left on hand, but specifically which were sold and which are left. This determination is made via one of four different approaches.

Specific identification—We record and identify each unit as it is acquired or sold.

First-in, First-out (FIFO)—We assume that the units acquired earlier are sold before units acquired later.

Weighted average (WA)—We assume that all units are indistinguishable and assign a weighted average cost to each unit.

Last-in, First-out (LIFO)—We assume that the last units acquired are the first ones sold, even if this implies sale of a unit prior to its acquisition. During periods of inflation there are tax savings associated with LIFO.

Eighteen
Cost Accounting

This chapter focuses on the terminology of cost accounting and how cost information can be used for improved managerial decisions. The role of cost accounting is to collect cost information to report what costs have been and to use that information for making decisions about the future. We must know how much our product costs us to make so that we can charge a high enough price to make a profit.

COST VS. EXPENSE: THE INVENTORY PROCESS

The words *cost* and *expense* are often casually used interchangeably. However, they are very distinct in their underlying meaning. From an accounting perspective, the cost of an item is what is paid to acquire it. Expense refers to resources that have been used up. In essence, an item is a cost before it becomes an expense. If we purchase clay to make statuettes, we can refer to the cost of the clay. However, if we have not yet used the clay to make the statuettes, nor sold any statuettes, then the matching principle of accounting does not allow us to consider that cost to be an expense. Using generally accepted accounting principles (GAAP), we can only treat a cost as an expense in the period in which we record the revenues associated with that cost. Until a cost becomes an expense, it is generally treated as an asset, such as inventory.

This creates some rather interesting problems. Assume that we started the hypothetical Statuette Corporation on the last day of 2001. The owners purchased common stock in exchange for $1,000 cash. Statuette purchased 100 pounds of clay in 2002 for $1 per pound. Each statuette it makes requires one pound of clay. By the end of 2002, it had started 80

EXHIBIT 18-1.
The Inventory Process

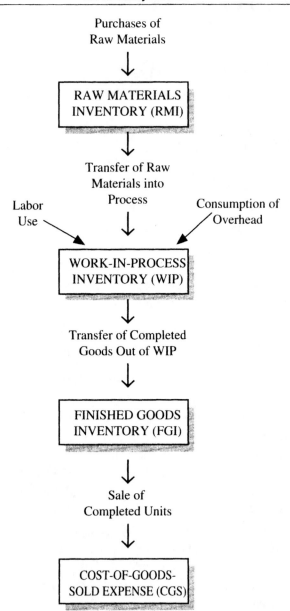

Purchases of
Raw Materials

RAW MATERIALS
INVENTORY (RMI)

Transfer of Raw
Materials into
Process

Labor
Use

Consumption of
Overhead

WORK-IN-PROCESS
INVENTORY (WIP)

Transfer of Completed
Goods Out of WIP

FINISHED GOODS
INVENTORY (FGI)

Sale of
Completed Units

COST-OF-GOODS-
SOLD EXPENSE (CGS)

statuettes and had 20 pounds of unused clay. Only 70 of the statuettes had been completed, and of those 70, a total of 60 statuettes had been sold for $2 each. What was the expense for clay for 2002?

The answer to this question requires an understanding of the inventory process. See Exhibit 18-1. When Statuette initially bought the clay, it was recorded as $100 of raw materials inventory (RMI). The 20 pounds that were not used remain as a $20 inventory balance for the raw materials account at the end of 2002. When we started to make statuettes, the clay was transferred from the raw materials inventory into production. From an accounting point of view, the cost of that portion of clay was transferred from the RMI account into a separate work-in-process (WIP) account. Thus, during 2002, $80 was transferred from RMI into the WIP account. Other production costs, such as labor and the various elements of overhead, also go into the WIP account and ultimately become expenses. Here, however, we are focusing only on how much of the cost of clay ultimately becomes an expense this year.

Of the clay put into production, work was finished on 70 pounds, causing a transfer from WIP into a finished goods inventory (FGI) account. Then 60 units were sold, so they were transferred into a cost of goods sold (CGS) expense account. It is the $60 related to the final transfer that becomes an expense. At the end of 2002, $40 of cost is still in the raw materials, work in process, and finished inventory accounts. We can trace through the journal entries involved in a manner similar to that presented in Chapter 7 based on the modified basic equation of accounting, as shown in Exhibit 18-2.

If we were to look at a ledger for the accounts involved in this inventory process, we would see the following:

		ASSETS			+ EXP.	+ DIV. = LIAB +	STK EQUITY		+ REV.
	CASH	RMI	WIP	FGI	CGS		C.S.	RE	REV.
Beg.	$1,000	$0	$0	$0	$0		$1,000	$0	$0
1	−100	100							
2		−80	80						
3			−70	70					
4	120			−60	60				120
End	$1,020	$20	$10	$10	$60		$1,000	$0	$120

EXHIBIT 18-2.
Inventory Journal Entries

ASSETS + EXPENSES + DIVIDENDS = LIABILITIES + REVENUES + CONTRIBUTED CAPITAL

1. Purchase of 100 pounds of clay for $100

Cash–100   = No change on right side

RMI +100

2. Transfer of 80 pounds of clay from RMI to WIP

RMI –80   = No change on right side

WIP +80

3. Transfer of seventy 1-pound statuettes from WIP to FGI

WIP –70   = No change on right side

FGI +70

4. Sale of sixty 1-pound statuettes for $2 each

FGI –60,   CGS +60   = No change on right side

Cash+120   =   Sales +120

The only portion of the cost that becomes an expense is the $60 that relates to the units that have been sold, thus generating $120 of revenue.

This process represents a manufacturing operation. For a wholesale or retail company, goods enter a merchandise inventory account when they are acquired. Their cost is transferred to cost of goods sold expense when the units are sold.

Cost of goods sold is generally shown separately on an income statement. Rather than simply using the format:

Sales
– Expenses

Net Income

it is more common to present the income statement as:

Sales
– Cost of Goods Sold

Gross Profit
– General and Administrative Expenses
– Other Expenses

Net Income

The Gross Profit measure becomes an important indicator of potential profitability for many companies.

PERIOD COSTS VS. PRODUCT COSTS

In the previous example, we looked only at the cost of direct materials. In fact, there is a wide variety of costs. We must be concerned with labor, rent, administration, and marketing. We divide all costs into two broad categories: period costs and product costs. All costs directly associated with the product itself are considered to be product costs. All other costs are period costs.

For a merchandising firm that simply buys and sells, the cost of the units purchased is the product cost. In a manufacturing firm, all costs associated with the manufacture of the product are considered to be product cost. This means that materials, labor, and factory rent are all treated as part of the cost of the product. Consider the implications of this for labor or factory rent. When we pay our factory workers, we cannot directly charge the labor expense account. This would imply that the labor generated revenue this period. However, it might be that the workers made units of product that have not yet been sold. To charge labor costs to expense directly would violate the matching principle. Instead, we add the cost of the labor to the WIP inventory account. Similarly, the factory rent will be added to WIP. In this way, only a proportionate share of the labor and rent winds up being an expense this period. This proportion depends on how much of the product that we work on this period is finished and sold. The remainder of these costs reside in the WIP and FGI accounts until all of this year's production is finally sold.

Any costs that are not product costs are automatically period costs. For all period costs, such as selling, general, and administrative costs, there is no matching. These costs are charged to expense in the year incurred. Generally this is because it would be too difficult to determine which future sales result from bookkeeping, administrative, and selling efforts of this year. Thus, all depreciation on an office machine is an expense in the year the depreciation is incurred. But not all of the depreciation on a factory machine is an expense this year, unless all of this year's production is sold. When we see cost of goods sold on an income statement, it represents all elements of product cost: direct labor (the hands-on labor in the production process), direct materials (the raw materials used to make the product), and factory overhead (all other elements of the production process such as supervisory labor, electricity, rent, depreciation, etc.).

COST SYSTEMS: PROCESS, JOB-ORDER, AND STANDARD COSTS

The main focus of cost accounting is to be able to come up with a figure for the cost of each unit produced or acquired. The two most rudimentary systems for calculating this cost per unit are process and job-order actual costing. In both of these methods, we collect actual cost information and assign it directly to the units. Standard costs are the next step in the costing picture. Standard costs can simplify the costing process substantially.

Let's first consider process costing. This approach represents one extreme costing method. Under this approach, a firm that makes a large quantity of an individual product keeps track of both the cost of the various components of the production process, and the number of units made. For example, an aspirin manufacturer could keep track of the total amount of acetylsalicylic acid, labor, and so on used for a batch, and the number of bottles of aspirin produced in that batch. By dividing the total costs by the number of units, we find the cost per unit. This calculation can be done on a batch basis, or for continuous operations, on a monthly basis.

At the opposite extreme is the job costing or job-order costing approach. Consider the manufacturer of customized items, such as furniture. We can think of a custom furniture house receiving an order for six rosewood tables and another order for six knotty pine tables. The rosewood lumber is far more expensive than the knotty pine lumber. We might use skilled workers on the rosewood tables and apprentices on the knotty pine tables. Clearly, the firm cannot get a good estimate of costs if it simply adds the total lumber and labor costs for the month and divides by twelve tables. Because each job is different, we need to gather information separately for each job.

Job-order costing is inherently more expensive from a bookkeeping standpoint than process costing. We need to keep track of how much of each type of lumber was used for each job. We need time cards to keep track of how much time each type of worker spent on each job. Pricing decisions cannot effectively be made without this information if the labor and materials truly are different for each job.

Many hybrid methods are possible. For example, it might well be that our furniture manufacturer has substantially different material costs depending on whether tables are oak, rosewood, or knotty pine. But if all tables are alike from the point of view of labor, then regardless of which lumber we use, the labor requirements are identical. In that case, we could use job-order cost accounting to keep specific track of the materials used on each job, but we could use process-cost accounting for labor. We could simply total our labor cost and divide by the number of tables to get the labor cost per table.

What about standard costs? In using process and job-order accounting, one approach is to collect costs as you go and assign them periodically (often monthly) to the units produced. This provides very accurate information. Information, however, is costly. Managerial accountants are always attempting to find ways to provide an adequate amount of information at a lower cost. Do we really need the accuracy gained from actual process or actual job-order costing? Standard costs are a simplification that often provide enough information, but at a lower cost.

Suppose that our aspirin manufacturer produces a wide variety of pharmaceuticals, and the workers are used interchangeably among the various products. Further, there are materials that are used in common by many of the products. Process costing is no longer reasonable because there are so many different products using the same resources. Job-order costing is expensive because of the extra detail of material records and time cards. The standard costing alternative uses industrial engineering estimates and past experience to determine how much of our various resources we expect each unit of each product to consume, and what we expect those resources to cost.

For example, we have a standard cost card for aspirin showing how much of each material and how much labor and how much overhead we expect each bottle (or hundred bottles or thousand bottles) to consume, and the price we expect to have to pay for each material, type of labor, and so on. At the end of any month, as long as we know the number of units we have produced, we can multiply the standard cost per unit times the number of units produced to get our total estimated production costs.

Use of standard costs does not relieve us from collecting actual cost information. The pharmaceutical house still needs to know the actual cost of labor, for instance. But, by using standards, we can estimate a cost for each product individually, yet collect labor costs for all of our production in total. This significantly lessens the cost of collecting information about our expenditure on labor. At the same time, it increases our ability to control our operations significantly. Now we can compare our labor cost to what it should have cost (according to the standard cost) for the quantity of production we actually had.

If we actually spent more than we expected for that volume (an unfavorable variance), we can investigate to determine what the cause was. Possible causes include unexpected overtime, use of inferior materials, pay raises not included in the standard, or simply laxity on the part of workers and supervisors. Variances between actual production costs and estimated production costs based on standards require adjustments to the income statement so that we correctly report based on actual expenses. However, the inventory shown at year-end on the balance sheet is generally shown at its standard cost. This is much simpler than trying to calculate the actual costs for each product line and assigning that value to year-end inventory. The ability to use standard cost information, both for financial reporting and as a tool to assess what has happened and improve control over future costs, makes it particularly valuable.

ACTIVITY-BASED COSTING (ABC)

At the end of the 1980s and the beginning of the 1990s, a growing literature developed that was critical of traditional cost accounting methods. One major criticism concerns accounting for overhead. Many have suggested solving the overhead problem by moving to activity-based costing (ABC). Activity-based costing proposes examination of overhead costs to see whether they can be directly related to specific activities.

Production costs are classified as being either *direct* or *indirect*. The direct costs generally consist of direct labor and direct materials. Direct labor is the labor directly associated with the production of a specific product. Direct materials are the materials specifically used to make a product. Anything that does not fall into a direct category is indirect, and is considered to be overhead. Direct costs for each product are measured and assigned directly to that product on a cause-and-effect basis. Indirect (overhead) costs are aggregated, and then allocated to products, not necessarily proportionately to the products that caused them to be incurred.

In determining the costs of a product, we would like to directly associate with the product all of the costs it is responsible for causing to be incurred. If more costs of production could be classified as direct, and fewer items as indirect, the costing would be more accurate. More accurate costs provide managers with better information for pricing and other product decisions. However, more accurate costing is usually more expensive.

For example, labor that is used to make a product or provide a service is often easily associated with the product. On the other hand, consider the labor of supervisors. Their labor is more difficult to associate with individual products. It might be extremely costly to track their time. Therefore their cost is considered to be indirect labor, and it is placed in an overhead pool. Overhead costs are then allocated to individual units of product.

Historically, most costs of production have consisted of direct materials and direct labor. Overhead has been a relatively minor component of total cost. As long as total overhead costs are relatively minor, the distortion caused by an arbitrary allocation of an overhead item is not important. In recent years, however, overhead has been a substantially growing portion of the overall cost of producing products and services. With the growth of the overhead component, a growing proportion of the cost assigned to each product is allocated arbitrarily rather than being directly measured.

For example, the cost of supervisory labor may be assigned to different products based on the proportion of direct labor hours worked on each project. Assume that a department's supervisory labor costs $100,000, and that in total the department's workers work 50,000 hours. The supervisory overhead cost is allocated at a rate of $2 per direct labor hour ($100,000 of cost divided by 50,000 direct labor hours). Assume further that the department makes 10,000 units of product A and 10,000 units of product B. Product A units each require 4 direct labor hours to make, and product B units each require 1 direct labor hour to make. Therefore, product A used 40,000 direct labor hours and product B uses 10,000 hours. At $2 per hour, product A is assigned supervisory labor overhead cost of $80,000, and product B is assigned $20,000 of overhead cost. This seems to be a fair allocation.

However, what if the supervisors spend most of their time setting up the production process? Suppose that they do an equal number of setups for A and B, and that they spend an equal amount of time for any setup. In other words, in terms of actual supervisor time consumed, each product has used the exact same amount of that resource. Then each product should be assigned $50,000 of supervisory cost (i.e., half of the total). The existing system, which allocates supervisory cost based on direct labor hours rather than based on the number of setups for each product, has created a distortion in the cost of each product.

The focus of ABC is to review the various elements of overhead to determine whether they are related to an activity that can be measured. If so, then those overhead elements can become direct costs rather than overhead costs. They can be assigned directly to products. If setups are a good activity measure for supervisors, then we can measure the number of setups for each product and assign supervisory costs on a direct basis, without having to keep constant track of each supervisor's time.

AVERAGE VS. MARGINAL COSTS

Average cost information should always be viewed with suspicion. Very often we hear someone speak of the average cost or "cost per unit" of a product. However, short-term decisions should be based on marginal costs. To understand this we first need to review *fixed* and *variable* costs. Fixed costs are those that do not change with changes in the volume of production. Variable costs change in direct proportion to production. For example, if we produce more units in our existing factory, the rent wouldn't rise, so rent would be a fixed cost. The amount of raw materials we use would increase, thus being a variable cost.

Suppose we currently are manufacturing 10,000 units at a cost of $10,000. Our cost per unit is $1. Suppose further that the variable costs for the 10,000 units are a total of $2,000, while the fixed costs are $8,000. If we are selling our units for 80 cents each, and they have a cost per unit of $1, then we are losing 20 cents on each unit we sell. We've all laughed at the story of the individual, faced by such a situation, who decided to increase production and make it up on volume! However, that is exactly the correct strategy. This is because our cost per unit is $1 *at a volume of* 10,000 units.

What happens to our cost per unit if we produce and sell 20,000 units? Our variable cost of $2,000 for 10,000 units doubles to $4,000 for 20,000 units, but the fixed cost remains $8,000. Thus the total cost for 20,000 units is $12,000, and the cost per unit is 60 cents. Suddenly our loss of 20 cents per unit becomes a profit of 20 cents per unit! This assumes that we could sell 20,000 units at the same price of 80 cents. The key is that, because some costs are fixed, the cost per unit declines as volume increases. Thus, some products that look unprofitable at certain volumes might be very profitable at higher volumes. Of course, this only helps if you can sell the higher volume of units.

We can go even one step further. What if we were making 10,000 units at a cost of $1 per unit at that volume. However, now suppose that we were selling them for $1.20, so we are making a profit. Along comes a potential high-volume customer who offers to buy 10,000 units for 50 cents per unit. We assume that this additional sale of 10,000 units does not affect our original sales at $1.20. Should we take the offer?

First we must understand how it might be possible for this new order not to affect our current sales. In order for this to be possible, we must be able to segment the market we face into distinct groups. This task generally belongs to the marketing department. The airlines have commonly charged several distinct prices for the same product. However, the lower super-saver fares usually have restrictions that make them undesirable to business traffic. Another form is separation by wholesale and retail or by purchase volume. For example, a firm normally selling a cleaner for home use might sell the same product at a substantially different price to a high-volume industrial user.

Assuming that we can segment our market adequately to prevent our current customers who are paying $1.20 from demanding and receiving a 70-cent discount, should we sell an extra 10,000 units at 50 cents each? At first thought, we might say no. Even if we double our production from 10,000 units to 20,000, our average cost only falls to 60 cents. We would lose 10 cents on every unit sold. Or would we?

We are already making and selling 10,000 units. What will happen to the firm if it accepts this order, versus what would happen if it rejects the order? For every extra unit produced, we are going to generate an additional 50 cents of revenue. For every extra unit we make, we are going to spend an extra 20 cents on variable costs. How about fixed costs? How much extra fixed cost will we have for each extra unit we make? By definition, fixed costs are fixed in total. Assuming that we have sufficient excess capacity of plant and equipment to make the extra 10,000 units without incurring any additional fixed cost, our total fixed costs will not change. In that case, the total extra cost of producing an extra unit is only 20 cents. This cost is often referred to as the out-of-pocket, or incremental, or *marginal* cost. As long as the extra revenue received from each unit sold exceeds the extra cost, we are better off to make the additional sales.

Basically this constitutes a short-run strategy. In the long run, the firm cannot survive unless it has some sales that not only cover variable cost, but also pay for the fixed costs. However, once the firm has committed itself to its fixed costs, all of the short-term decisions should consider those costs to be irrelevant. This is frequently referred to as marginal or incremental costing.

Thus, it should not be surprising that financial managers sometimes make decisions that seem perverse on the surface. They insist on allocating costs, even if those costs exist anyway. This is done because the financial reporting for historical purposes requires that total costs be shown. On the other hand, the same financial officers may require that you offer a product, even at a loss, because its revenue exceeds its marginal cost. Such marginal cost pricing will increase firm profits.

KEY CONCEPTS

Cost accounting—the collection of information related to the costs incurred for the acquisition or production of a product or service, and for making decisions regarding future production and product strategy.

The manufacturing inventory process—When inventory is acquired, its cost is recorded as raw materials inventory (RMI). The costs of RMI that enter into the production process are transferred into the work-in-process inventory account (WIP). Other production costs are also added to WIP. When production is completed, the costs in WIP related to that production are transferred to the finished goods inventory account (FGI). When goods are sold, their cost is transferred from FGI to the cost-of-goods-sold (CGS) account.

Product cost vs. period cost—Product costs are all of the costs of manufacturing or acquiring the product. These costs become an expense only in the year in which the units of product are sold. Period costs are all costs that are not product costs. They become expenses in the year in which they are incurred.

Cost systems:

Process costing—the determination of unit costs by comparing the number of units made to the total cost for large amounts of production, such as an entire month's output.

Job-order costing—The costs of each particular job are accumulated separately, and the cost per unit is assessed based on resources consumed for each particular job.

Standard costing—use of a predetermined estimate of the cost per unit for each product.

Activity-based costing (ABC)—a method of examining overhead costs to see whether they can be related to specific activities. If so, then they can be assigned to products as direct costs, rather than being arbitrarily allocated as part of general overhead.

Marginal costing—additional cost incurred to produce an additional unit; the appropriate cost measure for short-term decision making.

Nineteen

Accountability and Internal Control

A substantial part of this book has focused on various aspects of planning. Good plans are critical if an organization is to do as well as it can. However, to achieve the best possible results, the plans need to be carried out. To assure that this happens, departments and individuals must be held accountable for actions and results. That is the focus of this chapter.

MANAGEMENT CONTROL SYSTEMS

The centerpiece of an organization's attempts to accomplish its plans is its *management control system (MCS)*. A management control system is a set of policies and procedures designed to keep operations going according to plan. Such systems also detect variations from plans and provide managers with information needed to take corrective actions when necessary.

Management control systems have often been compared to thermostats. We might set a thermostat for 70 degrees. That is our plan. It is the temperature that we hope will exist in a room. However, a thermostat does more than just establish the desired temperature. It also monitors the existing temperature in the room. Similarly, an MCS assesses the actual *outcomes* for the organization. If the temperature in the room varies from the desired 70 degrees, the thermostat activates the furnace to send heat if it gets too cold, or turns off the furnace if it gets too hot. Similarly, the MCS must set in motion actions that are needed if it determines that there are variations from the plan.

251

Further, management control systems establish an environment in which it is likely that the organization will come as close to its plans as possible. This means that MCSs are proactive as well as reactive. They are reactive to the extent that they monitor, detect if something is going wrong, and then initiate actions to correct the problem. However, they are also proactive in that they put in place a set of incentives and controls that help the organization avoid having bad outcomes in the first place.

One proactive aspect of management control is that it should provide managers with a clear way to identify and capitalize on opportunities. Plans cannot possibly anticipate everything that might occur. Organizations need to be flexible enough to respond to unexpected opportunities. On the other hand, there needs to be control. The organization wants to walk a fine line between allowing anyone to use opportunity as an excuse to do whatever he or she wants, versus failing to take advantage of truly significant opportunities.

To accomplish these ends, MCSs use *responsibility accounting*. Responsibility accounting is the assignment of the responsibility for keeping to the plan and carrying out the elements of the MCS to managers of cost, revenue, or profit centers. Some MCSs employ rewards for managers and staff that meet or exceed budgets. Others take an approach of doling out punishments if targets are not achieved. In either case, responsibility accounting should not be primarily focused on assigning blame. The intent is not to have a ready scapegoat when things go wrong.

Rather, the philosophy is that individuals should have a clear understanding of their responsibilities. Given that knowledge, they are likely to act in a manner to achieve the best possible outcomes for the organization. Responsibility accounting is oriented toward clearly communicating expectations ahead of time and then tracking results to generate feedback after the fact. The most important reason for the feedback is to improve future outcomes.

The MCS has the potential to create severe problems if people are held accountable for things that they either could not control or were unaware they were responsible to control. The common result is low morale and a downward spiral in results, rather than the desired high level of achievement. It is people who make things happen in organizations, not plans or budgets. If we are not mindful of what people are likely to do and why, we are not likely to achieve our hoped-for results.

Motivation and Incentives

Even the most loyal employees, at times, focus on how various actions will affect them personally. It is human nature to act in your own self-interest. For example, it is quite likely that most employees would prefer a higher salary. When resources are limited, however, organizations must make choices. If higher salaries are given, less money is available to expand the range of products or services offered. The tension between the goals of the organization and those of its employees creates a phenomenon often referred to as *goal divergence*.

If unchecked, goal divergence can result in employees becoming demoralized and starting to work at odds with the organization. To achieve its goals the organization must overcome this natural divergence. Motivation of staff and managers cannot be overemphasized. If people are not motivated to achieve the organization's plans, then they are unlikely to achieve the targets of those plans.

Organizations need to find ways to get their employees to buy into the organization's plans. When the organization accomplishes its objectives, the employees must feel that they are the winners too. There are many ways to motivate employees to want to achieve the things the organization wants to achieve. However, it is up to management to find out what things work within the culture of a particular organization and to implement those things. Bringing the individuals' and organization's wants and desires together is referred to as *goal congruence*.

Bonuses are effective because the employee gets the bonus only if the targets of the organization are met or exceeded. Stock options provide a similar incentive. Employees are given the option to buy shares of stock at a certain price. The options are valuable only if the price of the company's stock increases. Therefore the employees are more likely to undertake the actions necessary to improve the stock price.

There are other approaches to motivating employees. Some employees may need Thursdays off because of child-care difficulties. Other employees may really want to take off President's week to travel with their children who have the week off from school. A manager needs to learn what employees really value so that those things can be given as rewards for quality work. In fact, even a letter from a manager to a subordinate employee commending a job well done can have a dramatic impact on attitudes and future performance.

MEASURES OF PERFORMANCE

The planning process provides goals for the organization. But how will it know if it has achieved its goals? Each organization must decide how to measure its performance. A simplistic approach is to focus solely on profits, or perhaps on revenues and profits. From a more sophisticated perspective, there are many objectives that each manager is attempting to achieve. If we can evaluate performance based on the accomplishment of those objectives, we are more likely to achieve long-term success.

For example, if we were to defer maintenance on critical equipment, we might save money and improve profits this year. However, if the equipment breaks down next year and is out of service for a long period, because we avoided routine maintenance this year, the result is not a good one for the organization. So one objective might be for each department to undertake certain routine maintenance activities each year.

SAFEGUARDING RESOURCES

Management control systems and performance measurement are two critical elements of *internal control*. Internal control refers to systems designed to ensure efficiency and effectiveness of operations, compliance with all relevant laws, and reliable reporting of financial results. As part of these goals, internal control works to ensure that assets are safeguarded.

The first step in safeguarding resources is to hire ethical people and create a culture that rewards ethical behavior and condemns unethical behavior. Unfortunately, no matter how hard you try to do that, it is still necessary to take additional steps to protect the resources of the organization. These include having an audit trail, separation of duties, proper authorization, adequate documentation, proper procedures, physical safeguards, bonding, vacations, rotation of duties, independent checks, and cost–benefit analysis. Each of these elements is discussed in turn.

Audit Trail

The first element in accounting control is to establish a clear *audit trail*. An audit trail refers to the ability to trace each transaction in an accounting system back to its source. For example, suppose that the Coffin Corporation spent $50,000 on travel expenses for the year. That might seem to be an inordinately large amount. Documentation should exist that would allow us to determine exactly what that $50,000 was spent on. Perhaps the expenses were legitimate approved expenses. But they might represent unauthorized travel.

The existence of the audit trail serves as a preventive device. If people knew that we did not have good audit trails, they might feel safer in misappropriating money. They might assume that we would never be able to backtrack and find where the money went. When people recognize that all spending is carefully documented and that an audit trail will allow the organization to retrace the steps in the accounting process back to the source of unusual expenditures, it serves to inhibit inappropriate spending.

In order for an audit trail to be effective, there must be regular use of the trail to identify and examine discrepancies or unusual spending patterns. If employees knew that a trail was kept, but investigations never took place utilizing that information, it would not have as strong a preventive influence as if it were used on a regular basis.

Separation of Functions

Activities that relate to the disbursement of resources should be separated so that no one individual controls too much of the process. The individual who approves bills for payment should not be the same person who writes checks, and the person who writes checks should not be the same person who signs the checks.

The benefit of such separation is that each individual may catch a problem that is missed by another. If a bill is not correct, the person approving payment should catch it. If that person doesn't, the person writing the check for payment may find the problem. Even if neither of them finds the problem, the person signing the check may raise a question about the payment, which leads to discovery of the problem. This system of separation is also an especially powerful tool for reducing the potential for embezzlement.

If the same person authorizes payments, writes checks, and signs them, that person has the ability to steal money with a minimum likelihood of detection. By separating functions, we make such activity more likely to be discovered and therefore less likely to occur.

Another example of separation is keeping operations separate from accounting. For example, Coffin Corporation has a central inventory department that tracks all of the coffin inventory. This department should not be the one responsible for making periodic checks of the number and models of coffins on hand (called "'taking an inventory"). The members of that department have access to these coffins, and there is the potential for theft. If the same individuals are responsible for counting them, they can falsify records to hide the theft. If they know that independent individuals from elsewhere in the organization will count them, they know there is a high likelihood of the theft being discovered, so theft is less likely to occur.

However, any control system can be defeated. Separation of functions will not protect resources if several individuals collude to steal from the organization. If the person approving payment, the person writing checks, and the person signing checks all agree to steal money and share it, it will be hard for the control system to prevent such actions. That is why hiring ethical individuals and having a corporate culture that stresses ethical behavior are critical elements of an internal control system.

Proper Authorization

Another control element is related to proper authorization. A system of authorization for spending helps the organization to set spending policies, and then adhere to them. For example, a policy decision might be that all air travel is done in coach. But the organization may have thousands of employees. What is to stop one of them from buying and using a first-class air ticket and charging the organization for the higher first-class airfare?

Organizations accomplish this by establishing formal authorization mechanisms. Expenditures will be reimbursed only if they have received the proper authorization. This can be stifling if every individual has to go through an elaborate process to get authorization to spend any amount on any item. Therefore, some items can qualify for *general authorization*. General authorization is a standing approval of certain spending. Items under a certain dollar limit or for certain purposes may fall under that general authorization. For example, air travel at the coach airfare rate for valid business reasons may fall under general authorization. General authorization may contain limits and prohibitions.

Items that cannot be acquired using general authorization require *specific authorization*. Specific authorization would require an individual to get written permission to override the general authorization policies.

Proper authorization is required for many things in addition to spending. For example, some employees can sign contracts committing the organization to provide specific services. Some employees can represent the organization with respect to legal matters. The ultimate source of authority rests with the Board of Directors. The Board provides letters of delegation to senior managers, providing them with the authority to undertake a variety of functions on behalf of the organization. These senior managers can, in turn, delegate authority to specific individuals who report to them.

Adequate Documentation

The audit trail discussed earlier requires an ability to provide detailed documentation of what was spent and why it was spent. Documents, however, do not have to be on paper. The computer age is pushing us more and more toward electronic record keeping.

For example, at one time, organizations maintained files with all canceled checks. If a discrepancy arose concerning whether a payment had been made or not, the organization could find the canceled check in its files and use the check to prove that payment had been made. More and more often, payments are made by electronic transfer rather than by check. In many organizations, for example, very few payroll checks are issued. Instead, payments to employees are deposited directly into the employees' bank accounts.

In light of such dramatic changes, it is essential that organizations carefully think out what documentation will be available to them to allow them to trace back, explain, and prove that transactions have occurred. It is also important to recognize that loss of electronic data (such as the loss or erasure of a computer tape) can be as devastating as a fire that destroys all of an organization's paper records.

Proper Procedures

Internal control systems rely heavily on standard operating procedures, often in the form of a procedures manual. Doing things "by the book" may seem rigid to some employees; but if we follow clearly documented procedures, we are likely to reduce the number of errors. Less time will have to be spent correcting those errors.

By the same token, the "book" should be current and relevant. Internal control procedures should be reviewed and updated on a regular basis. New approaches for increasing efficiency and protecting resources should be adopted.

Physical Safeguards

Common sense dictates the need for physical safeguards. Cash and blank checks should obviously be kept locked when not in use. Backup copies of computer records should be maintained in a separate location. Controls should be put in place to protect valuable inventory.

Bonding, Vacations, and Rotation of Duties

If individuals are in positions in which it would be possible for them to steal significant amounts from the organization, it is appropriate to bond them. *Bonding* means that the organization purchases insurance to protect itself against theft by the employee. Many organizations fail to bond, being reluctant to give the impression that they don't trust their employees. However, bonding is similar to fire insurance. You don't expect your building to burn down—you may even have a sprinkler system—but the potential loss is too great to risk. Just as it would be foolish to not buy fire insurance, it is foolish to fail to bond key employees.

What other controls go hand in hand with the bonding of employees? One approach is mandated vacations and rotation of staff. Many types of defalcation require constant supervision by the embezzler. If money is being stolen from the accounts receivable cash stream, checks received later are often used to cover the cash that has been taken.

By requiring vacations, we move another employee into each role periodically. That provides an opportunity for discrepancies to be uncovered. Similarly, a formal rotation system establishes the fact that no employee will be doing exactly the same job year after year. If it is well known that all employees must take vacations and that rotation in duties will occur from time to time with little advance notice, these controls can serve not only to discover problems, but to prevent them as well.

Performance Audits

Performance audits, sometimes called *operational audits*, are systems reviews that should take place on a regular basis. They generally are divided into two subcategories, *economy* and *efficiency audits* and *program audits*. Economy and efficiency audits are reviews that determine if the organization is acquiring, protecting, and using its resources efficiently. Essentially they check for waste. Program audits check for effectiveness. They determine whether the organization's programs are accomplishing their objectives.

Larger organizations have internal audit departments. These departments work year-round on performance audits that review the financial and operating systems of the organization. They seek out weaknesses in controls that might allow for theft of resources. They also try to improve systems to reduce the chances that errors will occur in the recording or reporting of financial information. At the same time, internal auditors focus their performance audits on trying to find ways that the organization can better achieve its mission. This will at times require them to evaluate the role and functioning of each unit or department of the organization.

Outside independent auditors also serve a crucial role. Independent auditors have the benefit of experience from reviewing control systems in many different organizations. As a result, these external auditors can often offer suggestions for improvement in internal controls. From an outsider's perspective, they are more likely to see flaws in the system that most insiders might not notice.

Cost–Benefit Analysis

Internal control systems can be quite simple or quite elaborate. The more careful we are to ensure that the organization's system catches all potential problems, the more it costs. Systems should be cost-effective. The organization should not spend more on the systems than they are worth. For example, one wouldn't spend $1,000 to prevent someone from possibly stealing $10. We should also be aware that no matter how careful we are with our control systems, fraud, embezzlements, and some inefficiencies can still take place.

LEGAL CONSIDERATIONS

There are important legal reasons for having an adequate system of internal control. In an attempt to reduce certain abuses, the Foreign Corrupt Practices Act (FCPA) became law in the 1970s. Although the law stemmed from certain international activities by American firms, it is poorly named since it applies to all public companies, even if their activities are all domestic. The law requires maintenance of a system of internal controls and maintenance of accurate accounting records. It is incumbent upon management to review their system, be explicit in the cost–benefit trade-offs made that limit the system, and evaluate the extent to which the internal control system works. The Enron bankruptcy of 2001–2002, will likely lead to additional laws and regulations tightening internal control.

KEY CONCEPTS

Management control system (MCS)—a set of policies and procedures designed to keep operations going according to plan.

Responsibility accounting—an attempt to measure financial outcomes and assign responsibility for those outcomes to an individual or department.

Goal divergence—the natural differences between the goals, desires, and needs of the organization and those of its employees.

Goal congruence—bringing together the goals, desires, and wants of the organization with those of its employees.

Internal control—a system of accounting checks and balances designed to minimize both clerical errors and the possibility of fraud or embezzlement. Includes an audit trail, separation of duties, proper authorization, adequate documentation, proper procedures, physical safeguards, bonding, mandatory vacations, rotation of duties, independent checks, and cost–benefit analysis.

Performance (operations) audits—review of the organization's operations, consisting of economy and efficiency audits and program audits.

Part 4

Financial
Statement
Analysis

Twenty

A Closer Look at Financial Statements

Earlier, we examined the source of financial statements. We discussed the basic definitions of assets, liabilities, stockholders' equity, revenues, and expenses. We traced through a variety of journal entries, and saw how ledger balances can be used to derive key financial statements. In order to understand financial information, it is vital to have an understanding of where this information comes from.

We now turn our attention to trying to get as much useful information as possible from a set of financial statements. There are a variety of reasons for wanting to be able to do this. First and foremost is to enable us to manage our firm better. Second, we want to be able to review the financial statements of close competitors to evaluate our performance as compared to theirs. Third, we may want to evaluate the financial statements of a firm in which we wish to invest. Fourth, we want to evaluate the financial statements of firms we are considering extending credit to.

We may be looking for different types of information in each case. Before extending credit, we want to assess a firm's liquidity and solvency. Before investing in a firm, we wish to know about its potential profitability. The goal of financial statement analysis is to derive from financial statements the information needed to make informed decisions.

We do this primarily through examination of the notes that accompany the financial statements, and through the use of a technique called ratio analysis. Generally accepted accounting principles (GAAP), in recognition of many of the limitations of financial numbers generated by accounting systems, require that clarifying notes accompany financial statements. The information contained in these notes may be more relevant and important than the basic statements themselves. Ratio analysis is a method for examining the numbers contained in financial statements to see if there are relationships among the numbers that can provide us with useful information.

Chapter 21 focuses on the notes to the financial statements. Chapter 22 discusses ratio analysis. In the remainder of this chapter we will present a hypothetical set of financial statements to use as a basis of discussion for the remainder of Part 4.

THE BALANCE SHEET

Exhibit 20-1 presents the balance sheet for the hypothetical Pacioli Wholesale Corporation (PW) that will be the subject of our analysis. The information is provided for two years. In recognition of the fact that information in a vacuum is not very useful, accountants generally provide comparative data. In the case of PW, the financial statements present the current fiscal year ending June 30, 2002 and the previous fiscal year ended June 30, 2001. Many financial reports contain the current year and the two previous years for comparison.

All the numbers on the PW financial statements are rounded to the nearest thousand dollars. For large corporations, it is not uncommon to round numbers to the nearest hundred thousand or even million dollars.

Current Assets

The first assets listed on the balance sheet are the current assets. These are the most liquid of the firm's resources. The current assets are presented on the balance sheet in order of liquidity. Cash, the most readily available asset for use in meeting obligations as they become due, is listed first. Cash includes amounts on deposit in checking and savings accounts as well as cash on hand. The next item is marketable securities that are intended to be liquidated in the near term. They can be converted to cash in a matter of a few days. Marketable securities that the firm intends to hold as long-term investments shouldn't be listed with current assets, but instead under a long-term investment category, after fixed assets.

The next current asset listed is accounts receivable, net of uncollectible accounts. It is usually the case that we do not expect to collect

EXHIBIT 20-1.
Pacioli Wholesale Corporation
Statement of Financial Position
As of June 30, 2002 and June 30, 2001

ASSETS	2002	2001
Current Assets		
Cash	$ 8,000	$ 7,000
Marketable Securities	12,000	9,000
Accounts Receivable, Net of Uncollectible Accounts	22,000	30,000
Inventory	49,000	40,000
Prepaid Expenses	3,000	2,000
Total Current Assets	$ 94,000	$ 88,000
Fixed Assets		
Buildings and Equipment	$150,000	$120,000
Less Accumulated Depreciation	40,000	30,000
Net Buildings and Equipment	$110,000	$ 90,000
Land	50,000	50,000
Total Fixed Assets	$160,000	$140,000
Goodwill	$ 45,000	$ 50,000
TOTAL ASSETS	$299,000	$278,000

LIABILITIES AND STOCKHOLDERS' EQUITY	2002	2001
Current Liabilities		
Wages Payable	$ 3,000	$ 2,000
Accounts Payable	29,000	25,000
Taxes Payable	15,000	12,000
Total Current Liabilities	$ 47,000	$ 39,000
Long-Term Liabilities		
Mortgage Payable	$ 45,000	$ 50,000
Bond Payable	100,000	100,000
Deferred Taxes	39,000	35,000
Total Long-Term Liabilities	$184,000	$185,000
Stockholders' Equity		
Common Stock, $1 Par, 1000 Shares	$ 1,000	$ 1,000
Common Stock—Excess over Par	24,000	24,000
Preferred Stock, 10%, $100 Par, 100 Shares	10,000	10,000
Retained Earnings	33,000	19,000
Total Stockholders' Equity	$ 68,000	$ 54,000
TOTAL LIABILITIES & STOCKHOLDERS' EQUITY	$299,000	$278,000

The accompanying notes are an integral part of these statements.

what is due us from all of our customers. Credit policies, discussed in Chapter 16, may have an impact on the level of bad debts.

Inventory is not as liquid as receivables because we first have to sell the goods in order to generate receivables. Prepaid expenses are generally small, relative to the rest of the balance sheet. They include such items as prepaid rent or insurance. Prepaid expenses are grouped with current assets even though they will not usually generate any cash to use for paying current liabilities.

Long-Term Assets

All assets the firm has that are not current assets fall into the general category of long-term assets. Prominent among the long-term assets are fixed assets, which include the property, plant, and equipment used to process or produce the firm's product or service. A variety of other long-term assets may appear on the balance sheet. There would be a category for investments if we had marketable securities that we anticipated keeping for more than one year.

In the case of PW, there is an asset called goodwill. Goodwill is an intangible asset that may arise through the acquisition of another company. Most firms have some goodwill: They have customer loyalty and a good relationship with their suppliers. However, goodwill is an intangible asset that accountants usually leave off the balance sheet because of the difficulty in measuring it. When one company takes over another, if it pays more for the company it is acquiring than can reasonably be assigned as the fair market value of the specific identifiable assets that it is buying, then the excess is recorded on the balance sheet of the acquiring company as goodwill. This follows the accountant's philosophy that people are not fools. If we pay more for a company than its other assets are worth, then there is a presumption that the various intangibles we are acquiring that can't be directly valued must be worth at least the excess amount we paid.

Liabilities

The firm's current liabilities are those that exist at the balance sheet date, which have to be paid in the next operating cycle—usually considered to be one year. Common current liabilities include wages payable, accounts payable, and taxes payable. The taxes payable include only the portion to be paid in the near term, not the taxes that have been deferred more than one year beyond the balance sheet date.

Long-term liabilities include any recorded liabilities that are not current liabilities. There may be a variety of commitments that the firm has made that will not be included with the liabilities. For example, if the firm has operating leases (see Chapter 14), they will not appear on the balance sheet, even though they may legally obligate the firm to make large payments into the future. The notes to the financial statements are especially important in disclosing material commitments.

Stockholders' Equity

The stockholders' equity section of the balance sheet contains a number of elements. Instead of simply having contributed capital and retained earnings, there are a number of separate items that comprise contributed capital. In addition, there is a distinction between amounts paid representing *par value* and amounts in excess of par. Par value is a new term that is discussed in this section.

In the case of PW, there are two general classes of stock. There is common stock and preferred stock. Both types of stock were discussed in Chapter 10.

Par value is a legal concept. In many states, firms are required to set an arbitrary amount as the par value of their stock. As was discussed in Chapter 10, one of the primary reasons many firms incorporate is to achieve a limited liability for their owners. Limited liability assumes that the corporation's stock was originally issued for at least its par value. If stock is issued below the par value—let's say that $10 par value stock is issued for $7—then the owner could be liable for the difference between the issue price and the par value should the firm go bankrupt. Given that situation, the par value of a corporation's stock is generally set low enough so that all stock is issued for at least the par value. Par value is an arbitrary value set by the firm.

There is no connection between the par value and any underlying *value* of the firm. There is no reason to believe that the arbitrarily selected par value is a good measure of what a share of stock is worth. In fact, because most firms are very careful to set par low enough so that there is no extra liability for the corporation's owners, par value has become almost meaningless. Therefore, some states now allow corporations to issue stock without assigning a par value.

From an accounting perspective, we wish to be able to show the user of financial statements whether there is some potential additional liability to the stockholders. To accomplish this, the accountant will have one account to show amounts received for stock up to the par value amount. Anything paid above par for any share will go into a separate account with a name such as "excess paid over par" or "additional paid-in capital."

In the case of PW, we see that it has 1,000 shares of $1 par value common stock. The balance in the common stock par account is $1,000, meaning that all 1,000 shares were issued for at least $1 each, the par value. There are 100 shares of $100 par value preferred stock and the balance in the preferred stock par account is $10,000, indicating that each of the 100 shares was issued for at least $100. Therefore, we know that the stockholders of PW have limited liability. They can lose everything they've paid for their stock, but if the firm goes bankrupt, the creditors cannot attempt to collect additional amounts from the stockholders personally.

As is quite commonly the case, PW's stockholders have paid more than the par value for at least some of the stock issued by the corporation. The common stock excess over par account has a balance of $24,000. Together with the $1,000 in the common stock par account, this indicates the investors paid $25,000 (or gave the firm resources worth $25,000) for 1,000 shares of stock. On average, investors have paid $25 per share for the common stock. There is no excess over par account for the preferred stock. Therefore, we know that the preferred stockholders each paid exactly $100 per share for the preferred stock.

The preferred stock is referred to as 10 percent, $100 par stock, indicating that the annual dividend rate on the preferred stock is 10 percent of the $100 par value. Each preferred share must receive a $10 dividend before the firm can pay any dividend to the common stock shareholders.

The retained earnings, as discussed earlier in the book, represent the profits that the firm earned during its existence that have not been distributed to the stockholders as dividends, and therefore have been retained in the firm. Remember that this category, like the others on the liability and owners' equity side of the balance sheet, represents claims on assets.

There is no pool of money making up the retained earnings. Rather, the profits earned over the years and retained in the firm have likely been invested in a variety of fixed and current assets.

Excel Exercise

You may use Template 21 to prepare a balance sheet for your organization. The template is on the CD that accompanies this book.

THE INCOME STATEMENT

The income statement of PW (Exhibit 20-2) does not overtly raise as many new concepts and issues as the balance sheet did. PW uses the common multiple-step statement in which various expenses are shown separately. For instance, product costs are all grouped under the heading "Cost of Goods Sold." The gross margin provides information about the margin of profitability when sales are compared to the direct product costs of the firm.

Subtracting the various other day-to-day operating costs from the gross margin results in operating income. By operating costs, we mean the various selling, administrative, and general costs of the firm. These costs include everything except product costs, financing costs, and taxes. Financing costs are isolated as a separate figure because of the specific financial leverage decisions (see Chapter 11) the firm makes. There is a much greater degree of control over whether interest expense exists than, say, selling expenses. Management can decide whether money is to be borrowed, thus generating interest expense, or whether money should be raised through the issuance of stock.

Management can choose to use a single-step statement in which far less information is given about individual types of expenses. In this latter case, less information is provided to stockholders and creditors. On the other hand, less information is also given to competitors. The single-step approach cannot be used if it would mask information that the auditor believes is necessary for a fair representation of the firm's position and results of operations.

EXHIBIT 20-2.
Pacioli Wholesale Corporation
Income Statement and Analysis of Retained Earnings
For the Years Ending June 30, 2002 and June 30, 2001

		2002		2001
Sales		$297,000		$246,000
Less Cost of Goods Sold		162,000		143,000
Gross Profit		$135,000		$103,000
Operating Expenses				
Selling Expenses	$30,000		$25,000	
General Expenses	12,000		10,000	
Administrative Expenses	49,000		40,000	
Total Operating Expenses		91,000		75,000
Operating Income		$ 44,000		$ 28,000
Interest Expense		12,000		10,000
Income Before Taxes		$ 32,000		$ 18,000
Income Taxes		13,000		7,000
Net Income		$ 19,000		$ 11,000
Earnings Per Share Common	$ 18.00		$ 10.00	
Less Dividends 2002 and 2001		5,000		3,000
Addition to Retained Earnings		$ 14,000		$ 8,000
Retained Earnings July 1,				
2001 and 2000		19,000		11,000
Retained Earnings June 30,				
2002 and 2001		$ 33,000		$ 19,000

The accompanying notes are an integral part of these statements.

The line following net income in Exhibit 20-2 contains earnings per share data. GAAP require inclusion of information on a per-share basis for common stock. It is felt that this type of information may be more relevant than net income for many users of financial information. Consider an individual who owns 100 shares of common stock of a large corporation. The corporation reports that its profits have risen from $25,000,000 to $30,000,000. On the surface, we would presume that the stockholder is better off this year. What if, however, during the year the firm issued additional shares of stock, thereby creating additional owners. Although total profits have risen $5,000,000 or 20 percent, because of the additional shares of stock outstanding, investors will find that their share of earnings increased by less than 20 percent. In fact, it is quite possible that the profits attributable to each individual share may have fallen, even though the total profit for the firm has increased.

Therefore, we must show not only net income for the firm, but also net income per share of common stock. Although there are 1,000 shares of common stock for PW, and the net income was $19,000, the earnings or income (the two terms are used interchangeably) per share is $18.00, rather than the expected $19.00. This is because $1,000 has to be paid as a 10 percent dividend to the preferred shareholders. This portion of the income of the firm doesn't belong to the common shareholders. The remaining $18,000 does.

Many corporations have outstanding securities that can be converted to common stock. For example, convertible debt represents loans that give the lender the option of taking shares of common stock instead of a cash repayment. This potential increase in the number of common shares outstanding can reduce the portion of total earnings owned by each of the current shareholders. If PW had such potential conversions, the earnings per share (EPS) of $18.00 would have been called *basic EPS* and the potential lower amount would also be shown and would be called *diluted EPS*.

For PW, the balance in the common and preferred stock accounts didn't change during the year (Exhibit 20-1). However, upon looking at the stockholders' equity section of the balance sheet, we see that the retained earnings has changed. Furthermore, the change is not exactly equal to the firm's income for the year. Somewhere in the financials we need some way of reconciling this change. In PW's case it has chosen one of the most common approaches—retained earnings are reconciled as part of the income statement.

In order to accomplish this reconciliation, the first step is to subtract any of this year's dividends from this year's net income. The difference is the amount of this year's earnings that are being retained in the firm. This year's earnings that are retained in the firm plus the balance of retained earnings at the start of the year gives us the retained earnings balance at year-end. This number should, and does, reconcile directly with the number that appears on the balance sheet as the year-end retained earnings.

Excel Exercise

You may use Template 22 to prepare an Income Statement and Analysis of Retained Earnings for your organization. The template is on the CD that accompanies this book.

THE STATEMENT OF CASH FLOWS

The statement of cash flows focuses on financial rather than operating aspects of the firm. Where did the money come from, and how did the firm spend it? While the major concern of the income statement is profitability, the statement of cash flows is very concerned with viability. Is the firm generating and will it generate enough cash to meet both short-term and long-term obligations?

PW's statement of cash flows is presented in Exhibit 20-3. The first element of the statement is cash flows from operating activities. This is a key focal point, because it provides information on whether the routine operating activities of the firm generate cash, or require a cash infusion. If the operating activities generate a surplus of cash, the firm is more financially stable and viable than if they consume more cash than they generate. This does not mean that negative cash from operating activities is bad. It may be indicative of a growing, profitable firm that is expanding inventories and receivables as it grows. However, it does provide a note of caution. Overly rapid expansion, without other adequate cash sources, can cause financial failure.

EXHIBIT 20-3.
Pacioli Wholesale Corporation
Statement of Cash Flows
For the Years Ending June 30, 2002 and June 30, 2001

	2002	2001
Cash Flows from Operating Activities		
Net Income	$ 19,000	$ 11,000
Add Expenses Not Requiring Cash:		
Depreciation	10,000	8,000
Impairment of Goodwill	5,000	0
Increase in Taxes Payable and Deferred Taxes	7,000	8,000
Other Adjustments:		
Add Reduction in Accounts Receivable	8,000	1,000
Add Increase in Wages Payable	1,000	0
Add Increase in Accounts Payable	4,000	0
Subtract Decrease in Accounts Payable	0	(3,000)
Subtract Increase in Inventory	(9,000)	(2,000)
Subtract Increase in Prepaid Expenses	(1,000)	0
Net Cash from Operating Activities	$ 44,000	$ 23,000
Cash Flows from Investing Activities		
Increase in Marketable Securities	$(3,000)	
Sale of Fixed Assets	0	$2,000
Purchase of New Equipment	(30,000)	(20,000)
Net Cash Used for Investing Activities	$(33,000)	$(18,000)
Cash Flows from Financing Activities		
Payment of Mortgage Principal	$ (5,000)	$ (5,000)
Payment of Dividends	(5,000)	(3,000)
Net Cash from Financing Activities	$(10,000)	$ (8,000)
NET INCREASE/(DECREASE) IN CASH	$1,000	$ (3,000)
CASH, BEGINNING OF YEAR	7,000	10,000
CASH, END OF YEAR	$ 8,000	$ 7,000

The accompanying notes are an integral part of these statements.

The cash flows from operating activities are first approximated by the net income of the firm. Revenue activities are generally generators of cash, and expenses generally consume cash. That is not always the case, however, and a number of adjustments are needed. First of all, there are certain expenses that do not consume cash. In Exhibit 20-3, note that there are several expenses that are added to net income. Depreciation reflects a current year expense for a portion of fixed assets that are being used up during the year. These assets were mostly purchased in earlier years, and paid for at that time. The income statement charges part of their cost as an expense in the current year. However, that does not necessarily require any cash. Similarly, a reduction in the value of goodwill (called Impairment of Goodwill) will often occur only years after payment was made to acquire that goodwill. Therefore, net income is an imperfect measure of cash flow. It treats all expenses as if they consumed cash. Since depreciation and impairment did not consume cash, they are added back. To the extent that cash was actually spent this year on fixed asset purchases, it will show up in the investing activity portion of the statement of cash flows.

Taxes are another expense that do not necessarily require cash. As noted earlier (Chapter 15), some tax expense may be deferred for a number of years into the future, requiring no current cash payment, even though they are currently recorded as an expense. Additionally, some taxes that are due for the current year may not actually be paid until the tax return is filed, several months after the end of the year. These taxes also show up as an expense, even though the cash payment has not yet been made. Thus, these increases in taxes that are recorded as expenses but don't require cash payments must be added back to net income to arrive at a clearer picture of actual cash flows.

In addition to these expense items, there are a variety of other activities related to operations that consume or provide cash, but are not adequately approximated by net income. For example, when the firm purchases more inventory than it uses, the extra inventory is not an expense. Nevertheless, we must pay for it, so there is a cash flow. Increases in inventory must therefore be subtracted to show that they consume cash. On the other hand, if wages payable increase, that indicates that less cash was currently paid than we would expect based on the labor expenses we had for the year.

These adjustments can become complicated. However, for the nonfinancial manager it is not necessary to be able to make the various adjustments. Nonfinancial managers should focus on interpretation of the numbers. It is more important to be aware of the fact that these components show us what is affecting cash from operating activities. For instance, increases in accounts receivable require a subtraction from net income. This is because net income assumes that all revenues have been received. If accounts receivable are rising, the firm is not collecting all of its revenues from the current year. If we note a large increase in accounts receivable, it warns the managers that perhaps greater collections efforts are in order.

The second part of the statement of cash flows is cash from investing activities. We note here that PW increased its marketable securities, using $3,000 of cash, and purchased new equipment for $30,000. In the prior year, some equipment had been purchased and some equipment had been sold.

The third section of the statement is cash flows from financing activities. In this case there were no cash inflows from financing activities in either year. The corporation issued no new stock, nor were there increases in debt. The only financing activities relate to paying off an existing mortgage to creditors and paying dividends to shareholders.

Combining the cash flows from operating, investing, and financing activities yields the net increase or decrease in cash for the year. Added to the cash balance at the beginning of the year, this provides the cash balance at the end of the year. This is the same balance as that appearing on the balance sheet (Exhibit 20-1).

For PW the final cash balance has not been varying substantially. At the end of 2002 the balance is $8,000. The prior year it was $7,000. More important than the stability in the closing balance each year is the fact that the investments made by PW are being financed from operating activities. Not only are operations generating a positive cash flow, but further this cash flow is generally sufficient, or nearly sufficient, to cover the firm's investing and financing needs.

Right now, PW is relatively stable. It is growing and profitable, has twice as much in current assets as current liabilities, and has sustained its cash balance. On the other hand, as growth continues it must carefully monitor this statement. Increases in fixed assets, inventory, and receivables that normally accompany growth may prevent the firm from remaining in balance. Managers should consider whether the cash being generated from activities will be sufficient to sustain planned growth. If not, they should start to plan for either increases in long-term debt or the issuance of additional stock. A specific focus on the statement of cash flows can be a tremendous aid to management in preparing an orderly approach to meeting the financial needs of the firm.

Excel Exercise

You may use Template 23 to prepare a Statement of Cash Flows for your organization. The template is on the CD that accompanies this book.

THE NOTES TO THE FINANCIAL STATEMENTS

This chapter introduced you to the financial statements of PW. We discussed these statements in somewhat more detail than the statements we looked at in earlier chapters. However, no matter how closely you read the numbers in the financial statements nor how well you understand the detail presented on the financial statements, in themselves they are an inadequate picture of the firm.

The balance sheet, income statement, and statement of cash flows of an audited set of financial statements all refer the reader to the "notes" that follow or accompany the financial statements. Accounting is not a science. It is a set of rules containing numerous exceptions and complications. Financial analysis requires an understanding of what the firm's financial position really is and what the results of its operations and cash flows really were. It is vital that the user of financials not simply look to the total assets and net income to determine how well the firm has done. The notes that accompany the financial statements really are an integral part of the annual report. It is to those notes for PW that we turn in Chapter 21.

KEY CONCEPTS

Financial statement analysis—techniques of analyzing financial statement information to find out as much about the firm's financial position and the results of its operations and its cash flows as possible. The focus is on the financial statements, the notes to the financial statements, and ratio analysis.

Par value—a legal concept related to limited liability of stockholders. There is no relationship between par value and a fair or correct value of the firm's stock.

Earnings per share—Rather than focus simply on net income or total earnings, GAAP require disclosure of the earnings available to common shareholders on a per-share basis.

Twenty-One

Notes to the
Financial Statements

The financial statements for Pacioli Wholesale (PW) Corporation tell a great deal about the company. We have information about the firm's resources, obligations, net worth (stockholders' equity), profitability, and cash flows. Yet financial statements are extremely limited in their ability to convey information. Therefore, audited financial statements must be accompanied by a set of *notes*. These notes explain the company's significant accounting policies and provide disclosure of other information not contained in the balance sheet, income statement, and statement of cash flows, but that is necessary for the statements to be a fair representation of the firm's financial position and the results of its operations.

This chapter presents a hypothetical set of notes for the financial statements of PW. We will first present each note and then discuss it before moving on to the next note. This discussion will not be exhaustive. Each firm has notes that apply to its own unique circumstances.

SIGNIFICANT ACCOUNTING POLICIES

The notes section generally begins with a statement of accounting policies. This is particularly important because of the alternative choices of accounting methods allowed, even within the constraints of generally accepted accounting principles (GAAP). In cases in which the firm has a choice of methods, that choice will likely have an impact on both the balance sheet and the income statement and possibly on the statement of cash flows. The financial statement figures are not meaningful unless we know what choices the firm has made.

NOTE A: Significant Accounting Policies

1. *Sales—Sales are recorded when title passes; for most sales this is at the time of shipment.*

For some businesses, revenue can be recorded prior to the final sale. For example, a construction company can record some revenue on a partially completed building if it has a sales contract. Even though the title has not yet passed to the buyer, some revenue and expense might be reported in that situation. On the other hand, for some sales for which there is great uncertainty about the collection of the sales price, revenue recognition is deferred until the time of cash receipt. For example, if a company sells swampland in Florida for a vacation or retirement home, it can generally only record revenue as cash installments are received, because of the uncertainty surrounding receipt of future installments. For PW, which is a wholesale company, the normal rules of accrual accounting require revenue recognition when title passes, which is normally when the goods are shipped.

2. *Short-term investments—Short-term investments are stated at their fair market value.*

PW has $12,000 of marketable securities at the end of fiscal year 2002 (see Exhibit 20-1). Your expectation might well be that these securities cost PW $12,000 because that would correspond with the *cost* principle of accounting. However, objective market prices for stocks and bonds are available from many sources. We can determine the price at which identical securities were actually sold. Therefore, marketable securities are generally shown on the balance sheet at their fair market value.

3. *Inventories—Inventories are stated at cost, not to exceed market. Cost is calculated using the last-in, first-out (LIFO) method.*

Here the principle of recording at cost (based on objective evidence) conflicts with that of conservatism (adequate consideration of relevant risks). In this case, GAAP requires use of lower of cost or market value (LCM). If the market value exceeds cost, we use the cost. If the cost exceeds market value, we use the market value. Essentially, we are willing to value inventory below its cost, but not above it.

So, inventories are stated using LCM because of the GAAP of conservatism. But how does PW measure the cost of its inventory? This note tells us that PW uses the LIFO method to determine inventory cost. LIFO/FIFO is a choice the firm is allowed under GAAP.

> 4. *Property, plant, and equipment—Property, plant, and equipment are recorded at cost, less depreciation. Depreciation taken over the useful lives of plant and equipment is calculated on the straight-line basis.*

For tax purposes, law largely mandates our depreciation choices. For financial reporting, however, we have a fair degree of latitude. We could use a declining balance or sum-of-the-years-digits approach as an alternative to straight-line depreciation. For PW in 2002, operating costs included $10,000 of depreciation calculated on a straight-line (STL) basis. Suppose that the double-declining balance (DDB) depreciation would have been $18,000, and that the sum-of-the-years-digits (SYD) depreciation would have been $14,000.

The firm's reported net income can be greatly affected by the choice of accounting methods. Disclosure of choices, such as the inventory and depreciation methods used, provides users with a greater ability to understand the firm's financial situation.

> 5. *Taxes on income—Income taxes reported on the income statement differ from taxes paid as a result of deferred income taxes. Deferred income taxes arise when there are differences between the year in which certain transactions, principally depreciation, affect taxable income and the year they affect net income.*

This note discusses deferred taxes. Based on our discussion in Chapter 15, we are already familiar with that issue. See Note B (page 282) for additional discussion.

OTHER NOTES

In addition to a summary of accounting policies, the annual report contains other notes that provide additional disclosure of information needed for the financial statements to provide a fair representation of the financial position of the firm and the results of its operations.

Part 5 of Note A was concerned with the calculation of the amount of tax expense reported on the financial statements. Note B concerns the difference between taxes actually paid and the tax rate. PW is assumed to be in a 41 percent and 39 percent combined federal and state average tax bracket for 2002 and 2001, respectively, after adjusting for the federal tax benefit. This benefit arises from the tax deductibility of state and local income taxes on the federal tax return. Because our 2002 pretax income is $32,000 (Exhibit 20-2), we would expect tax payments of $13,000. However, PW did not pay $13,000 in 2002. Note B explains why.

NOTE B: Tax Payments

Differences between the effective tax rate and the statutory federal income tax rate are reconciled as follows:

IMPACT ON PRETAX INCOME	2002	2001
Statutory federal income tax rate	34%	34%
State and local income taxes net of the federal income tax benefit	7%	5%
Deferred tax increase	(13%)	(17%)
Taxes paid as a percentage of pretax income (effective tax rate)	28%	22%

We note from Exhibit 20-1 that deferred taxes increased by $4,000 in 2002. Based on Note A, Part 5, this must be attributed primarily to the use of accelerated depreciation for tax return purposes. In other words, only $9,000 of the $13,000 tax expense was paid or payable for 2002. $9,000 is only 28 percent of pretax income. This note makes it clear that the effective tax rate for PW for 2002 was not the statutory combined federal and state rate of 41 percent that was reported on the income statement as tax expense, but instead was only 28 percent.

NOTE C: Inventory

If the first-in first-out (FIFO) method of inventory had been used, inventories would have been $9,000 and $5,000 higher at June 30, 2002 and June 30, 2001, respectively.

The Internal Revenue Service (IRS) allows a firm to use LIFO on its tax return only if it uses LIFO for its income statement and balance sheet, which are included in its annual report to its stockholders. However, the Securities and Exchange Commission (SEC) requires publicly held firms to disclose their inventory on a FIFO basis if it differs significantly from inventory on a LIFO basis. This practice allows a financial analyst to convert income calculated on a LIFO basis to what it would have been if the firm were on a FIFO basis.

NOTE D: Commitments and Contingent Liabilities

Lease commitments and contingent liabilities stemming from pending litigation are not considered to be material in the opinion of management.

The firm is required to disclose any material obligations under noncancelable long-term leases, or other potential liabilities that are significant in amount. Recall that a financial transaction is not recorded unless there has been exchange. If PW has signed a contract raising its president's salary from $5,000 to $500,000 and guaranteeing that new salary for the next ten years, there would be no journal entry to record the new $5,000,000 total obligation. However, if that amount is material, disclosure would be required as a commitment or contingent liability.

NOTE E: Goodwill

The goodwill recorded on the balance sheet arose as a result of the acquisition of another company for more than the fair market value of the identifiable assets of that company. It has been determined that due to permanent changes in market conditions, the goodwill has lost 10 percent of its value during 2002. Therefore, goodwill has been reduced from $50,000 to $45,000 on the balance sheet and a $5,000 expense has been charged.

When one firm acquires another for more than the value of the specific identifiable resources, the excess is grouped under the category of goodwill. It is very common for goodwill to arise when acquisitions occur. If the ongoing firm being acquired wasn't worth more than its specific assets, the purchaser might simply buy similar assets rather than acquiring the firm. Many intangibles arise over a firm's life, such as reputation for quality products and creditworthiness. Goodwill remains as an asset on the balance sheet indefinitely under current GAAP. Goodwill is only reduced when there is a clear impairment to its value. At such time the entire impairment is treated as a one-time reduction in the value of good-will. This differs from tax treatment that allows the organization to deduct the cost of goodwill as an expense over a fifteen-year period.

NOTE F: Industry Segment Information

The firm has only one major type of operation—that of selling con-sumer goods to retail outlets. All of the firm's operations are domestic.

One of the requirements of financial reporting is industry segment information. A major reason for this requirement is that many firms have diversified substantially, making it difficult for stockholders and other users of financial information to determine just what business the company is in. Therefore, firms are required to disclose financial information about components of a business for which separate financial information is available and is used for making decisions. While the intent is to protect and inform stockholders, the information provided can, in fact, hurt stockholders.

The type of information disclosed for a business with multiple types of operations includes not only a description of each type of business, but also sales, operating profit, net earnings, and assets for each segment. This means that a competitor can examine your financial statements (or for that matter, you can examine a competitor's financial statements) to determine which segments are the most profitable. This information can be a tremendous aid in planning competitive strategy. The same is true of geographic data. If it is disclosed that our growth is occurring primarily in Latin America, our competitors may use that information to decide that it is time for a push in Asia.

Management is far more answerable to the firm's stockholders about its mistakes if the mistakes aren't buried among the successes. If the firm is losing some money in Latin America or in one major line of business, it is harder to hide that fact from the firm's owners when disclosure is required by the line of business and geographic location. Therefore this disclosure is required for the benefit of stockholders and creditors, despite the potentially negative impact on the firm's competitive position.

SUMMARY

This chapter does not present an all-inclusive listing of required notes to the financial statements. Depending on the exact circumstances of different companies, a wide variety of disclosures are required by GAAP and by requirements of the SEC. The most important learning issue in this chapter is not the information contained in the notes discussed here. Rather, it is that the reader should have an awareness of the importance of the information that is contained in the notes to the financial statements.

The notes to the financial statements may at first seem both overwhelming and boring. They certainly don't make for light reading. You have to work through them slowly and carefully to understand the information that each note is trying to convey. Exactly which choices has the firm made, and what are the implications of each choice? Is the company reliant on one key customer? If so, that fact would have to be disclosed somewhere in the notes. Can the company use all of its cash, or does it have a "compensating balance" agreement with its bank that requires it to maintain a minimum balance? If the latter, the firm's liquidity is somewhat overstated in the balance sheet. Compensating balance arrangements must be disclosed. Are there securities outstanding, such as convertible bonds that can be converted into common stock? If so, then the firm's net income might have to be shared among more stockholders. Such potential dilution, if significant, is discussed in the notes.

We could continue with examples of the types of information relevant to creditors, investors, and internal management contained only in the notes to the financials. Not all notes are relevant to all readers. Some items are of more concern to employees than to stockholders. Some items help creditors more than internal managers. Whatever your purpose in using a financial report, the key is that the financial statements by themselves are incapable of telling the full story. To avoid being misled by the numbers, it is necessary to supplement the information in the statements with the information in the notes that accompany the statements.

KEY CONCEPTS

Significant accounting policies—Whenever GAAP allow a firm a choice in accounting methods, the firm must disclose the choice that it made. This allows the user of financial statements to better interpret the numbers, such as net income, contained in the financial statements.

Other notes—The firm must disclose any information that a user of the financial statements might need in order to have a fair representation of the firm's financial position and the results of its operations in accordance with GAAP. This information should be included in either the financial statements themselves or the notes that accompany the financial statements.

Twenty-Two

Ratio Analysis

One of the most widely used forms of financial analysis is the use of ratios. Ratios can provide information that is useful for investment decisions such as, "Should we acquire XYZ Corporation?" Ratios can provide information regarding whether we should sell to XYZ or lend money to XYZ. They can also help internal management of an organization gain an awareness of their company's strengths and weaknesses. And, if we can find weaknesses, we can move to correct them before irreparable damage is done.

What is a ratio? Basically, a ratio is simply a comparison of any two numbers. In financial statement analysis, we compare numbers taken from the financial statements. For instance, if we want to know how much Pacioli Wholesale Corporation (PW) had in current assets as compared to current liabilities at the end of fiscal 2002, we would compare its $94,000 in current assets (Exhibit 22-1) to its $47,000 in current liabilities. Or more briefly, it had $94,000 compared to $47,000. Mathematically, we could state this as $94,000 divided by $47,000, which is equal to two. This means that there are two dollars of current assets for every one dollar of current liabilities. This would be referred to either as a ratio of 2 or a ratio of 2 to 1. This particular ratio is called the current ratio. In this chapter, we discuss many widely used ratios, but the discussion is not all-inclusive. Each industry may have many ratios specially suited to its needs.

EXHIBIT 22-1.
Pacioli Wholesale Corporation
Statement of Financial Position
As of June 30, 2002 and June 30, 2001

		2002		2001
	ASSETS			
Current Assets				
Cash	2.7%	$ 8,000	2.5%	$ 7,000
Marketable Securities	4.0%	12,000	3.2%	9,000
Accounts Receivable,				
Net of Uncollectible Accounts	7.4%	22,000	10.8%	30,000
Inventory	16.4%	49,000	14.4%	40,000
Prepaid Expenses	1.0%	3,000	.7%	2,000
Total Current Assets	31.4%	$ 94,000	31.7%	$ 88,000
Fixed Assets				
Buildings and Equipment	50.2%	$150,000	43.2%	$120,000
Less Accumulated Depreciation	13.4%	40,000	10.8%	30,000
Net Buildings and Equipment	36.8%	$110,000	32.4%	$ 90,000
Land	16.7%	50,000	81.0%	50,000
Total Fixed Assets	53.5%	$160,000	50.4%	$140,000
Goodwill	15.1%	$ 45,000	18.0%	$ 50,000
TOTAL ASSETS	100.0%	$299,000	100.0%	$278,000

The accompanying notes are an integral part of these statements.

		2002		2001
LIABILITIES AND STOCKHOLDERS' EQUITY				
Current Liabilities				
Wages Payable	1.0%	$ 3,000	.7%	$ 2,000
Accounts Payable	9.7%	29,000	9.0%	25,000
Taxes Payable	5.0%	15,000	4.3%	12,000
Total Current Liabilities	15.7%	$ 47,000	14.0%	$ 39,000
Long-Term Liabilities				
Mortgage Payable	15.1%	$ 45,000	18.0%	$ 50,000
Bond Payable	33.4%	100,000	36.0%	100,000
Deferred Taxes	13.0%	39,000	12.6%	35,000
Total Long-Term Liabilities	61.5%	$184,000	66.5%	$185,000
Stockholders' Equity				
Common Stock, $1 Par,	.3%	$ 1,000	.4%	$ 1,000
Common Stock—Excess over Par	8.0%	24,000	8.6%	24,000
Preferred Stock, 10%,				
$100 Par, 100 Shares	3.3%	10,000	3.6%	10,000
Retained Earnings	11.0%	33,000	6.8%	19,000
Total Stockholders' Equity	22.7%	$ 68,000	19.4%	$ 54,000
TOTAL LIABILITIES				
& STOCKHOLDERS' EQUITY	100.0%	$299,000	100.0%	$278,000

BENCHMARKS FOR COMPARISON

Is the PW current ratio of 2 good or bad? Is it high enough? Is it too high? We don't want to have too little in the way of current assets, or we may have a liquidity crisis—that is, insufficient cash to pay our obligations as they become due. We don't want to have too much in the way of current assets because this implies that we are passing up profitable long-term investment opportunities. But there is no correct number for the current ratio. We can only assess the appropriateness of our ratios on the basis of some benchmark or other basis for comparison.

There are three principal benchmarks. The first is the firm's history. We always want to review the ratios for the firm this year, as compared to what they were in the several previous years. This enables us to discover favorable or unfavorable trends that are developing gradually over time, as well as pointing up any numbers that have changed sharply in the space of time of just one year.

The second type of benchmark is to compare the firm to specific competitors. If the competitors are publicly held companies, we can obtain copies of their annual reports and compare each of our ratios with each of theirs. This approach is especially valuable for helping to pinpoint why your firm is doing particularly better or worse than a specific competitor. By finding where your ratios differ, you may determine what you are doing better or worse than the competition.

The third type of benchmark is industrywide comparison. Dun and Bradstreet and the Risk Management Association are a few examples of firms that collect financial data, compute ratios by industry, and publish the results. Not only are industry averages available, but the information is often broken down both by size of firm and in a way that allows determination of relatively how far away from the norm you are.

For example, if your current ratio is 2, and the industry average is 2.4, is that a substantial discrepancy? Published industry data may show that 25 percent of the firms in the industry have a current ratio below 1.5. In this case, we may not be overly concerned that our ratio of 2.0 is too low. We are still well above the bottom quartile of firms in our industry. On the other hand, what if only 25 percent of the firms in the industry have a current ratio of less than 2.1? In this case, over three-quarters of the firms in the industry have a higher current ratio than we do. This might be a cause for some concern. At the very least, we might want to investigate

EXHIBIT 22-2.

MANUFACTURING—WOOD OFFICE & STORE FIXTURES, PARTITIONS, SHELVING, & LOCKERS SIC# 2541 (NAICS 337127, 337212, 337215)   325

Comparative Historical Data				Current Data Sorted By Sales					
			Type of Statement						
37	21	13	Unqualified				2	3	8
58	31	30	Reviewed		7	2	10	11	
45	25	24	Compiled	2	9	6	6	1	
7	8	8	Tax Returns	1	4	1	1	1	
65	26	34	Other	6	5	6	8	6	3
4/1/97-3/31/98	4/1/98-3/31/99	4/1/99-3/31/00			23 (4/1-9/30/99)		86 (10/1/99-3/31/00)		
ALL	ALL	ALL		0-1MM	1-3MM	3-5MM	5-10MM	10-25MM	25MM & OVER
212	111	109	**NUMBER OF STATEMENTS**	9	25	15	27	22	11
%	%	%	**ASSETS**	%	%	%	%	%	%
8.1	6.2	8.1	Cash & Equivalents		11.3	7.4	8.8	8.3	3.6
32.0	34.9	32.9	Trade Receivables - (net)		40.5	32.7	30.6	35.1	29.3
22.0	22.4	22.0	Inventory		16.5	23.2	21.7	27.0	28.9
2.4	2.2	2.2	All Other Current		.8	5.8	2.1	2.1	1.5
64.5	65.6	65.2	Total Current		69.1	69.1	63.3	72.6	63.4
27.2	26.9	26.5	Fixed Assets (net)		22.7	27.8	29.0	22.3	26.5
2.9	2.6	1.6	Intangibles (net)		1.4	.3	2.1	.3	4.3
5.4	4.9	6.7	All Other Non-Current		6.8	2.8	5.7	4.8	5.8
100.0	100.0	100.0	Total		100.0	100.0	100.0	100.0	100.0
			LIABILITIES						
10.7	15.2	12.8	Notes Payable-Short Term		18.1	11.0	12.4	12.0	10.3
3.9	4.7	2.9	Cur. Mat.-L/T/D		2.4	2.8	3.5	2.2	3.0
14.8	17.2	15.9	Trade Payables		20.2	18.7	13.1	16.1	10.6
.4	.4	.2	Income Taxes Payable		.2	.2	.0	.1	.5
10.1	12.6	12.9	All Other Current		18.1	11.2	14.5	11.5	9.6
39.9	50.1	44.6	Total Current		59.1	43.8	43.5	41.9	33.9
13.1	14.5	17.3	Long Term Debt		21.3	18.8	11.8	8.3	15.3
.5	.4	.1	Deferred Taxes		.1	.1	.3	.0	.0
2.8	2.3	4.0	All Other Non-Current		2.0	5.7	3.0	4.1	4.0
43.7	32.7	34.0	Net Worth		17.5	31.7	41.5	45.6	46.7
100.0	100.0	100.0	Total Liabilities & Net Worth		100.0	100.0	100.0	100.0	100.0
			INCOME DATA						
100.0	100.0	100.0	Net Sales		100.0	100.0	100.0	100.0	100.0
28.6	29.3	31.7	Gross Profit		38.7	26.8	29.7	26.4	26.6
23.4	24.7	26.1	Operating Expenses		33.2	23.0	24.0	20.1	20.0
5.2	4.6	5.7	Operating Profit		5.5	3.8	5.7	6.3	6.6
.8	.9	1.0	All Other Expenses (net)		1.3	.0	1.0	.7	1.5
4.4	3.6	4.7	Profit Before Taxes		4.2	3.7	4.7	5.5	5.1
			RATIOS						
2.6	2.0	2.6			3.4	2.0	2.2	3.3	3.6
1.6	1.5	1.8	Current		1.8	1.8	1.6	1.7	1.8
1.1	1.2	1.2			1.0	1.2	1.0	1.2	1.5
1.6	1.4	1.7			2.4	1.3	1.5	2.5	1.5
.9 (110)	.9	1.0	Quick		1.3	.9	.9	.9	1.1
.7	.6	.6			.7	.7	.6	.6	.8
30 12.0	29 12.7	30 12.4			30 12.1	27 13.4	28 13.1	29 12.6	41 8.8
45 8.1	45 8.2	43 8.5	Sales/Receivables		42 8.6	39 9.4	42 8.7	46 8.0	52 7.1
60 6.1	62 5.9	56 6.5			66 5.5	60 6.1	55 6.6	54 6.8	54 6.8
22 16.7	20 18.1	27 13.5			11 34.6	28 13.2	19 19.5	28 13.2	41 8.8
42 8.7	40 9.2	40 9.1	Cost of Sales/Inventory		29 12.8	35 10.5	46 7.9	41 8.8	66 5.5
70 5.2	60 6.1	63 5.8			53 6.9	61 6.0	56 6.5	64 5.7	93 3.9
14 25.5	17 21.5	17 22.1			16 23.5	22 16.7	13 28.5	15 24.1	21 17.6
25 14.4	25 14.3	24 15.0	Cost of Sales/Payables		33 11.2	28 13.0	21 17.3	24 15.3	24 15.3
39 9.4	38 9.6	41 9.0			62 5.9	42 8.7	29 12.7	33 10.9	26 14.2
5.8	8.5	6.9			6.5	7.2	7.0	5.6	4.3
10.9	12.7	9.7	Sales/Working Capital		13.0	14.3	12.8	9.2	8.5
41.2	44.2	33.6			537.6	30.2	193.6	29.5	10.3
16.3	10.1	17.3			21.5	9.0	26.5	28.2	
(200) 4.1	(104) 4.2	(102) 4.5	EBIT/Interest		(23) 4.1	2.3	(25) 8.8	7.7	
1.7	1.4	1.7			1.3	1.6	2.5	2.6	
7.2	5.8	5.2	Net Profit + Depr., Dep.,						
(78) 3.5	(42) 2.8	(26) 2.8	Amort./Cur. Mat. L/T/D						
1.5	1.4	.3							
.3	.4	.3			.3	.2	.3	.3	.2
.6	.7	.6	Fixed/Worth		.5	1.1	.9	.5	.6
1.3	1.5	1.5			3.8	1.5	1.4	1.1	1.5
.6	.9	.8			1.1	1.0	.7	.6	.5
1.5	1.8	2.0	Debt/Worth		2.2	2.1	2.0	1.1	.9
3.6	3.3	3.6			23.6	4.0	3.2	2.5	3.1
46.2	54.6	58.7			57.3	42.8	62.8	58.2	68.5
(200) 23.5	(100) 25.0	(101) 22.5	% Profit Before Taxes/Tangible Net Worth		(21) 17.4	(14) 17.0	29.7	26.8	(10) 39.6
7.2	12.0	8.1			10.3	-6	8.6	8.4	9.4
18.6	17.4	21.0			19.0	13.4	23.0	31.1	17.1
8.9	10.0	8.0	% Profit Before Taxes/Total Assets		7.7	5.1	6.5	11.1	13.8
2.3	3.1	2.5			1.3	1.2	3.9	3.7	5.4
22.9	26.7	25.7			55.2	26.0	24.2	28.9	14.8
11.3	13.3	12.7	Sales/Net Fixed Assets		16.9	15.1	11.4	16.4	8.6
5.5	6.7	6.3			6.6	6.5	5.5	8.7	5.5
3.3	3.6	3.7			3.9	4.3	3.7	3.9	2.6
2.4	2.9	2.6	Sales/Total Assets		2.8	2.9	2.8	2.8	2.3
1.8	2.1	2.1			2.2	2.2	2.1	2.3	1.7
1.1	1.1	1.1			.9	.5	1.3	.9	1.5
(200) 1.9	(103) 1.7	(102) 1.7	% Depr., Dep., Amort./Sales		(23) 1.7	(13) 2.0	1.8	(21) 1.2	(10) 2.1
3.1	2.6	2.5			3.1	2.9	2.5	2.0	2.5
2.6	2.2	2.7			6.7		2.2	1.2	
(83) 4.6	(59) 4.5	(53) 5.6	% Officers', Directors', Owners' Comp/Sales		(19) 9.5		(13) 3.9	(10) 2.5	
7.1	6.5	9.4			11.2		7.1	4.0	
3719693M	1212123M	1205044M	Net Sales ($)	5927M	49712M	54631M	192743M	311266M	590785M
1973376M	546773M	494954M	Total Assets ($)	3195M	18425M	20293M	79607M	110134M	263300M

why our ratio is particularly low, compared to our industry. Exhibit 22-2 presents one page from the Risk Management Association's *Annual Statement Studies 2000–2001 Edition*. Note that this page provides information about the balance sheet and income statement as well as a variety of ratios for firms in one industry. The firms are broken down by size, and ratio values are given for the mean firm and also the 25th and 75th percentiles.

There are five principal types of ratios that we examine in this chapter. They are 1) common size ratios; 2) liquidity ratios; 3) efficiency ratios; 4) solvency ratios; and 5) profitability ratios.

COMMON SIZE RATIOS

Common size ratios are used as a starting point in financial statement analysis. Suppose that we wished to compare our firm to another. We look to our cash balance and see that it is $10,000, while the other firm has cash of $5,000. Does this mean we have too much cash? Does the other firm have too little cash? Before we can even begin to consider such questions, we need more general information about the two firms. Are we twice as big as the other firm? Are we smaller than the other firm? The amount of cash we need depends on the size of our operations compared to theirs. Comparing our cash to their cash does not create a very useful ratio.

However, we can "common size" cash by comparing it to total assets. If our cash of $10,000 is one-tenth of our total assets and their cash of $5,000 is one-tenth of their total assets, then relative to asset size, both firms are keeping a like amount of cash. This is much more informative. Therefore, the first step in ratio analysis is to create a set of common size ratios. Usually common size ratios are converted to percentages. Thus, rather than referring to cash as being one-tenth of total assets, we would refer to it as being 10 percent of total assets.

To find our common size ratios, we need a key number for comparison. On the balance sheet, the key number is total assets or total equities (that is, liabilities plus stockholders' equity). We calculate the ratio of each asset on the balance sheet as compared to total assets. We calculate the ratio of each liability and stockholders' equity account as compared to the total equities. For the income statement, all numbers are compared to total sales. Once we have calculated the common size ratios, we can use them

EXHIBIT 22-3.
Pacioli Wholesale Corporation
Income Statement
For the Years Ending June 30, 2002 and June 30, 2001

	2002		2001	
Sales	100.0%	$297,000	100.0%	$246,000
Less Cost of Goods Sold	54.5%	162,000	58.1%	143,000
Gross Profit	45.5%	$135,000	41.9%	$103,000
Operating Expenses				
Selling Expenses	10.1%	$ 30,000	10.2%	$ 25,000
General Expenses	4.0%	12,000	4.1%	10,000
Administrative Expenses	16.5%	49,000	16.3%	40,000
Total Operating Expenses	30.6%	$ 91,000	30.5%	$ 75,000
Operating Income	14.8%	$ 44,000	11.4%	$ 28,000
Interest Expense	4.0%	12,000	4.1%	10,000
Income before Taxes	10.8%	$ 32,000	7.3%	$ 18,000
Income Taxes	4.4%	13,000	2.8%	7,000
Net Income	6.4%	$ 19,000	4.5%	$ 11,000

to compare our firm to itself over time, to specific competitors, and to industrywide statistics.

The common size ratios for PW's balance sheet and income statement are presented in Exhibits 22-1 and 22-3.

The Balance Sheet: Assets

Looking at the balance sheet (Exhibit 22-1), we can begin to get a general feeling about PW by comparing the common size ratios for two years. Note that there will typically be some rounding errors in ratio analysis. We could eliminate them by being more precise. For example, in 2002 the ratio of cash to total assets really is 2.6756 percent. We generally don't bother with such precision. Ratios can't give their users a precise picture of the firm. They are meant to serve as general conveyors of broad information. Our concern is if a number is particularly out of line—either unusually high or low. It is virtually impossible to interpret minor changes.

For PW, current assets have remained relatively stable, falling from 31.7 percent to 31.4 percent of total assets. Note, however, that accounts receivable have fallen while inventory has risen. Is this good or bad? If accounts receivable have fallen because sales are down this year or because there are more bad debts, and inventory has risen because PW is left with a lot of unsold goods, then this is bad. On the other hand, if accounts receivable are down because the firm has been successful in its efforts to collect more promptly, and inventory is up because it is needed to support growing sales, then this is a good sign.

Clearly, ratios can't be interpreted in a vacuum. The ratio merely points out what needs to be investigated. The ratio doesn't provide answers in and of itself. In the case of PW, the income statement (Exhibit 22-3) shows us that sales did indeed rise during the fiscal year ending June 30, 2002. It would appear that the changes in accounts receivable and inventory represent a favorable trend.

Fixed assets (Exhibit 22-1) for PW have increased, not only in absolute terms, but also as a percentage of total assets. After accounting for depreciation that has accumulated on buildings and equipment over their lifetime, we see a rise in net buildings and equipment from 32.4 percent to 36.8 percent of total assets.

The Balance Sheet: Equities

The current liability common size ratios have remained fairly constant over time (Exhibit 22-1). Each has risen slightly, which might well have been anticipated given the rise in sales and inventory noted earlier. As our operations grow and become more profitable, we might expect some growth in current liabilities to match the increases in inventory. In any case, the changes here appear to be modest.

Long-term liabilities (Exhibit 22-1) have fallen as a percentage of total equities. This is primarily because the firm has not needed to raise funds from the debt market to finance its fixed asset growth. Deferred taxes have risen modestly, an indication that we are taking advantage of the Modified Accelerated Cost Recovery System, which in effect creates interest-free government loans as we acquire additional equipment (see Chapter 15).

The common size ratio for stockholders' equity (Exhibit 22-1) has risen from 19.4 percent for 2001 to 22.7 percent for 2002. This is not surprising considering the absolute growth in profits retained in the firm (Exhibit 20-2).

Excel Exercise

Template 24 may be used to calculate common size ratios for your organization's balance sheet. The template is on the CD that accompanies this book.

The Income Statement

For the income statement (Exhibit 22-3), sales is the key figure around which all common size ratios are calculated. This year the cost of goods sold has fallen in relation to sales. Assuming that quality has been maintained, this is a favorable trend. By keeping production costs down relative to the selling price, profits should rise. Internal management of a firm should, nevertheless, be very interested in determining why this occurred. If the causes were related to improved efficiency, we want to know that so we can reward the individuals responsible and maintain the higher level of efficiency. On the other hand, if the improvement is caused by use of poorer quality raw materials, the long-run impact may be to hurt our reputation and long-run profits.

Therefore, even favorable trends such as reduced cost of goods sold should be viewed with caution. Investigation is needed to determine why that change occurred.

For PW, other operating expenses have remained fairly stable, increasing in relative proportion to the dollar increase in overall sales. Gross profit has risen from 41.9 percent to 45.5 percent, and operating income has risen from 11.4 percent to 14.8 percent, both as a result of the change in the cost of goods sold expense. The firm is making more profit on each dollar of sales than it had in the prior year. Of course, greater profits are associated with greater taxes. Because the pretax profit per dollar of sales has risen from 7.3 percent to 10.8 percent, the tax per dollar of sales has also risen from 2.8 percent to 4.4 percent.

> **Excel Exercise**
>
> Template 25 may be used to calculate common size ratios for your organization's income statement. The template is on the CD that accompanies this book.

Common Size Ratios: Additional Notes

The common size ratios give a starting point. You can quickly get a feel for any unusual changes that have occurred, adjusted for the overall size of assets and the relative amount of sales. Comparison with specific and industrywide competition would point out other similarities and differences. For example, our firm has 31.4 percent of its assets in the current category. (See Exhibit 22-1). Is that greater or less than the industry average? If it's substantially greater or less, then you might want to investigate why. Are we in a peculiarly different situation relative to other firms in our industry? From Exhibit 22-2 we see that the office furniture manufacturing industry tends to have about 65 percent of total assets in the current category. For some industries that is a very high proportion. In other industries, that is quite common. As mentioned earlier, the key to interpretation of ratios is benchmarks. Without a basis for comparison, it is impossible to reasonably interpret the meaning of a ratio.

LIQUIDITY RATIOS

Liquidity ratios attempt to assess whether a firm is maintaining an appropriate level of liquidity. Too little liquidity raises the possibility of default and bankruptcy. Too much liquidity implies that long-term investments with greater profitability have been missed. Financial officers have to walk a tightrope to maintain enough, but not too much, liquidity.

The most common of the liquidity ratios is the current ratio (see Exhibit 22-4), discussed earlier in the chapter. This ratio compares all of the firm's current assets to all of its current liabilities. A common misleading rule of thumb is that the current ratio should be 2. A manufacturing industry needs inventories and receivables. Both of those items result in significant amounts of current assets. An airline, on the other hand, collects most payments in advance of providing service, so its receivables are low. Its product isn't inventoriable, so except for spare parts and supplies, its inventory is low. You would expect the airline industry to have a very low current ratio.

A second liquidity ratio exists that places even more emphasis on the firm's short-term viability—its ability to stay in business. This ratio is called the quick ratio. It compares current assets quickly convertible into cash to current liabilities (see Exhibit 22-4). The concept here is that while not all current assets become cash in the very near term, most current liabilities have to be paid in the very near term. For example, prepaid rent is a current asset, but it is unlikely that we could cash in that prepayment to use to pay our debts. Inventory, while salable, takes time to sell.

EXHIBIT 22-4.
Liquidity Ratios

$$\text{Current Ratio} = \frac{\text{Current Assets}}{\text{Current Liabilities}}$$

$$\text{Quick Ratio} = \frac{\text{Cash} + \text{Marketable Securities} + \text{Receivables}}{\text{Current Liabilities}}$$

The quick ratio compares the firm's cash, plus marketable securities, plus accounts receivable to its current liabilities. Accounts receivable are considered to be "quick" assets because there are factoring firms that specialize in lending money on receivables or actually buying them outright, so they can be used to generate cash almost immediately. For PW, the quick ratio fell from 1.2 in 2001 to .9 in 2002.

Both of these ratios have commonly been used as measures of the firm's risk—how likely it is to get into financial difficulty. However, you should be extremely cautious in using these ratios. No one or two ratios alone can tell the entire story of a firm. They should be used like clues or pieces of evidence for the financial analyst who is really acting as a detective. Any one clue can point in the wrong direction.

For example, suppose a firm has large balances in cash and marketable securities, and its current ratio is 4 or 5. Is this an extremely safe company? The current ratio by itself leads us to believe that it is. The quick ratio might be 3. This ratio also leads us to believe that the firm is very safe. However, what if the company is losing money at a rapid rate, and the only thing that staved off bankruptcy was the sale of a major plant or investment? The sale generated enough cash to meet immediate needs and left an excess, resulting in the high current and quick ratios. How long will this excess last? If the cash and securities are large relative to current liabilities, but small relative to operating costs or long-term liabilities, then the firm may still be extremely risky.

On the other hand, a profitable firm, with careful planning, may be rapidly expanding. Due to cash payments related to the expansion, perhaps the current ratio falls to 1.5 and the quick ratio to .6 at year-end. However, within a month or two after the year-end, the firm may be receiving cash from the issuance of stock or debt that has already been arranged. This firm is probably stable. The point is that all of the ratios when taken together can supplement the financial statements and the notes to the financial statements. They can point out areas for specific additional investigation. No one or two ratios by themselves can, in any way, replace the information in the financial statements, the notes to the financial statements, and the other information possessed by management.

Excel Exercise

Template 26 may be used to calculate liquidity ratios for your organization. The template is on the CD that accompanies this book.

EFFICIENCY RATIOS

The firm wants to maximize its profits for any given level of risk. This requires the firm to operate efficiently. A number of ratios exist that can help a firm to assess how efficiently it is operating and allow for comparison between firms and over time. These ratios are sometimes referred to as *activity ratios*. The principle efficiency or activity ratios measure the efficient handling of receivables, inventory, and total assets.

Receivables Ratios

One problem faced by most firms is the timely collection of receivables. Once receivables are collected, the money received can be used to pay off loans or it can be invested. This means that once the money is received, either we would be paying less interest, or we would be earning more interest. Therefore, we want to collect our receivables promptly.

The receivables turnover ratio (Exhibit 22-5) is a very common indicator of efficiency in collecting receivables. It measures how many times during the year our receivables are generated and then collected. To measure the turnover of receivables, we compare our sales on credit to our average accounts receivable balance. The average accounts receivable is simply the balance in accounts receivable at the beginning and the end of the year divided by two. In the case of PW, the average accounts receivable is $22,000 plus $30,000 divided by two, or $26,000. The turnover ratio for 2002 is sales of $297,000, divided by $26,000, which equals 11.4. This number by itself is not very meaningful.

EXHIBIT 22-5.
Efficiency Ratios

$$\text{Receivables Turnover Ratio} = \frac{\text{Credit Sales}}{\text{Average Receivables Balance}}$$

$$\text{Days Receivable} = \frac{365}{\text{Receivables Turnover}}$$

$$\text{Inventory Turnover Ratio} = \frac{\text{Cost of Goods Sold}}{\text{Average Inventory Balance}}$$

$$\text{Days Receivable} = \frac{365}{\text{Inventory Turnover}}$$

$$\text{Total Asset Turnover Ratio} = \frac{\text{Total Sales}}{\text{Total Assets}}$$

We often think of receivables in terms of how long it takes from the sale to the collection. A useful aid in analysis is to convert our receivables turnover into a statistic referred to as "days receivable," or more simply, the average age of receivables (Exhibit 22-5). We arrive at this statistic by dividing the 365 days in a year by the receivables turnover ratio. For PW, the average age of receivables is thirty-two days (365/11.4).

This is much easier to relate to. Consider whether thirty-two days is a reasonable average length of time to wait for collection of receivables. If the industry average is forty days we might be pleased with ourselves. If the industry average is twenty days we may be concerned. However, like the current ratio, we want the turnover of receivables or the average age to be neither too low nor too high. We are really striving for a middle ground, rather than as far to one extreme as possible.

The problem is that, in order to keep the age of receivables low, our credit manager may attempt to deny credit to any firm that typically pays slowly. This is not necessarily in the best interests of the company. The sales may create enough profits that we benefit even if the customer is slow to pay.

Therefore, we not only want to calculate the receivables turnover and age of receivables, but we also need to investigate that ratio to see if a short average age of receivables indicates too restrictive a credit policy on whom we sell to, or if a long age indicates too loose a credit policy or a lack of sufficient efforts to collect on a timely basis.

Inventory Ratios

The same type of ratios calculated for receivables can also be calculated with respect to inventory (Exhibit 22-5). The inventory turnover ratio is the cost of goods sold divided by the average inventory (beginning plus ending inventory divided by two). For PW for 2002, the inventory turnover ratio is $162,000 (cost of goods sold from Exhibit 22-3) divided by the average of $49,000 and $40,000 (2002 and 2001 ending inventory balances from Exhibit 22-1), which is equal to 3.6. The average age of PW's inventory is 100.3 days, calculated by dividing 365 days in a year by the inventory turnover.

If we keep inventory on hand for too long a period, we are wasting money through lost interest that could have been earned, or through extra interest paid on money borrowed to maintain the inventory. Excessively large inventories also result in unnecessarily high warehousing costs, property taxes, and spoilage. On the other hand, if we don't maintain a sufficiently large inventory, we may lose sales or have production-line stoppages due to stock-outs of finished goods or raw materials, respectively.

Industrywide statistics are usually available for total inventory turnover. However, it is especially useful to compute the turnover and age of inventory separately for raw materials, work in process, and finished goods for manufacturing concerns. For example, a common response to why inventory turnover is slow is that the business is seasonal, and the firm must stockpile *finished goods* for the busy season, often Christmas. On the other hand, if we examine the inventory ratios on a more detailed basis, we may find it is, in fact, *raw materials* that are being held for excessive periods of time.

Total Asset Turnover

A final efficiency ratio is the total asset turnover ratio. This ratio compares sales to total assets. The more sales an organization can generate per dollar of assets, the more efficient it is, other things being equal. If we divide 2002 sales of $297,000 (from Exhibit 22-3) by total assets of $299,000 (from Exhibit 22-1) the ratio of .99 indicates nearly $1 of sales for each dollar invested in assets. This is an improvement compared to the .88 ratio for the prior year.

Excel Exercise

Template 27 may be used to calculate efficiency ratios for your organization. The template is included in the CD that accompanies this book.

SOLVENCY RATIOS

One of the primary focuses on the firm's riskiness occurs through examination of its solvency ratios. Unlike the liquidity ratios that are concerned with the firm's ability to meet its obligations in the very near future, solvency ratios take more of a long-term view. They attempt to determine if the firm has overextended itself through the use of financial leverage. That is, does the firm have principal and interest payment obligations exceeding its ability to pay, not only now, but into the future as well? These ratios are sometimes referred to as *leverage* or *capital structure* ratios.

Two of the most common of the solvency ratios are the interest coverage ratio and the debt to equity ratio (Exhibit 22-6). The former focuses on the ability to meet interest payments arising from liabilities. The latter focuses on the protective cushion owners' equity provides for creditors. If a bankruptcy does occur, creditors can share in the firm's assets before the

owners can claim any of their equity. The more equity that the owners
have in the firm, the greater the likelihood that the firm's assets will be
great enough to protect the claims of all the creditors.

EXHIBIT 22-6.
Solvency Ratios

$$\text{Interest Coverage} = \frac{\text{Operating Income}}{\text{Interest Expense}}$$

$$\text{Debt to Equity} = \frac{\text{Total Liabilities}}{\text{Total Liabilities} + \text{Stockholders' Equity}}$$

The interest coverage ratio compares funds available to pay interest
to the total amount of interest that has to be paid. The funds available for
interest are the firm's profits before interest and taxes. As long as the profit
before interest and taxes (the operating income) is greater than the amount
of interest, the firm will have enough money to pay the interest owed.
Therefore operating income is divided by interest expense to calculate this
ratio. The higher this ratio is, the more comfortable creditors feel. For PW
in 2002, the operating income is $44,000, and the interest is $12,000
(Exhibit 22-3). The interest coverage ratio therefore is 3.7. This is a relative improvement from 2001 when the operating profit was $28,000 and
interest was $10,000. In that year, the interest coverage was 2.8.

However, we should be careful in our use of the term *improvement*.
From a creditor's point of view, this is an improvement because profits are
up relative to interest, creating a greater cushion of safety. From the firm's
point of view, whether this is an improvement or not depends on its atti-
tude toward risk and profits. If the firm desires to be highly leveraged, this
rise in the interest coverage ratio indicates that the firm could have paid
more dividends to its owners and financed more of its expansion through
increased borrowing. This would have increased the rate of return earned
by the owners, although they would have incurred a greater risk because
of the increased leverage. (Review Chapter 11 for a discussion of financial leverage and its implications.)

There are several different debt/equity ratios. For example, we can
compare long-term debt to stockholders' equity, or total liabilities to
stockholders' equity. One common form of the debt/equity ratio compares

the firm's total liabilities to its total equities (both liabilities and stock-holders' equity). The greater the liabilities relative to the total, the more risky the firm.

For example, at the end of fiscal 2002, PW has $299,000 of total equities—liabilities plus stockholders' equity (Exhibit 22-1). By defini-tion, this is equal to the total assets. These assets are available to repay our liabilities. The total liabilities of PW are $231,000, which consists of $47,000 of current liabilities and $184,000 of long-term liabilities. The debt to equity ratio of $231,000 to $299,000 is .77. If PW were to have financial difficulty, and perhaps even go bankrupt and sell off all of its assets, it would have to realize, on average, 77 cents on every dollar of assets in order to fully pay its creditors.

It is important to bear in mind that the nature of the firm and its industry have a lot to do with what is an acceptable level of debt, relative to equity, and what level of interest payments can be considered reason-ably safe. For a business with very constant sales and earnings, more debt is relatively safer than for a firm that has wide swings in profitability. Therefore, any arbitrary rules of thumb commonly used, such as a debt to equity ratio of .5, are not terribly valuable.

Excel Exercise

Template 28 may be used to calculate solvency ratios for your organization. The template is included on the CD that accompanies this book.

PROFITABILITY RATIOS

When all is said and done, the key focus of accounting and finance tends to be on profits. Profitability ratios attempt to show how well the firm did, given the level of risk and types of risk it actually assumed during the year.

If we compare net income to that of the competition, it is an inade-quate measure. Suppose that the chief competitor of PW had earnings of $57,000 this year, while PW made only $19,000. Did the competitor have a better year? Not necessarily. It earned three times as much money, but perhaps it required four times as much in resources to do it. Even earnings per share is inadequate. Suppose that PW's earnings per share of $18.00

were only one-third of the competitor's $54.00. If the investors in PW's competitor invested four times as much to buy each of their shares, they would have been better off investing an equal total amount of money in PW. Therefore, a number of profitability ratios exist to help in evaluating the firm's performance.

Margin Ratios

Margin ratios are one common class of profitability ratios. Firms commonly compute their gross margin, operating margin, and profit margin as a percentage of sales (sometimes referred to as *Return on Sales*). These ratios (Exhibit 22-7) are nothing more than common size ratios we calculated earlier in the chapter. For PW in 2002, the gross margin was 45.5 percent, the operating margin was 14.8 percent, and the profit margin was 6.4 percent. These margins are often watched closely, as changes can be early warning signals of serious problems. A slacking off of a percentage or two in the gross margin can mean the difference between healthy profits or a loss in many industries. For instance, in the supermarket industry the profit margin is rarely more than 1 or 2 percent. A 2 percent change in the gross margin can totally wipe out the supermarket's profit.

EXHIBIT 22-7.
Profitability Ratios

MARGIN RATIOS

$$\text{Gross Margin} = \frac{\text{Gross Profit}}{\text{Sales}} \times 100\%$$

$$\text{Operating Margin} = \frac{\text{Operating Income}}{\text{Sales}} \times 100\%$$

$$\text{Profit Margin} = \frac{\text{Net Income}}{\text{Sales}} \times 100\%$$

RETURN ON INVESTMENT (ROI) RATIOS

$$\text{Return on Assets (ROA)} = \frac{\text{Net Income}}{\text{Total Assets}}$$

$$\text{Return on Equity (ROE) or Return on Net Assets (RONA)} = \frac{\text{Net Income}}{\text{Stockholders' Equity}}$$

Return on Investment (ROI) Ratios

Another broad category of profitability measures falls under the heading of return on investment (ROI). There are many definitions for return on investment, although individual firms usually select one definition and use that as a measure of both individual and firm performance. Because we cannot know the specific definition a firm has chosen, we will discuss a variety of ROI measures in this section. Even if none of the ones discussed here is exactly the same as that chosen by your firm, you should gain enough from the discussion to understand the strengths and weaknesses of whatever ROI measure(s) your firm uses.

Return on assets (ROA) is an ROI measure that evaluates the firm's return or net income relative to the asset base used to generate the income. If we could invest $100 in each of two different investments, and one generated twice as much income as the other, we would prefer the investment generating twice as much income (assuming the levels of risk had been the same).

Therefore, the firm that generates more income, relative to the amount of investment, is doing a better job, other things equal. If we divide the profit earned by the amount of assets employed to generate that profit, we get the ROA. A high ROA is better than a small one. The ROA measure is particularly good for evaluating division managers. It focuses on how well they used the assets entrusted to them.

Is that what the firm's owners want to know? Not really. They are not as interested in the use of assets as they are with the return on their investment. They want to focus on how well the firm did in earning a return on the stockholders' equity. This is commonly called the return on equity (ROE) or the return on net assets (RONA). (See Exhibit 22-7.) Note that net assets are defined as being the assets less the liabilities. Net assets are equivalent to the firm's book value or net worth or stockholders' equity.

While ROA is good for evaluating managers but inadequate for evaluating the firm, ROE is good for evaluating overall firm performance but not for manager evaluation. Except for the very top officers of the firm, managers don't control whether the firm borrows money or issues stock to raise funds. Most managers are simply trying to use the funds that the finance officers have provided them most efficiently. If two managers operated their firms exactly the same, except that one firm was financed substantially with debt, while the other was financed almost exclusively with equity, the firms would have substantially different ROEs for two reasons. First of all, the stockholders' equity will be different for the two firms, because one firm issued more stock than the other, so the denominator of the ratio will be different. Second, the interest expense will differ because one firm borrowed less than the other, so the net income will not be the same. Therefore, the numerator of the ratio would be different. How can we evaluate what part of the firm's results was caused by reasons other than the leverage decision, and what part was caused by the specific decision regarding financial leverage?

ROE is a useful measure of the income that the firm was able to generate relative to the amount of owners' investment in the firm. ROE includes the effect caused by the firm's degree of leverage. To remove the impact of leverage from our evaluation, we should use ROA. This eliminates the problem with respect to the denominator of the ROE ratio. The asset base or denominator of the ROA ratio is the same whether the source of the money used to acquire the assets is debt or equity. However, ROA leaves a problem with the numerator. The return, or numerator (that is, the net income) is affected by the amount of interest the firm pays. For this reason, the measure of ROA often used for evaluation abstracting from the leverage decision is calculated using something called delevered net income.

Delevered net income means recalculating the firm's income by assuming that it had no interest expense at all. In doing this, we can put firms with different decisions regarding the use of borrowed money vs. owner-contributed funds all on a comparable basis. We can see how profitable each firm was relative to the assets it used regardless of their source. We have completely separated any profitability (or loss) created by having used borrowed money instead of owner-invested capital. The way we delever net income is to take the firm's operating margin (income before interest and taxes) and calculate taxes directly on that amount, ignoring interest. The result is a net income based on the assumption that there had been no interest expense.

This should not lead the reader to believe that all firms calculate ROA in exactly the same way. Some firms use assets net of depreciation as the basis for comparison. This is how the assets appear on the balance sheet. Some firms ignore depreciation and use gross assets as a base. The reason for this is to avoid causing a firm or division to appear to have a very high return on assets simply because its assets are very old and fully depreciated. Such fully depreciated assets cause the base of the ratio to be very low and, therefore, the resulting ratio to be very large. Along the same lines, some firms use replacement cost instead of historical cost to place divisions in an equal position.

Despite any of these adjustments, use of any of the ROA measures for evaluation of managers creates undesired incentives. Suppose the firm and its owners are happy to accept any project with an after-tax rate of return of 20 percent. One division of the firm currently has an ROA of 30 percent, and a proposed project that would have a 25 percent ROA is being evaluated. The manager of the division wants to reject the project entirely if he or she is evaluated based on ROA. The 25 percent project, even though profitable, and perhaps better than anything else the firm's owners could do with their money, will bring down that division's weighted average ROA, which is currently 30 percent. Even though the project is good for the firm and its owners, it would hurt the manager's performance evaluation.

For this reason we recommend an ROI concept called residual income (RI). Under this approach, the firm specifies a minimum required ROA rate, using one of the various approaches previously discussed. For each project being evaluated, we would multiply the amount of asset investment required for the project by the required ROA rate. The result would be subtracted from the profits anticipated from the project. If the project is expected to earn more than the proposed investment multiplied by the required rate, then there will be a residual left over after the subtraction. A division manager would be evaluated on the residual left over from all his or her projects combined.

For example, suppose that 20 percent was considered to be an acceptable rate to the firm. Currently all projects for the division earn 30 percent. Suppose further that a project requiring an investment of $100,000 of assets was proposed. If this new project would earn a profit of $25,000, or 25 percent ROA, it would be rejected by a manager evaluated on an ROA basis and accepted by a manager evaluated on an RI basis. From an ROA basis, the 25 percent would lower the currently achieved 30 percent average. For RI, we would multiply the $100,000 investment by the 20 percent ROA required rate, getting a result of $20,000. When the $20,000 is subtracted from the profit of $25,000, there is a $5,000 resid-

ual income. The manager is considered to have increased his or her RI by
$5,000.

The advantage of this method is that if the firm would like to undertake any project earning a return of more than 20 percent, division managers will have an incentive to accept all such projects. This is because all
projects earning more than 20 percent will cover the minimum desired 20
percent ROA and have some excess left over. This excess adds to the manager's total residual income. Thus, RI motivates the manager to do what is
also in the best interests of the firm.

The reader can readily see that ROI is not a simple topic. The finance
officers of most firms spend a fair amount of time considering the implications of various forms of ROI for both motivation and evaluation.
Unfortunately, many firms use just one ROI measure for the firm and its
managers. In attempting to make the measure serve multiple roles, the
ROI measures used often are so complex that they are difficult to understand. The net result often is that ROI measures do not motivate the way
they are intended to and do not provide fair measures of performance.

Excel Exercise

Template 29 may be used to calculate profitability ratios for your
organization. The template is included on the CD that accompanies
this book.

KEY CONCEPTS

Ratio—any number compared to another number. Ratios are calculated by dividing one number into another.

Benchmarks—A firm's ratios can be compared to ratios for the same
firm from prior years and to ratios of a specific competitor and to
ratios for the entire industry.

Common size ratios—All numbers on the balance sheet are compared to total assets or total equities, and all numbers on the income
statement are compared to total sales. This makes intercompany or
interperiod comparison of specific numbers such as cash more
meaningful.

Liquidity ratios—Assess the firm's ability to meet its current obligations as they become due.

Efficiency ratios—Assess the efficiency with which the firm manages its resources, such as inventory and receivables.

Solvency ratios—Assess the firm's ability to meet its interest payments and long-term obligations as they become due.

Profitability ratios—Assess how profitable the firm was and how well it was managed by comparing profits to the amount of resources invested in the firm and used to generate the profits earned.

Part 5

Getting Your Own Finances in Order

Twenty-Three
Personal Finance

This chapter provides an overview of personal finance issues. For a more in-depth discussion, Eric Tyson's *Personal Finance for Dummies: A Reference for the Rest of Us*, 3rd edition (IDG Books Worldwide, 2000) is an excellent source.

THE BASICS

Just as a business needs a balance sheet in order to have a sense of its financial position, individuals should prepare a personal balance sheet, or *net worth statement*. Net worth is simply another term for owner's equity. For an individual, the fundamental equation of accounting would be:

$$\text{Assets} = \text{Liabilities} + \text{Net Worth}$$

or

$$\text{Assets} - \text{Liabilities} = \text{Net Worth}$$

By tracking your net worth from year to year, you can assess whether you are making progress in terms of achieving your personal financial goals. (See Chapters 4 and 20 for a further discussion of balance sheets.)

Individuals should also consider developing personal budgets. This is especially true if your net worth has not been increasing as much from year to year as you would like. A budget can give you a clearer sense of the money that is available to you, and how you are using it. (Budgets were discussed in Chapter 12.)

For all personal financial decisions, take the time value of money into account. The timing of cash receipts and payments dramatically

313

affects many personal decisions, especially investment decisions. Unless the time value of money is considered, you stand to make some poor decisions. (Time value of money was discussed in Chapter 13.)

EMERGENCY RESERVES

A high priority for individuals should be the establishment of an emergency reserve. Hopefully, you will never need to dip into this reserve. However, life holds all kinds of unexpected surprises in store for us. They are not all good. The strongest of employers sometimes fall on hard financial times. The most secure employee may be suddenly laid off.

Reserves should be kept in T-bills, money-markets accounts, or other secure and highly liquid investments. If you feel quite secure in your job, your income is stable, you have substantial amounts in retirement funds, and you have family members to turn to for financial assistance in a difficult time, then a reserve equal to three months worth of living expenses is generally considered adequate.

A six-month cushion is more sensible if you would be unwilling or unable to get assistance from family members, your retirement account balances are more limited, or your job is not totally secure. If your income tends to fluctuate widely from year to year, then a reserve large enough to cover one year's worth of expenses should be maintained.

THE PRIMARY REASONS FOR ACCUMULATING WEALTH

Much of personal finance focuses on the accumulation of wealth. As you make your spending or investment decisions it is worthwhile to reflect on the goals that you are trying to achieve. Home ownership, education for your children, retirement, and consumer purchases—vacations, a giant-screen TV, or a nicer car—are typical reasons that people save money.

One thing that should be kept in mind as one deals with personal finances is that if you buy consumer items before you have cash accumulated to pay for them, you will typically pay high amounts of interest on those purchases. Alternatively, if you delay purchases and save money, you will be earning interest. The difference between paying 15 percent interest on a charge card versus earning 5 percent interest on a savings account is 20 percent. This means that you will be able to afford substantially fewer consumer goods in your lifetime if you buy on credit, instead of saving first and buying with cash.

CONTROLLING YOUR DEBTS

One key to successful accumulation of wealth is to control your debts. As the example above implies, it is much better to earn interest than to pay it. And if you do have to pay interest, the lower the rate the better. The implications are that you should try to completely avoid credit card debt, auto loans, and other consumer loans. Such loans carry high interest rates, and are often accompanied by other costs.

Credit Cards

If you are like most people, offers for credit cards flood your mailbox. Credit cards are huge profit makers. If they're so good for the companies that issue them, there's a good chance they're not so good for you. The primary problem with credit cards is that they charge high interest rates.

The offers often sound good—no annual fee and low interest rates. However, if you read the fine print you often find that there are annual fees starting the second year, or that interest rates jump up after six months.

At this point you must think that I am against using credit cards. Not at all. I love credit cards. They can be great if you religiously do two things. First, shop around for the best deal. Second, pay off the credit card balance in full each month.

What is the right deal? First and most importantly, the card should allow you to incur zero charges if you pay off your balance in full by the end of the *grace period*. Each card allows you a period of time to make payment. This period, usually two to three weeks, is called the grace period. If you pay the full balance each month by the end of the grace period you enjoy an interest-free loan referred to as *credit card float*. The interest-free loan is not just from the time you receive the invoice, but actually from the date of your purchases until the day your check to the credit card company clears your bank account. Sometimes this may just be a few weeks, but on some purchases the interest-free loan may be several months. But you must pay the full balance on the statement. Allow for mail delays to be sure to avoid interest and late charges.

The second thing to look for in the right deal is the right rebate. Many consumers have credit cards that give "airline miles" that can eventually be used for free flights. Other credit cards offer a variety of other types of rebates. For example, some car manufacturers will give you up to 5 percent back on the purchases you make using their card. The catch? You can use that money only to purchase one of their cars. But if you always buy General Motors (GM) cars, a GM 5 percent rebate credit card may be a great deal for you.

Some credit cards will literally give you cash back. For example, Exxon/Mobil has a card that gives a 3 percent rebate on all Exxon or Mobil purchases (gas, tires, auto repairs, etc.), and 1 percent back on all other purchases. Discover offers cash back, up to 2 percent. That's okay, but you start out at a much lower percent, and have to spend quite a bit to reach the 2 percent level. Shop around. One of my credit cards gives me 2 percent cash back on *all* purchases up to $15,000 a year.

What if you just can't get your act together to pay off all your charge card balances in full by their due dates? Avoid the cards with high interest rates. And negotiate a better rate anytime you see a really good offer. For example, if you see another card with a six-month introductory low rate, call your credit card company and tell them you plan to cancel your card with them. In many cases they will match that rate or perhaps even do better to keep you as a customer. If you are paying 15 percent on your balance and can bring that down to 4.9 percent for six months with a simple phone call, why not do it?

Debit Cards

Debit cards are growing in popularity. When you use a debit card the money is immediately taken out of your account, the same as if you wrote a check and it cleared the moment you gave it to the merchant. This is convenient and a good way to control yourself if you can't stop accumulating credit card debt. But it has drawbacks as well. First, you lose the entire credit card float. Second, if you are writing checks and using the debit card on the same account, you may lose track of your balance and bounce checks. People are not as careful about recording debit purchases in their checkbook as they are with checks. Bouncing checks is both expensive and embarrassing.

When to Use Debt

Although consumer debt is expensive and often destructive, there are appropriate uses for debt. Borrowing money for the purchase of a home, for education, or to start a business, represents long-term investment rather than consumption. It often makes sense to borrow for such reasons, and the types of loans associated with these types of investments often carry much lower rates of interest than consumer debt.

In fact, at times it makes sense to take a mortgage or even a second mortgage on your house to eliminate credit card debt. The mortgage on your house will usually carry a much lower interest rate than credit cards, and the home mortgage interest is tax-deductible, while the credit card interest is not. On the other hand, you should not make a habit of borrowing against your home to pay for current consumption. Such living beyond your means can only lead to disaster, which brings us to the next section.

Filing for Bankruptcy

First of all, if you do have to file for bankruptcy, always keep in mind that it's not the end of the world. Over one million households file for bankruptcy every year. As a result of a bankruptcy filing, you can generally cancel credit card, medical, auto, utility, and rent debt. On the other hand, bankruptcy cannot cancel child support, alimony, student loans, taxes, and court-ordered damages.

Bankruptcy stays on your credit report for a number of years. It is also not without cost—there are court filing costs and legal fees, not to mention emotional stress. On the other hand, some states will allow you to keep your house or some portion of the equity in your house, furniture, clothing, pensions, and other retirement accounts.

Much as you might want to avoid it, in some cases bankruptcy is a sensible alternative. You may be better off starting over than trying to cope with an endless stream of collection agencies and a level of debt that you may never overcome.

CONTROLLING YOUR TAXES

Chapter 2 provided a background on taxes that applies to both businesses and individuals. In addition to the information in that chapter, there are some basic things that individuals can do to control their taxes.

First, it is important to try to avoid receiving a big refund each year. Many taxpayers love receiving that nice big refund check. However, a refund means that all year long you were paying too much tax. The government was holding your money, but not paying any interest to you. A simple solution to this problem is to fill out a new W-4 form at work. Your employer can show you how to fill it out to reduce the withholding from your paycheck. You will have more cash each pay period, and can start investing that extra cash so that it earns money for you, rather than for Uncle Sam.

Next, be aware of the possible benefits from shifting income between tax years. For example, suppose you have a choice of taking a bonus in December of this year or January of next year. If you anticipate being in a lower tax bracket in one of the two years, you should try to shift the receipt of the bonus into that year.

The same approach should be applied to deductions. Suppose that you are making quarterly estimated income tax payments for both federal and state taxes. You will likely have a state tax payment due on January 15. If you pay that tax in late December of this year, you can deduct that tax on your federal return for this year. Or you can wait to make the payment in January and deduct it next year. You need to consider the benefit of taking the deduction this year to reduce taxes immediately versus the impact of any possible changes in your tax bracket. This is especially true if any Alternative Minimum Tax (AMT) is due. State taxes are not deductible for AMT purposes.

Another reason for shifting deductions relates to the standard versus itemized deduction. If your deductions are low, you are better off taking the standard deduction. However, if the standard deduction and itemized deduction give you about the same benefit, it may pay to alternate back and forth between the standard deduction one year and the itemized the next. If you do that, you should shift as much of your deductions as possible into the year you itemize.

For example, suppose you usually make all your charitable donations around Christmas each year. In 2003 you could delay those payments for a week, until the beginning of 2004. In December of 2004 you still make your usual donations. This will cause you to alternate between years of zero contribution and years of double contributions. In the years with high contributions you would itemize your deductions. In the years of zero contributions you would take the standard deduction. The only impact on the charities you support is that every other year they will receive your contribution around January 3 instead of December 27, or

about a week later than usual. Be sure to get a receipt at the time of donation for any contributions of $250 or more. The IRS will not accept a can-
celed check as adequate evidence of a donation.

Another strategy for lowering taxes is to trade consumer debt for
mortgage debt. In addition to getting a lower interest rate, mortgage interest on home equity loans (up to $50,000 in loans for individuals and
$100,000 for married couples filing joint returns) is deductible, while con-
sumer interest is not. Also, be sure to consider whether you are paying
taxes on property (not only real estate tax, but also things such as a portion of the registration fee on cars), or state disability and unemployment
insurance which may be deductible. Casualty losses and work-related
expenses may also be deductible.

Capital gains represent another area for tax planning. For example,
if you sell shares of stock for a gain just a few days less than a year after
you purchased them, your tax will be much higher than if you sell the
same shares more than a year after you purchased them, because long-
term gains (held longer than one year) are taxed at a much lower rate.

Congress periodically makes major revisions to the tax code, so it is
important to check the current rules. You can do that at *www.irs.gov* or by
using one of the many tax books written for the lay user that are updated
each year, such as J. K. Lasser's *Your Income Tax* or *The Ernst and Young
Tax Guide*.

This discussion has barely scratched the surface of the many issues
that individual taxpayers should consider. Individual circumstances vary
tremendously and affect issues such as whether you can deduct the cost of
a home office. I strongly recommend that you either work with a competent tax preparer who can walk you through some of these issues, or
acquire and read through one of the tax books mentioned in the last paragraph, or the excellent *422 Tax Deductions for Businesses & Self-
Employed Individuals*, 3rd Edition, by Bernard B. Kamoroff (Bell Springs
Publishing Co., 2001).

RETIREMENT PLANS

Another important opportunity to control taxes is by making contributions
to retirement plans. These plans are critical not only because of their tax
advantages, but also because they help you accumulate the money you
will need to retire.

How much money will you need in retirement? The correct answer varies tremendously from individual to individual. Some individuals live modest lives in retirement. Without earned income, their taxes drop. They don't need as much clothing or that extra car. Their commuting costs go away. The kids are out of the house and done with college.

Other individuals consider retirement the time to spend all that money they have worked so hard to earn, but never had any time to spend. They may actually spend more each year than they did when they were working. Developing a pro forma retirement budget can help you assess what you expect to do in retirement and how much you expect to spend.

The more you earn, the lower the percentage you are likely to need. For example, if you earn $20,000 a year before retirement, you may need nearly that much each year in retirement. But suppose you earn $300,000 each year, pay $100,000 a year in taxes, and save $100,000 a year. That means you are currently consuming $100,000 per year. You can probably live on less than half of your current $300,000 income in retirement.

Where will your retirement income be coming from? Social Security is one, although not necessarily the largest, source of retirement income. You may automatically be receiving an annual statement from Social Security indicating the likely benefits that you will receive in retirement. If you aren't, call 800-772-1213 for Form SSA-7004-SM, or go to *www.ssa.gov* and request a statement.

You may also gradually liquidate your savings that are in a variety of different types of investments. Some people want to be able to live on the income from their investments, without having to liquidate a portion each year. If you can do that, you can afford to live forever!

The third major source is from *tax-advantaged retirement plans*. Tax-advantaged plans give the taxpayer some tax benefit not available for ordinary savings. This might be deductibility of the initial investment, the ability to accumulate earnings without current tax payment, or even the ability to avoid taxes on investment earnings completely. These include both IRAs and a number of different employer-sponsored plans.

In general, contributions to tax-advantaged plans are deductible from your taxable income in the year of the contribution and earnings are not taxed until withdrawal.

Generally, you cannot withdraw money from tax-advantaged accounts until you are at least $59^1/2$ years old, and you must start to withdraw by the time you are 70$\frac{1}{2}$ years old. There are penalties for early withdrawal, but there are exceptions that avoid the penalties related to using the money for medical or educational expenses, first-time home purchase, or due to disability. It is also possible to avoid the penalties if you are retiring and taking out an equal annual installment based on your life expectancy.

Individual Retirement Accounts (IRAs)

IRAs are available to anyone with employment income. Each year, you can put an amount up to the lower of $3,000 or your earned income into an IRA for yourself, and also an equal amount for a nonworking spouse. The $3,000 limit rises to $4,000 in 2005 and to $5,000 in 2008. These amounts can be deducted on your tax return, unless your income exceeds certain levels. However, you can deduct the IRA investment even if your income is high, if you are not participating in any other retirement plan.

When you withdraw money from an ordinary IRA later in life, the full amount withdrawn is taxable as ordinary income (not as long-term capital gains). If your income is too high for a regular IRA, you may still be able to contribute to a *Roth IRA*. This type of IRA has income limitations that are higher than those for regular IRAs. Contributions to a Roth IRA are not deductible. However, it is still a good deal because earnings accumulate tax-free and retirement withdrawals from the account are tax-free.

Consider Table 23-1, which compares regular savings, a regular IRA (typical of many of the other types of retirement accounts discussed later), and a Roth IRA. We will assume that you are currently in a 33 percent marginal tax bracket, and will be in a 23 percent bracket when you take the money out of the IRA. Presumably you will be in a lower tax bracket once you retire and your earned income drops.

We will also assume that you put your money in the stock market and earn an average of 10 percent per year. Assume that before taxes you have $3,000 available to invest. One alternative is to invest that entire amount in a regular IRA. Alternatively you can invest in regular savings or a Roth IRA, but you will have to pay $990 in taxes (33% × $3,000) before making those investments, so you will have only $2,010 to invest.

The example further assumes, for simplicity, that you pay short-term capital gains tax annually on the return on regular savings. Thus, of the 10

TABLE 23-1.

Comparison of Regular Savings, Regular IRA, and Roth IRA

	Regular Savings	IRA Regular	IRA Roth
Initial Investment 12/31/02	$2,010	$3,000	$2,010
Balance on 12/31/03 after Taxes	2,145	2,541	2,211
Balance on 12/31/04 after Taxes	2,288	2,795	2,432
Balance on 12/31/32 after Taxes	14,064	40,308	5,073
Balance on 12/31/42 after Taxes	26,901	104,549	90,971

percent increase each year, only 6.7 percent is left after taxes. This may not precisely reflect reality. It depends greatly on the specific approach to investing (e.g., frequency of trading), but it is a reasonable approximation for comparison purposes.

Table 23-1 calculates the value for the regular IRA at *each* future date as if the money were withdrawn and taxed on that date. That explains why the accumulated value on December 31, 2003 is less than the value on December 31, 2002.

From Table 23-1 we can see that the two IRAs' ability to accumulate earnings without paying taxes each year results in much greater appreciation than regular savings. The regular IRA has a better result than the Roth IRA, even though the entire amount of the regular IRA was taxable at the end, while none of the Roth IRA accumulation was taxable at the end. This is because the regular IRA had a larger initial investment accumulating earnings over a long time period.

Regular savings pale in comparison to tax-advantaged accounts. And looking at Table 23-1, we can really feel the impact of compounding over long periods of time. Just one single IRA investment can grow to be more than $100,000 over a forty-year period. If you make IRA investments every year, you can accumulate a substantial amount for retirement. IRAs, however, are among the most limited of the retirement plans available. Other plans allow you to set aside greater amounts than IRAs, and may not be taxed as heavily if you die before withdrawing all accumulated amounts.

Excel Exercise

Use Template 30 to calculate the future value of an IRA based on either a single invested amount or annual contributions. The template is included on the CD that accompanies this book.

Employer-Sponsored Plans

At one time most pensions were *defined-benefit plans*. Defined-benefit plans are generally paid for by the employer, who guarantees to pay a specific amount each year after the employee retires. The defined benefit is based on a formula such as 2 percent multiplied by years of service, multiplied by the average salary for the last five years before retirement. Such plans must fully vest within five years of full-time work. *Vesting* means that the worker becomes entitled to the pension, even if he or she leaves the organization.

Today 401(k) plans are common. These are *defined contribution* plans that withhold some of the employee's wages to put into the pension. Defined contribution plans specify the amount that goes into the plan, but not the amount one gets upon retirement, which depends on investment results. Often employers will match the employee contribution up to a specific percentage such as 5 percent. This allows you to accumulate an amount of money tax-free each year up to a limited amount ($11,000 in 2002, increasing gradually to $15,000 by 2006) plus the employer match. Funds are fully taxed when withdrawn, similar to the regular IRA. Not-for-profit organizations can use a 403(b) tax-sheltered annuity plan that is similar to the 401(k).

Self-Employment Plans

Simplified employee pension individual retirement accounts (SEP-IRAs) and Keogh plans allow a self-employed individual to invest a substantial amount on a tax-deductible basis. Keogh plans are broken down into profit sharing plans, money purchase plans, and paired plans that contain both profit sharing and money purchase plans. Profit sharing plans have the same limits as SEPs, but allow more flexibility in giving different benefits to different employees. Money purchase plans have higher contribution limits, but the contribution amounts are fixed and must be paid each year. Paired plans provide the ability to make higher contributions, with some flexibility in terms of giving different benefits to different employees.

Keogh plans allow even higher limits for defined-benefit plans. However, such plans are quite complicated and require input from an actuary. Generally such plans are of greatest value to older (over 50 years of age) owner-employees.

Annuities

Annuities are one additional type of retirement investment worth noting. These are insurance-backed contracts. Money put into these accounts is not deductible, but earnings accumulate without tax until withdrawal. However, the fees for annuities are often high. As a result, it generally doesn't pay to go this route unless you've maxed out on other retirement accounts, and expect a long investment period.

INVESTING

When many individuals think of personal finances, they think of investing. The first rule of investing is that there is usually a direct trade-off between risk and return. Safer investments tend to have lower returns than riskier investments. Historical averages indicate that on an overall basis, stocks and real estate earn about 10 percent/year, bonds earn around 5 percent, and savings accounts around 4 percent. However, individual investments may do much better or worse than those averages. It is essential that you choose a set of investments that provides you with a comfort level. If you can't sleep at night because you are worried about your investments, your portfolio is probably too risky.

It is also important to consider how soon you will need to use funds. Riskier investments tend to be very volatile. Over a period of twenty years they will have ups and downs, and overall are likely (although not guaranteed by any means) to be much higher at the end of that time period than at the start. But if you need to use the money in that investment in two or three years, you may find that its value at that point has fallen sharply from the amount invested.

A related factor concerns the allocation of funds between fixed income securities (e.g., bonds that pay interest every six months) versus growth investments (e.g., stocks). Fixed income securities tend to be safer, but have less potential for appreciation. Growth investments have more appreciation potential, but more risk.

A rule of thumb often employed is to use your age as the percent of your investments to put into fixed income securities. For example, at age 40 you might want to be 40 percent in bonds and 60 percent in stocks. By age 60 you want to be 60 percent in bonds and 40 percent in stocks. However, this is a fairly arbitrary guide. Many reasonable investment advisors would argue that 20-year-olds should have all of their money in stocks. Obviously, money needed for college tuition would be excluded from the stock portfolio and should reside in something such as a money market fund or CDs or a short-term bond fund. Conversely, 80-year-olds might put all of their money into bonds to avoid a stock market plunge that could wipe out a huge chunk of their assets overnight.

In choosing your portfolio of investments, remember that no one investment is the correct choice for everyone. You must understand your attitudes toward risk and return, and you must consider when you will need the money.

Lender Investments

We can broadly think of all investment opportunities as falling into one of two classes: lending investments and equity investments. If you put money in a bank account, CD, T-bill, bond, or similar investment you are a lender. Your goal is to earn interest and eventually recover your principal investment.

In some cases, you might make some appreciation on your original investment if interest rates fall and you sell the instrument before maturity. For example, as interest rates fall, bond prices rise (because you have a bond that pays a higher interest rate than currently issued bonds, so yours is more valuable). On the other hand, if interest rates rise and you need to sell your bond before maturity, you will probably lose some of your principal.

The worst that could happen is that the borrower goes bankrupt and you get neither interest nor your principal back. This extreme is unlikely with highly safe investments such as government or insured bonds. It is a greater risk with bonds of companies having financial difficulty. Another potential risk is that inflation erodes the value of the interest and principal over time.

Equity Investments

Equity investments are those in which your role is that of owner rather than lender. Stock represents ownership of part of a company, while a bond just represents a loan. However, there are many equity investments aside from stock. You may own real estate, gold, baseball cards, and an infinite number of other items. Your potential gain is appreciation in value, and in some cases receipts such as dividends or rental income.

Investing in Stocks

An investor purchases stock with the hope that, over time, the underlying business is successful in producing and selling products and services. As profits grow, the price of the stock will grow as well.

Many investors focus on the ratio of a stock's price to earnings per share, called the price/earnings (PE) ratio. A stock in a stable industry may typically sell with a PE of 10. This means that if the stock earns $2 of profits per share, the stock price will probably be around $20. Suppose you believe that next year the company will earn $2.30 per share. If the company's PE is stable, the price of the stock will rise to $23.

However, earnings might fall short of expectations, or broad economic conditions may affect the entire market, including that stock. There is a chance the price of the stock might fall. If it is really a solid company with excellent long-term earnings prospects, it should do fine over the long run. You must be willing to incur volatility in exchange for a potential return.

However, even fine companies sometimes have unexpected problems and go bankrupt. Investing in just one or a few companies increases your risk. This doesn't mean investing in stocks is a bad idea. It does mean that you should diversify. Broad diversification and holding investments for long periods have been shown to reduce volatility and increase returns.

Avoid frequent stock trading. Commissions eat away at profits, and short-term trades are more likely to result in high capital gains tax. Pick an asset allocation (a split between lending and equity investments); pick some good diversified, no-load (no sales charge) investments (e.g., Vanguard Total Stock Market Index Fund, Vanguard Total Bond Market Index Fund); invest on a regular basis (e.g., each month); include some global investments (such as a broad global mutual index fund); and let your investments grow over time.

It won't be all smooth sailing. You may have some wildly successful years and some horrible years. Don't watch gains of 30 percent a year for several years and start to think it will last forever. Don't be depressed when your entire portfolio drops 20 percent in one year. And don't try to time the market. Many think that they can figure when the market will go up or down, but few ever have. If you try to move your money in and out of the market based on when you think it will go up or down, there is a good chance you will miss the days that account for most stock market gains.

Be extremely cautious in dealing with investment brokers. Most of them are working on commissions, and you can often invest directly, avoiding those commissions. Stockbrokers are not all-knowledgeable gurus. They are likely to push the investments that pay them the highest commissions. And don't listen to gurus either. So many people are making stock predictions that it's just the law of chance that someone will make correct predictions several years in a row. If a coin comes up heads five times in a row, how much of your life's savings would you bet on it coming up heads a sixth time? And would you consider that bet to be an investment or a gamble?

Be extremely hesitant to focus on past performance. You will often see mutual fund companies advertising a fund that has done great the last few years. Is that because it has really smart managers? More likely it's because the company has many different funds. The odds are that in any given year some will beat the market and some will do worse. Which ones do you think they advertise?

The broad stock market has historically done better over the long run than most of the vast majority of individual stock pickers, brokers, gurus, newsletters, and mutual funds. Following the stock picks of those sage advisors usually leads to high current taxes due to portfolio turnover, high management or advisement fees, and high transactions costs. How can you possibly win after paying for all that?

Investing in Mutual Funds

A *mutual fund* is a portfolio of securities that is managed by an investment company. When you buy a share of a mutual fund, you own a proportional piece of all of the securities held by that fund. Mutual funds are great investments for most investors because they give you the ability to be broadly diversified at low cost. With $500 you could not buy a broad range of individual stocks, to give you the safety that diversification provides. However, by investing that $500 in a stock mutual fund, you own a little bit of stock in many different companies.

There are three main classes of mutual funds: money market, bond, and stock funds. Money market and bond funds are lending investments. Money market funds lend to businesses on a short-term basis. The investment is not insured, as it would be in a bank deposit, but these funds tend to be highly liquid and reasonably safe. Stock funds buy stocks and bond funds invest in bonds.

Mutual funds may be either *load* or *no-load* funds. Load funds charge a sales fee. That fee may be substantial—3 to 5 percent or even more of your initial investment. No-load funds do not charge sales fees. There is no reliable evidence that indicates that load funds have better annual returns. In many cases, load funds charge more so that they can pay a commission to an agent who sells the fund to you.

Mutual funds come in all shapes and sizes. There are funds whose income is taxable, and some that are free of federal and state tax. Bond funds may focus on short, intermediate, or long-term bonds; and on extremely safe or risky (called junk) bonds. A triple-A rating is the best bond rating. Bonds rated below BB are considered to be below investment grade (i.e., speculative). (Different bond rating companies use slightly different scales, but AA is always better than A that is better than B, etc.)

There are stock funds that invest only in United States companies (domestic), only in companies outside the United States (international), or in companies here and abroad (global). They may be large cap, medium cap, or small cap. This refers to the size of the companies they invest in, measured by capitalization—i.e., the market price per share of common stock multiplied by the number of shares outstanding. There are funds for growth stocks (companies with rapidly expanding revenues and profits and high PEs), or value stocks (low PEs relative to assets and profits). There are sector (technology, health, banking, etc.) funds. There are index funds that seek to match broad market indexes, such as the Wilshire 5000. That index approximates the movement of the stock market as a whole.

Some mutual fund companies have high management fees. You should shop around for one with low annual fees. Some specialize in certain types of funds, although in recent years there has been a trend in which many companies offer a very wide range of funds. For example, The Vanguard Group, one of the largest mutual fund companies (*www.vanguard.com*), specializes in index funds that have low management fees. However, they offer many nonindex funds as well.

How can you choose the right fund for you? As an investor, your interest in the stock market is as an investment in the economy—in the success of the businesses of this country and the world. Trying to pick individual stocks or groups of stocks is probably not fruitful whether you pick them one at a time or in a cluster, such as a technology stock fund.

It is very time-consuming to pick stocks or mutual funds. Your emotions mess you up. Diversification is not easy to accomplish. The more stocks or mutual funds you own, the more tax and bookkeeping hassles you will have. We suggest that you consider the Bogle philosophy of investing.

John Bogle, founder of The Vanguard Group of mutual funds, recommends that investors simplify, diversify, and bear in mind that costs matter. Simplify, just to make life more pleasant, since you will do just as well with a simple, limited set of investments. Diversify, because broad diversification has been shown to lead to better results. And focus on costs, because the management fees charged can dramatically lower your long-term return.

Bogle argues that beating the market on a consistent basis is extremely difficult to do. Investors picking individual stocks or picking specific mutual funds are likely to underperform the overall market before paying management fees, and do even worse after considering those fees. The best approach? Invest in a broadly diversified index fund that has extremely low trading costs because of low stock turnover, and extremely low management costs because there are few decisions to be made. Rather than contributing to the seven-figure bonuses received by traders on Wall Street, Bogle argues that your returns will be better if you just select a broad-based bond fund and a broad-based stock fund with low costs, invest on a regular basis, and ignore them. His excellent book, *Common Sense on Mutual Funds* (John Wiley & Sons, 2001), provides facts to support his contention that attempting to beat the market is a fruitless exercise.

Investing in Real Estate

Real estate is another equity investment alternative. Real estate ownership can provide rental payments for current income, as well as potential appreciation in property value. However, property values may also go down. Even though real estate does well over time on average, any particular property or geographic area may see declines in value.

Buying your own home can be a useful hedge against inflation—your fixed mortgage payments don't rise, but the value of your house does. If you rent your home, your monthly rent payments will rise over time due to inflation.

Buying rental property is somewhat more problematic. While residential housing (single family homes, apartment houses) can be an attractive investment, it can also be time-consuming. Tenant complaints about plumbing, heat problems, and so on can be a constant headache. You can hire a company to manage the property, but that takes away a portion of your potential profits.

Real estate has traditionally been an area where investors borrow a substantial portion of the total purchase price. The risk of required interest and principal payments should be carefully considered.

One strategy for making money in real estate is to buy a run-down property and fix it up. Such an approach can be very profitable, but usually requires a fair amount of personal sweat equity along the way.

If you want to invest in real estate without many of the headaches of day-to-day management, you can invest in a real estate investment trust (REIT) that sells shares in the stock market, or you can buy shares in a real estate mutual fund.

Investing in Small Business

Even Microsoft was small once. Many of the richest individuals in our society started their businesses in a garage. Ben and Jerry's ice cream company started in a garage. Apple Computer started in a garage. One way to have a substantial share of equity in a business is to invest at the ground (garage) level.

You can start a business, investing your own money in it. Or you can invest in a friend's small business. Friends and relatives often provide the first capital for a new business. The risks are high, but so are the potential returns.

Investing in Gold

Gold has historically been seen as an investment. It is needed for jewelry and for industrial purposes. But does it have an intrinsic value? That is not clear. What we do know for sure is that it is expensive to buy and sell, has high storage costs, earns no interest while it is owned, has no guarantee of appreciation, and has the possibility for a decline in value.

Investing in Collectibles

Collectibles have been a growing investment area. Artwork has long been an investment vehicle. The same is true of stamps and coins. Today, a sweaty Barry Bonds jersey worn when he hit a record-breaking home run, a Pokemon card, or a gown worn in an academy-award-winning movie are seen as investment items as well. If you acquire collectibles it is important to realize they often have no intrinsic value at all. Buy them and enjoy them. But be aware that fads come and go, and in many cases these memorabilia can lose all their value overnight.

Speculation

Many so-called investors are really speculators. In contrast to investors who hope to gain as a result of a company's growing profitability over time, speculators are typically looking for quicker and more dramatic results. Day trading—purchasing a stock in the morning and selling it later that same day—is speculation in the short-term movement of the stock price rather than investment in the company.

There is nothing inherently bad about speculation. It helps provide liquidity to the market. More people trading stocks means there will be more potential buyers if you want to sell a stock. However, speculation is not something that is safe for the unsophisticated investor. Many would argue that it probably isn't safe for sophisticated investors either.

Short Sales

Selling short is a practice of selling securities you don't own, in the hopes that they will fall in value. For example, you borrow 100 shares of Microsoft stock from a broker and sell those shares for $80 per share. If Microsoft later falls to $50 per share, you buy 100 shares and give them to the broker to cover the shares you had borrowed. Since you bought shares for $50 and sold shares for $80, you have made a profit. And you didn't even invest any of your own money since you sold and received cash before you bought! Of course, if the stock goes up, the broker will likely ask you to buy at that higher price to return the shares you owe. Since prices can go up indefinitely, your potential loss is unlimited.

Buying on Margin

Some investors buy securities on *margin*. Margin refers to using an investment as collateral to borrow money for its purchase. For example, you could invest $2 of your own money to buy a $10 share of stock. The brokerage firm lends you $8. If the share goes up in value to $12, your $2 investment will have doubled (less the interest on the loan) rather than going up 20 percent. If the share goes down in value to $8, you will have lost 100 percent of your investment (plus interest), rather than just 20 percent. This is an example of leverage (See Chapter 11). Note that there are limits on the tax-deductibility of investment interest expenses.

Buying on margin borders between speculation and investment. Some investors who can tolerate a higher level of risk do employ margin. However, unless you are a sophisticated investor, you should avoid margin purchases because of the high degree of risk.

Derivatives, Calls, and Puts

One type of speculation is the use of *derivatives*. A derivative is anything that derives its value from something else. Derivatives are commonly used in the stock market, and are also used to hedge foreign currency (reduce the risk related to currency fluctuations), or the exposure to other types of risks. They are sometimes, but not always, used for speculation.

Suppose that you wanted to invest $10,000 in a portfolio of ten stocks. One choice would be to buy $1,000 worth of each of the ten stocks. Another option would be to buy $10,000 worth of a derivative based on that portfolio. The value of the derivative would move in direct proportion to changes in the value of the stocks.

Why would anyone buy a derivative instead of the stocks themselves? One reason is that it is possible that derivatives have lower transaction costs. It is easier and less expensive to buy and maintain one security than ten, or perhaps one hundred or one thousand. Thus you get the benefits of diversification while keeping costs down. Another reason is that derivatives can more easily be used as defensive tools to offset risk, or as aggressive tools to magnify profits (and risks).

Assume that you have $10,000 and you really believe that the stock of a corporation is badly undervalued. You are considering buying 1,000 shares at $10 each. If the stock price goes to $20 you will double your money. The 1,000 shares will rise in value from $10,000 to $20,000 and you will have earned a profit of $10,000. Alternatively, you can buy *call options*. A call option gives the buyer the right to purchase a stock at a given price for a specific period of time.

Suppose that you can buy options for $1 each that give you the right to purchase a share of that company's stock for $10 anytime during the next three months. You could use the $10,000 you have to buy 10,000 options. What happens if the stock price rises to $20 within that three-month period? You can exercise the options, buying 10,000 shares for $10 each and immediately selling them for $20 each. After subtracting the $10,000 cost of the options, you have a profit of $90,000, as compared to the $10,000 profit you would have earned if you had purchased the stock.

What if the price of the stock had stayed at exactly $10? If you had purchased 1,000 shares of stock for $10,000 you would have no loss or gain. If you had purchased 10,000 call options for $1 each, they would have expired, and you would have lost your entire $10,000 investment.

Put options are defensive tools. A put option gives you the right to sell stock at a particular value for a period of time. For example, suppose that you already own 1,000 shares of stock in a company. The stock is currently worth $10 a share, and you think it will go up in value, so you don't want to sell your shares. But you are afraid to lose money. You fear the possible loss of a sizable portion of your investment if the company were to have trouble, or if the entire stock market were to fall.

You might be able to buy a put option on the stock for 15 cents per share. The put option will give you the right to sell a share for $10 for a period of time, such as three months. If you pay $150 to buy 1,000 puts, you are protected. If the stock price falls to $2, you will still be able to sell your shares for $10 each. If the price of the stock stays at $10 or goes up, you will let the puts expire, and you effectively will have paid $150 for insurance to protect yourself against a loss. Note that a put is usually less expensive than a call because a stock can only fall to zero, while it potentially could rise an unlimited amount.

TAX SHELTERS

Many investments are sold based on their ability to act as tax shelters. For example, there are definite tax advantages to real estate investments. Business property may be depreciated. That depreciation expense offsets current rental income, thereby reducing current taxes. Meanwhile, the property may actually be rising in value. Eventually when you sell the property you will pay tax on the gain, but that will be in the future. The key to most tax shelters is not avoidance of tax, but rather deferral of tax payments. Tax shelters allow the investor to benefit from the time value of money. (See Chapter 13.)

Be extremely careful about tax shelters that are real estate limited partnerships. This once popular form of tax shelter promised high tax deductions, but often delivered only high sales commissions and management fees. Many investors lost huge amounts of money in such partnerships, and they should be considered only with extreme caution.

The Tax Reform Act of 1986 introduced the concept of passive investments. Unless you are an active participant in the management of an investment, it is much harder now to benefit from losses on investments on your tax return. The IRS also will look at whether investments make economic and financial sense, aside from their tax implications. If not, the IRS may disallow any tax benefits you might hope to realize.

In general, tax shelter investments tend to have high sales commissions and high risk. They also tend to be quite illiquid. The average investor should be extremely cautious and skeptical about such investments.

INSURANCE

Adequate and appropriate insurance is one key to protecting your financial well-being. The first lesson about insurance is that you should buy insurance for things that probably won't happen, not things that probably will happen.

Insurance usually requires a lot of paperwork, and also a fair amount of profit for the insurance company. If you insure an event that is likely to happen, you will have to pay the insurance company enough to cover the losses they have to pay out, as well as the cost of their paperwork and profits. You will almost certainly be worse off by buying the insurance.

Similarly, it doesn't pay to insure for small losses, even if they are unlikely to occur. Suppose you buy an auto insurance policy with a $100 deductible for comprehensive coverage. Your car is broken into and someone steals your brand new $150 DVD player. You can file a claim for $50 (you must absorb the deductible amount of the loss). It costs an insurance company a lot to process a $50 claim. Your premium will reflect that paperwork cost.

In contrast, if you purchase a policy with a $1,000 deductible, your premiums will be much lower, since you are less likely to file a claim. You might save $100 in premiums each year because of the higher deductible. You would lose the right to claim the $50 on the DVD loss, but still come out ahead. Besides, who wants the hassle of dealing with an insurance company to recover $50? And even if you do have a loss of $200 or $300, will it change your life?

Insurance is best employed to prevent a catastrophic loss. Try to avoid the complications of having to deal with insurance companies for minor amounts, but be sure that you are protected against potential substantial losses. Too often people overpay to keep their low $100 deductibles on their car insurance, and then fail to have fire insurance on their houses. Yet it is the loss of the house that could have a dramatic negative impact on their financial position, not the loss of a DVD player.

Life Insurance

Having a large life insurance policy is something that often makes sense. Not always? No. Not always. Since everyone dies, the premiums for life insurance have to be great enough to cover insurance company profits, paperwork costs, and the payout when you die. To win at life insurance you have to die early, before you have paid too many years of premiums. And that's hardly anyone's idea of winning.

Nevertheless, you can get a sensible policy at a reasonable cost if you consider why you really need it. Life insurance allows you to ensure that money will available for certain purposes if you do, unfortunately, die early.

You may want your spouse to have enough money to pay off the mortgage on the house. Or you may want there to be enough money to pay college tuition for your kids. When you are 25 or 30 years old, have young children, a large mortgage, and little savings, life insurance makes great sense. When the mortgage is paid off, the kids are out of college, and you have savings in the bank, life insurance no longer serves as much of a purpose. Perhaps you need some to supplement your spouse's income from your retirement accounts, but not nearly as much as you needed earlier in your life.

Given this declining need for insurance, it turns out that *term* life insurance, and specifically decreasing term insurance, is the most sensible insurance to buy. When you are young (and least likely to die), insurance companies will give you a great amount of coverage for a relatively small premium.

With a term policy, such as a five-year policy, we no longer have a situation in which every insured individual is going to collect. Most people won't die in the next five years. Therefore the premiums are much lower than those on *whole life*, which continues in force as long as you pay premiums until you do die.

A problem with term insurance is that, each time your policy ends and you renew it, you are older and therefore more likely to die. So the premiums rise with each renewal. However, decreasing term policies overcome this problem by allowing the coverage to gradually decline each year, rather than having the premiums rise. As the coverage declines, typically so do your needs for life insurance. If you choose a one- or five-year term policy, be sure to consider a policy that allows guaranteed renewability without a physical exam.

If you buy term instead of other forms of life insurance, you will likely spend many thousands of dollars less on insurance over your lifetime. And you will have greater amounts of coverage than you would otherwise have been able to afford when you need it most.

Other types of policies are much more common because they pay higher commissions. Whole life, universal, and other policies are generally a combined insurance policy and savings instrument. But the rate of return on the savings is not competitive with other types of investments.

As you listen to an insurance sales pitch, bear in mind that insurance agents work on commission. In many cases 50 to 100 percent of the first year's premium on a whole life policy is a commission for the salesperson. For the same annual premium you may be able to purchase ten times as much coverage or more with a term policy than with a whole life policy. Keep in mind that you want insurance that's best for you, not best for the sales agent. Buy direct from companies that don't pay commissions to their salespeople.

Disability Insurance

What if you are seriously disabled and can't earn a living? It is likely that you would need the same amount of money as if you died, if not more. Without an income coming in, you can't pay your mortgage or send your kids to that expensive college. For all the reasons that you need life insurance, you need disability insurance as well. The concern is not with a short-term injury or illness, but some catastrophe that will keep you from working for a long period of time—several years or longer.

If your spouse earns a good income, or you have substantial savings, disability insurance is less critical. Social Security provides some limited disability benefits. Workers' compensation may help as well, but only if you are injured on the job. Many disabilities result from off-the-job injuries.

If you buy disability insurance, the benefits you receive are tax-free. So if you currently earn $1,500 a week and take home $1,000 after federal and state taxes, you would only need a policy that pays $1,000 per week to maintain your current income. However, if your employer provides disability insurance for you at its expense, the benefits are taxable, so you would need a higher level of benefits.

Health Insurance

Most readers of this book are well aware of the need for health insurance, and probably have coverage in the form of either a now-rare *indemnity plan* or a *managed care* policy such as an HMO.

Health insurance generally provides coverage for care provided by both physicians and hospitals. Indemnity plans are the traditional health insurance policies that allow you to see any doctor or go to any hospital. Under such plans the insured typically pays a *deductible* and a *copayment*, and the insurance company pays the balance. The deductible is the amount paid before the insurance company has any obligation. The copayment is the share of any amount above the deductible that you must also pay.

For example, you might have to pay the first $200 a year of medical bills yourself. Then, you would also be responsible for a "copay" of 20 or 30 percent of the amount above the deductible. The insurance company pays the balance.

Usually there is also a maximum out-of-pocket for the insured. For example, the policy might pay 80 percent of the first $10,000, and 100 percent above that up to $1,000,000. You should always get a policy with high deductibles, because that will reduce your need to file claims, and will lower premiums substantially. Also, try to avoid the $1,000,000 cap if possible. It may seem like a lot, but if you become seriously ill, it is not unheard of to surpass that amount.

Managed care plans often have small copayments such as $5 or $10 per visit, no deductible, and no ceiling. However, they generally limit your choice of health care provider. Managed care companies negotiate aggressively with providers to get lower rates and to try to limit unnecessary care. Some argue that managed care companies go too far, limiting necessary care as well.

In retirement, most people get their health care insurance from Medicare. Part A of Medicare covers hospital care. It is a benefit all Medicare enrollees get. Part B covers physician care, and is available for a fee that is deducted from Social Security benefits. Many insurance companies offer Medigap policies to fill in the gaps in Medicare coverage—paying deductibles, copays, and some other noncovered expenses.

Long-term care insurance is more controversial. It pays for nursing home care for extended stays. Medicare will pay for a few months of rehabilitation in a nursing home. But if you enter a nursing home as a long-term patient, it is likely that you will have to pay for the care, and go on Medicaid once your assets have been depleted.

Most people do not stay in nursing homes long. One to three years is probably typical. But nursing homes may easily cost $200 to $300 per day now, and that cost will undoubtedly rise. At $65,000 to $100,000 per year, your assets can rapidly be depleted.

If you are interested in long-term care insurance, consider getting it early. The younger you are when you start a policy, the lower the annual premium. Even though you may not anticipate needing nursing home care while you are young, that is perhaps when it is most important. Suppose you were have an injury that were to leave you in a vegetative state. You might wind up in a nursing home for ten years or longer.

You should also consider buying automatic inflation protection. Most policies will allow you to choose to add more insurance year by year. However, each time you add you are adding at a higher premium rate because of your more advanced age. Or you can get an automatic increase every year. Such policies have a flat premium. It is likely to appear to be expensive at first, but as each year goes by, the premium stays the same. At the same time, your coverage is increasing in compound fashion.

Nevertheless, long-term care insurance is really beneficial only if you have substantial assets you wish to protect and if you are quite uneasy about the possibility of having to apply for Medicaid to pay your long-term care costs.

Protecting Assets

We insure assets primarily for two reasons. First, we don't want to lose what we have. Second, we don't want to lose the assets we don't even have yet. We insure a car and house so that if there is an auto accident or a house fire, we don't lose those valuable assets.

Just as important is insurance to protect you from a lawsuit. Liability judgments can not only wipe you out, but may place claims against your future as well. And bear in mind that legal judgments generally cannot be wiped out by bankruptcy filing. Therefore, they can be a financial disaster.

When you purchase renter's or homeowner's insurance, you want to make sure you will be adequately reimbursed for losses such as those due to fire. You can buy insurance that reimburses the cost of your dwelling, or that reimburses the cost to replace your dwelling. Usually replacement-cost insurance is a bit more expensive, but it provides much better protection. Homeowner's insurance typically protects the property you have in your house as well.

However, it is critical to make sure that your insurance also covers liability. If someone gets hurt in your house, you might be sued. If you own your home, people can trip on your sidewalk and sue you for negligence.

Auto insurance should similarly protect not only against the loss of your car, but also bodily injury and liability. The cost of the car itself often is small relative to the medical, legal, and liability costs that may be associated with a serious accident.

Most homeowner and auto policies have maximum liability limits of perhaps $300,000 or $500,000. In today's litigious society, that doesn't go far. In order to protect your current and future assets, it is quite worthwhile to purchase an umbrella or excess liability policy. These policies are essentially liability policies with very high deductibles—typically $300,000. Often they require you to maintain that level of liability insurance as part of your homeowner's and car insurance.

Umbrella policies kick in only if you have a loss that exceeds that level. Because of the high deductible, these policies are quite inexpensive. They cost only a few hundred dollars for the first million dollars of protection, and get less expensive for each additional million in coverage. Even if you don't have millions of dollars in assets, you probably don't want to wind up with millions of dollars in liabilities. Maintaining an umbrella policy for a few million dollars at a cost of a few hundred dollars a year is a wise investment.

How Safe Is Your Insurance Company?

You may pay premiums on long-term care insurance and life insurance policies for decades without filing a claim. Will the insurance company still be in business when you do have a claim?

Insurance companies are rated by A.M. Best, Moody's, Standard & Poor's, and other companies. The best rating is typically AAA or A, depending on the rating company. As you reduce the number of As in the rating or move from A to B to C, the financial strength of the company is declining. The longer the time before you expect to need a payout from your insurer, the more important it is that you ask the insurance companies you are considering to disclose their ratings to you.

ESTATE PLANNING

If you find thinking about life insurance and long-term care insurance depressing, you are unlikely to find this section any more pleasant. Estate planning focuses on what will happen to all the assets you have accumulated when you die. To start on a cheery note, the Economic Growth and Tax Relief Reconciliation Act of 2001 reduced the top federal estate tax rate to 50 percent and repeals the tax completely in 2010. However, that is also the year that the provisions of the Act expire unless renewed by Congress. In the meantime, the amount exempted from the tax will gradually rise and the rate will fall.

Nevertheless, estate planning is still necessary. For starters, you really should have a will if you have children who are minors. A will doesn't just focus on inheritance of assets. It specifies the guardian for your children. If you and your spouse both die *intestate* (without a will), the state gets to decide who raises your children. And if you don't have children you will probably want to have a will to specify who gets your assets.

When you have a will prepared you should also have a living will prepared. This document specifies your wishes regarding which life-support measures should or should not be used under various conditions.

You should also consider whether it is worthwhile for you to establish living trusts. Such trusts allow your assets to pass to your heirs without going through probate, a costly and lengthy legal process.

KEY CONCEPTS

Net worth statement—balance sheet. Assets – Liabilities = Net Worth.

Emergency reserves—money kept in cash or secure, liquid investments to serve as a cushion if you suddenly lose a major source of income.

Credit card float—the interest-free use of money during the period of time from the date of a credit card purchase until the check for payment clears your bank account.

Control of debt—Shop around for the best deal on credit cards; pay credit cards by the end of the grace period to avoid high interest charges; avoid auto and other consumer loans; use debt for long-term investments such as a home or for education.

Controlling taxes—Avoid large refunds; shift income to years you are in a lower tax bracket; shift deductions to years you are in a higher tax bracket; trade consumer debt for mortgage debt on which interest is deductible; take advantage of holding periods to lower capital gains tax; and liberally contribute to tax-advantaged retirement plans.

Tax-advantaged retirement plans—investments that give the taxpayer some tax benefit not available for ordinary savings. Include individual retirement accounts (regular and Roth), employer-sponsored plans (401(k) and 403(b) plans), self-employment plans (SEP-IRAs and Keoghs), and annuities.

Investing—Choose a portfolio of lender and equity investments that consider your attitudes toward risk and return, when you will need the money, and the need to diversify your holdings.

Tax shelters—investments that are sold at least partly based on their ability to reduce the investor's taxes.

Insurance—contracts that provide payments to you when certain events occur. Includes life, disability, health, homeowner, auto, and umbrella (excess liability) policies.

Estate planning—planning related to taxes, guardianship of your children, and inheritance of your assets in case of your death; and medical instructions should you become incapacitated.

Twenty-Four
Summary and Conclusion

This book has covered quite a bit of ground. In completing this book, you should have gained an improved understanding of the nature of accounting and finance. You should have a wealth of vocabulary and should be aware of many concerns of financial managers, as well as some of the tools they use to manage their concerns. For example, by now you are well aware of the emphasis on profitability, but should also have an awareness of the risks that go along with profits, and the fact that financial managers are attempting to balance the level of profit with the level of risk.

You should be aware of the financial manager's concern for liquidity, and the many measures of liquidity that the accountant builds into financial statements. This information helps the financial officer compute ratios on liquidity and solvency to monitor the firm's viability and to enable adjustments to be made if problems arise.

Accounting and finance go hand in hand in the financial process of the firm. The accountant provides information, both historical and prospective, and the finance officer uses that information to make crucial decisions regarding how much the firm will invest and from where the invested resources will come.

This book is not a comprehensive handbook on all the issues of accounting and finance. Such completeness in all detail was not the goal of this book. What the author hopes is that you have been taught a vocabulary, a language—the language of business. Obviously a book such as this one can't answer all the specific questions of all the many readers of the book. But if it helps you formulate specific questions for further exploration, that in itself is an accomplishment. You should now also be in a better position to understand your financial managers' answers to your questions.

A final caveat: You are not a financial analyst after having read this book. Don't think of this book as a how-to-do-it book. Don't attempt to do your own tax planning based on the tax discussions contained in this book. Accounting and finance are highly complex areas.

This doesn't mean that they should simply be left to the experts. Nonfinancial managers have a need to be able to understand the basic goals and techniques of financial officers. You should be able to understand what is going on and what is being said. Don't, however, gain an overconfidence that, "That's all there is to financial management." Rather, think of it this way: Hopefully someone soon will write a book on operating management for staff and financial managers. It won't teach them all there is to know about line management, but they certainly could use it—communication, after all, is a two-way street.

GLOSSARY

accelerated depreciation: techniques that allocate a higher portion of a long-term asset's cost as an expense in the earlier years of its useful lifetime and a smaller portion in the later years.

accounting: system for keeping track of the financial status of an organization and the financial results of its activities.

accounts payable: amounts owed to suppliers.

accounts receivable: money owed to an **entity** for goods and services it has provided.

accrual basis: accounting system that records revenues in the year in which they become earned (whether received or not).

accumulated depreciation: total amount of depreciation related to a fixed asset that has been taken over the years the organization has owned that asset.

acid test: see **quick ratio**.

aging schedule: management report that shows how long receivables have been outstanding since an invoice was issued.

allowance for uncollectible accounts: estimated portion of total **accounts receivable** that is not expected to be collected because of **bad debts**; also called allowance for bad debts.

amortization: allocation of the cost of an asset over its lifetime.

annuity: series of payments or receipts, each in the same amount and spaced at even time periods.

assets: tangible or **intangible** resources.

audit: examination of the financial records of the organization to evaluate the internal control system and to determine if financial statements have been prepared in accordance with **GAAP**.

auditor's report: a letter from a Certified Public Accountant providing an expert opinion about whether an organization's financial statements provide a fair representation of its financial position and the results of its operations, in accordance with **GAAP**.

audit trail: a set of references that allows an individual to trace back through accounting documents to the source of any number.

bad debts: amounts that are owed to the organization that are never collected.

balance sheet: financial report that indicates the financial position of the organization at a specific point in time; officially referred to as the **statement of financial position**.

bondholder: creditor of the organization who owns one of the organization's **bonds payable**.

bond payable: formal borrowing arrangement whereby a transferable certificate represents the debt.

bonding of employees: insurance policy protecting the organization against embezzlement and fraud by employees.

break-even analysis: technique for determining the minimum volume of services or goods that must be provided to be financially self-sufficient.

break-even volume: the volume just needed to break even. Losses would generally be incurred at lower volumes and profits at higher volumes; sometimes called the break-even point.

budget: a formal, quantitative expression of management's plans and intentions or expectations.

business plan: detailed plan for a proposed program, project, or service, including information to be used to assess financial feasibility.

capital acquisitions: see **capital assets**.

capital assets: assets with useful lives extending beyond the year in which they are purchased or put into service; also referred to as long-term investments, capital items, capital investments, or capital acquisitions.

capital budgeting: process of proposing and analyzing the purchase of **capital assets**.

capital cost: see **cost of capital**.

capital lease: form of long-term financing in which a long-term, noncancelable contractual arrangement is made to lease a **capital asset**.

carrying costs of inventory: capital (interest) costs and out-of-pocket costs related to holding inventory. Out-of-pocket costs include such expenses as insurance on the value of inventory and obsolescence of inventory.

cash basis: accounting system under which revenues are recorded when cash is received and expenses are recorded when cash is paid.

cash budget: plan for the cash receipts and disbursements of the organization.

cash equivalents: items that are quickly and easily convertible into cash, such as checking accounts and **commercial paper**.

cash flow statement: financial statement that examines the organization's sources and uses of cash.

cash management: active process of planning for borrowing and repayment of cash or investing excess cash on hand.

certificate of deposit: bank deposit with a fixed maturity term.

chart of accounts: accounting document that defines an identifying number for each possible element of a financial transaction.

collateral: specific asset pledged to a lender as security for a loan.

collection period: amount of time from when a bill is issued until the cash payment for that bill is collected.

commercial paper: form of short-term borrowing in which the borrower issues a financial security that can be traded by the lender to someone else.

common size ratio: class of ratios that allows one to evaluate each number on a financial statement relative to the size of the organization.

compound interest: method of calculating interest in which interest is earned not only on the original investment but also on the interest earned in interim periods.

conservatism principle: GAAP stating that financial statements must give adequate consideration to the risks faced by the organization.

contingent liabilities: obligations that will exist in the future if certain events occur, such as if the organization loses a lawsuit.

contra asset: an asset that is used to offset or reduce another asset.

contributed capital: amounts that individuals have paid directly to the firm in exchange for shares of ownership such as common or preferred stock; also called **paid-in-capital**.

contribution margin: amount by which the price exceeds the variable cost.

corporation: business form in which the owners (shareholders or stockholders) have limited liability—they are not liable for more than the amount they invested in the firm.

cost accounting system: any coherent system designed to gather and report cost information.

cost allocation: the process of taking costs from one area or cost objective and allocating them to others.

cost convention: GAAP that requires most assets to be valued at their cost at the time of acquisition.

cost driver: an activity that causes costs to be incurred.

cost-effectiveness: a measure of whether costs are minimized for the desired outcome.

cost of capital: the cost to the organization of its long-term debt and equity financing.

credit (cr.): bookkeeping term for an increase in an item on the right side of the **fundamental equation of accounting** or a decrease in an item on the left side.

creditors: entities to whom the organization owes money.

current: within one year; short-term or near-term.

current assets: resources the organization has that are cash, that can be converted to cash within one year, or that will be used up within one year. Often referred to as short-term or near-term assets.

current liabilities: obligations due to be paid within one year.

current ratio: current assets divided by **current liabilities**; this **liquidity ratio** assesses the ability of the organization to meet its current obligations as they come due.

days of inventory on hand: 365 divided by the **inventory turnover** ratio; this **efficiency ratio** assesses how many days' supply of inventory is kept on hand.

days receivable: 365 divided by the **receivables turnover** ratio; this **efficiency ratio** indicates the average number of days from the issuance of an invoice until a receivable is collected.

debit (dr.): bookkeeping term for an increase in an item on the left side of the **fundamental equation of accounting** or a decrease in an item on the right side.

debt: liability; an amount owed by one **entity** to another.

debt service: required interest and principal payments on money owed.

debt to equity: leverage ratio that considers the relative magnitude of debt to equity to assess the risk created by the use of **leverage**.

decision package: all information and analysis related to a **zero-based budgeting** review.

deficit: the excess of cash spending over cash receipts or of **expenses** over **revenues**.

defined-benefit plan: pension plan in which the organization is required to make specific defined payments to participants during their retirement.

defined-contribution plan: pension plan in which the employer's only obligation is to put into the plan a set amount of money each year.

depreciation expense: the portion of the original cost of a **capital asset** allocated as an expense each year.

derivatives: securities whose value is derived from the value of something else.

direct costs: a) costs incurred within the organizational unit for which the manager has responsibility; b) costs of resources used for direct provision of goods or services.

disbursement: cash payment.

discounted cash flow: method that compares amounts of money paid at different points of time by **discounting** all amounts to the present.

discounting: reverse of **compound interest**; a process in which interest that could be earned over time is deducted from a future payment to determine how much the future payment is worth at the present time.

discount rate: interest rate used in **time value of money** analysis.

dividend: distribution of profits to owners of the **entity**.

double-entry accounting: whenever a change is made to the **fundamental equation of accounting**, at least one other change must be made to keep the equation in balance.

economic order quantity (EOQ): technique that determines the optimal amount of inventory to order at one time.

efficiency ratios: ratios that examine the efficiency with which the organization uses its resources. Examples are **receivables turnover**, **days of inventory on hand**, and **total asset turnover**.

efficiency variance: see **quantity variance**.

employee benefits: compensation provided to employees in addition to their base salary; for example, health insurance, life insurance, vacation, and holidays.

entity: specific individual, organization, or part of an organization for which we are accounting.

equities: liabilities and owners' equity; the right-hand side of the balance sheet.

equity: ownership; e.g., the share of a house that is owned by the homeowner free and clear of any mortgage obligations is the homeowner's equity in the house.

expense: the cost of services provided; expired cost.

external accountant: accountant who is not an employee of the organization, often hired to perform an audit.

face value: see **maturity value**.

factoring: selling the organization's accounts receivable.

favorable variance: variance in which less money was spent or more money was earned than the budgeted amount.

finance: field that focuses on the alternative sources and uses of the organization's financial resources such as cash, marketable securities, and debt.

financial accounting: system that records historical financial information, summarizes it, and provides reports of what financial events have occurred and of what the financial impact of those events has been.

financial management: the subset of management that focuses on generating financial information to improve decision making.

financial statement analysis: analysis of the financial condition of an entity by reviewing financial statements including the accompanying notes and **auditor's report**, performing **ratio analysis**, and using comparative data.

financial statements: reports that convey information about the **entity's** financial position and the results of its activities.

financing accounts receivable: using the organization's accounts receivable as security or collateral for a loan.

first-in, first-out (FIFO): inventory-costing method that assumes the oldest inventory is used first.

fiscal: financial.

fiscal year: one-year period defined for financial purposes. A fiscal year may start at any point during the calendar year and finish one year later. Fiscal year 2003 with a June 30 year-end refers to the period from July 1, 2002, through June 30, 2003.

fixed assets: those assets that will not be used up or converted to cash within one year.

fixed costs: costs that do not change in total as volume of goods or services changes within the **relevant range**.

flexible budget: budget that is adjusted for volume of output.

flexible budgeting: process of developing a budget based on different workload levels.

flexible budget variance: difference between actual results and the flexible budget.

float: the interim period from when a check is written until the check is cashed and clears the bank.

fringe benefits: see **employee benefits**.

full disclosure: GAAP that requires notes to financial statements to convey all information necessary for the user to have a fair understanding of the financial position of the organization and the results of its operations.

fundamental equation of accounting: assets equal liabilities plus owners' equity.

fungible: interchangeable.

future value (FV): the amount money paid or received will grow to be worth at some point in the future.

GAAP: see **Generally Accepted Accounting Principles**.

general journal: first place that financial transactions are entered into the accounting records.

general ledger: book of **accounts**, listing the balances and all changes in each account.

Generally Accepted Accounting Principles (GAAP): set of rules that must be followed for the organization's financial statements to be deemed a fair presentation of the organization's financial position and results of operations.

goal congruence: bringing together the goals, desires, and wants of the organization with those of its employees.

goal divergence: natural differences between the goals, desires, and needs of the organization and those of its employees.

goals: broad, timeless ends of the organization meant to aid the organization in accomplishing its **mission**.

going-concern principle: GAAP that requires an explicit note in the auditor's opinion letter if there is a significant possibility that the organization will not be able to continue operations for the entire coming year.

goodwill: the value of the organization above the value of its specific physical assets.

hurdle rate: see **required rate of return**.

income: excess of revenues over expenses.

income statement: financial statement that reports the results of operations over a period of time.

incremental budgeting: an approach to resource allocation that simply adds an additional percentage or amount onto the prior year's budget allocation.

incremental costs: additional costs that will be incurred if a decision is made that would not otherwise be incurred.

indirect costs: a) costs assigned to an organizational unit from elsewhere in the organization; b) costs within a unit that are not incurred for direct provision of goods or services.

indirect expenses: see **indirect costs**.

inputs: resources used for producing the organization's output. Examples are labor and supplies.

intangible asset: asset without physical substance or form.

interest coverage ratio: operating income divided by interest expense; a measure of the organization's ability to meet its required interest payments.

interim statements: financial statements covering a period of time less than one year.

internal accountant: accountant who works as an employee of the organization.

internal control: a system of accounting checks and balances designed to minimize clerical errors and the possibility of fraud or embezzlement.

internal rate of return (IRR): discounted cash-flow technique that calculates the rate of return earned on a specific project or program.

inventory: materials and supplies held for use in providing services or making a product.

inventory-carrying costs: see **carrying costs of inventory**.

inventory costing: the process of determining the cost to be assigned to each unit of **inventory**.

inventory management: refers to the appropriate ordering and storage of supplies.

inventory-ordering costs: see **ordering costs**.

inventory turnover: efficiency ratio that evaluates the relative number of times that the organization's inventory has been consumed and replaced during the year.

investments: primarily stocks and bonds that the organization does not intend to sell within one year.

IRR: see **internal rate of return**.

journal entry: entry into the **general journal** or a **subsidiary journal**.

just-in-time (JIT) inventory: an approach to inventory management that calls for the arrival of inventory just as it is needed, resulting in zero inventory levels.

last-in, first-out (LIFO): inventory valuation method that accounts for inventory as if the most recent acquisitions are used first.

lease: agreement providing for the use of an asset in exchange for rental payments.

leasehold asset: the **balance sheet** title for the asset on a **capital lease**.

leasehold liability: the **balance sheet** title for the liability on a **capital lease**.

ledger: accounting record that tracks changes in each asset, liability, revenue, expense, and equity account.

leverage: a) the use of debt as a source of financing, increasing risk because of the requirement to make interest payments; b) the use of fixed costs to increase profits if the volume of goods or services sold is high.

leverage ratios: ratios that examine the relative amount of debt the organization has; sometimes referred to as **solvency** ratios.

liabilities: legal financial obligations the organization has to outsiders.

line item: any item listed as a separate line on a budget.

line of credit: prearranged loan to be made when and if needed by the **entity** in an amount up to an agreed limit.

liquid: able to be quickly converted to cash.

liquidate: convert into cash, by sale if necessary.

liquidity ratios: class of ratios that examine the ability of the **entity** to meet its obligations in the coming year.

lockbox: post office box that is emptied directly by the bank, with receipts immediately deposited into the organization's account.

long-range plan: plan that covers a period longer than one year, focusing on general objectives to be achieved by the organization.

long-term: period longer than one year.

long-term assets: see **capital assets**.

long-term financing: the various alternatives available to the organization to get the money needed to acquire **capital assets**.

long-term investment: see **capital assets**.

long-term liabilities: obligations that are not due until more than one year has passed.

management control system: complete set of policies and procedures designed to keep operations going according to plan.

management letter: letter from the CPA to the management of the **entity** discussing weaknesses in the internal control system that were revealed as part of an audit.

management's discussion: section of an annual report in which the organization's management discusses the organization's performance.

managerial accounting: subset of accounting that generates financial information that can help managers to manage better.

marginal cost analysis: process for making decisions based on the costs that change as a result of the decision rather than on the full or average costs.

marginal costs: variable costs plus any change in fixed costs incurred because of a change in activity.

marketable securities: investments in stocks and bonds that the organization intends to sell within one year.

master budget: set of all the major budgets in the organization; generally includes the operating, long-range, program, capital, and cash budgets.

matching: recording the revenues from the sale of a unit in the same period as the expenses incurred to generate the revenue.

material: amount substantial enough that an error of that magnitude in the financial statements would affect a decision made by a user of the statements.

maturity: due date or end date of a loan arrangement.

maturity value: the principal amount of a loan to be repaid at the ending date or maturity date of the loan.

mission statement: statement of the purpose or reason for existence of an **entity**.

monetary denominator: **GAAP** that requires resources be stated on financial statements in terms of an amount of money.

money market: the market for short-term marketable securities or the market for short-term debt instruments.

mortgage payable: a loan secured by specific property.

near-term: within one year; current or short-term.

negotiable certificate of deposit: certificate of deposit that can be transferred from one party to another.

net book value: the original cost of the asset less the total **accumulated depreciation** for that asset.

net cash flow: difference between cash receipts and payments.

net income: revenue less expense; profit.

net present value (NPV): **present value** of a series of receipts, less the present value of a series of payments.

net working capital: **current assets** less **current liabilities**.

net worth: **owners' equity**.

note payable: written document representing a loan.

NPV: see **net present value**.

objective evidence: **GAAP** that requires assets to be valued based on objective, rather than subjective, information.

objectives: specific targets to be achieved to attain goals.

operating: related to the normal routine revenue and expense activities of the organization.

operating budget: plan for the day-in and day-out operating revenues and expenses of the organization.

operating expenses: costs of the organization related to its general operations.

operating lease: lease that is either short-term or cancelable.

operating margin: **profitability ratio** that compares operating profit to operating revenue.

operating revenues: revenues earned in the normal course of providing the organization's goods or services.

operating statement: compares the **entity's revenues** and other **support** to its **expenses** for a period of time. Also called the income statement, activity statement, profit and loss (P&L) statement, or earnings report.

operations: routine activities of the organization related to its **mission** and the provision of goods or services.

opinion letter: letter providing a CPA's expert opinion as to whether a set of financial statements are a fair presentation of the financial position and results of operations of the organization, in accordance with **GAAP**.

ordering costs: those costs associated with ordering inventory, such as clerical time to prepare a purchase order.

output: the number of units of service or product produced.

overhead: indirect costs allocated to a unit or department from elsewhere in the organization.

owners' equity: residual value, owned by the owners, left over when the liabilities of an organization are subtracted from its assets.

paid-in-capital: see **contributed capital**.

partnership: type of business form in which a group of people (partners) have unlimited liability.

payback: evaluation approach that calculates how long it takes for a project's revenues to exceed all costs including the initial cash outlay.

payroll payable: amounts owed to employees.

period costs: costs that are treated as expense in the accounting period when they are incurred, regardless of when the organization's goods or services are sold.

periodic inventory: inventory method under which the organization uses a count of inventory to determine how much has been sold and how much is left on hand.

perpetual inventory: inventory method under which the organization keeps a record of each unit removed from inventory.

planning: selecting a course of action from a range of possible alternatives.

plant: building.

posting: process of recording all parts of a journal entry in the specific ledger accounts affected by the entry.

prepaid expenses: assets that have been paid for, but not yet used, e.g., rent paid in advance.

present value: value of future receipts or payments **discounted** to the present.

price variance: variance caused by spending a different amount per unit of resource than had been anticipated.

principal: the amount of money borrowed on a loan.

product costs: expenses that are directly related to the production of goods and services.

profit: excess of revenues over expenses.

profit center: responsibility unit that is accountable for both revenues and expenses.

profit margin: see **return on sales**.

profitability ratios: ratios that assess the profitability of the organization; examples are the **operating margin** and **total margin** ratios.

profit-sharing plan: an incentive arrangement under which some or all employees receive a portion of an organization's profits that exceed a certain threshold.

pro forma financial statements: forecast of what financial statements will look like if results are as expected.

program audits: reviews of the organization's operations to check for effectiveness.

proprietorship: business owned by one individual, who has unlimited liability.

quantity variance: variance caused by using more input per unit of output than had been budgeted.

quick ratio: cash plus marketable securities plus accounts receivable, all divided by current liabilities. Sometimes called the **acid test**.

rate variance: price variance for labor inputs.

ratio analysis: comparison of one number to another in order to gain insight from the relationship.

receivables: see **accounts receivable**.

receivables turnover: revenues divided by **accounts receivable**; see **average collection period**.

registered bonds: bonds whose ownership is tracked by the borrower.

relevant range: that range of activity that might reasonably be expected to occur in the budget period.

repurchase agreements (repos): short-term investment collateralized by securities.

required rate of return: the rate of return that must be achieved for a capital project to be considered financially worthwhile. Also called the **hurdle rate**.

responsibility accounting: attempt to hold individuals or departments accountable for outcomes.

responsibility center: part of the organization for which a manager is assigned responsibility.

retained earnings: the portion of the profits of a for-profit corporation that have not been distributed to the owners in the form of dividends.

return on assets (ROA): a measure of the amount of profit earned for each dollar invested in the organization's assets.

return on investment (ROI): a ratio that assesses the profitability of the investment.

return on sales (ROS): a ratio that determines the amount of profit generated by each dollar of revenue.

revenue: amounts of money that the organization has received, or is entitled to receive, in exchange for goods and services that it has provided.

revenue to total assets: ratio measure of the amount of revenue generated per dollar of assets used.

revenue variances: variance resulting from changes in the total demand, an organization's share of total demand, mix of products or services, and the prices for each class of product or service.

safety stock: minimum level of inventory that an organization would always attempt to maintain on hand.

sensitivity analysis: recalculations using varying assumptions and predictions, often referred to as "what-if" analysis.

short-term: within one year; current or near-term.

sinking fund: segregated assets to be used for replacement of plant and equipment or the repayment of a long-term loan.

solvency: ability to meet current and future obligations.

solvency ratios: class of ratios that evaluates the organization's ability to meet its obligations as they come due over a time frame longer than one year.

specific identification: inventory valuation method that identifies and tracks each unit of inventory.

statement of financial position: financial report that indicates the financial position of the organization at a specific point in time.

straight-line depreciation: technique that allocates an equal portion of a long-term asset's cost as an expense each year.

strategic plan: see **long-range plan**.

strategies: broad plans for the attainment of **goals**.

subsidiary journal: detailed journals in which original entries are first made, with only a summary total entry being made to the **general journal**.

subsidiary ledger: ledgers in which detailed information is recorded, with only a summary being posted to the **general ledger**.

tangible: having physical substance or form.

terms: refers to when an account payable is due and the discount for early payment.

time-series: forecasting approach that uses past trends and seasonal patterns as predictors for the future.

times interest earned: solvency ratio that assesses the ability of the organization to make interest payments.

time value of money: recognition of the fact that an amount of money in the future is less valuable than that same amount today.

total variance: difference between the actual results and the originally budgeted amount.

total asset turnover: efficiency ratio that assesses the number of dollars of revenue generated for each dollar invested in assets.

total margin: profitability ratio that determines profits per dollar of revenues.

trade credit: accounts payable.

uncollectibles: see **allowance for uncollectible accounts**.

unfavorable variance: variance in which more was spent than the budgeted amount.

unregistered bonds: bonds for which the borrowing organization does not have a record of whom the lenders are. Often called bearer bonds.

unsecured notes: loans that do not have any collateral.

use variance: quantity variance.

variable costs: costs that vary in direct proportion with volume.

variance: difference between the budget and actual results.

variance analysis: investigation by managers to determine why actual results varied from the budget.

vendor: supplier who sells to the organization.

viability: ability to continue in existence.

volume variance: variance caused by a change in the workload level.

wages payable: amounts owed to employees.

working capital: current assets less **current liabilities**.

write-off: entry to eliminate an asset from the accounting records by treating it as an expense.

zero balance accounts: a system in which automatic bank account transfers leave certain accounts with a zero balance at the end of each day.

zero-base budgeting (ZBB): budgeting approach that requires an examination and justification of all costs, rather than just the incremental costs, and that requires examination of alternatives rather than just one approach.

zero-coupon bonds: bonds that do not pay interest until the maturity date, when all accumulated interest and principal is paid.

Appendix

Annotated List of Web Sites Related to Finance and Accounting

Below is an extensive list of Web sites related to finance and accounting. These sites have been specifically chosen for their relevance to nonfinancial managers. Click on each link to be taken directly to that Web site.

    Please note that we do not specifically endorse any products offered at any of these sites. Also note that, unfortunately, many Web sites disappear over time. We apologize if any of the links below are no longer functioning.

1. GENERAL ACCOUNTING PORTALS

Portals are Web sites that primarily provide links to other sites. The following are two of the best sites for accounting and finance links.

http://www.geocities.com/WallStreet/Floor/6295/acct.html
This portal provides links to FASB, AAA, IMA, and many other useful accounting-related Web sites.

http://accounting.rutgers.edu/
Rutgers University is rapidly building an unsurpassed accounting Web site infrastructure, with links to numerous accounting sources and resources.

2. BUSINESS NEWSPAPERS AND MAGAZINES

A number of business newspapers and magazines provide a variety of useful information on financial issues. Articles are often relevant for both business and personal finance. Although subscriptions are required for some services, the sites below all provide extensive information for free.

http://public.wsj.com/home.html
This is the home page for the *Wall Street Journal*.

http://news.ft.com/home/us/
This is the home page for the *Financial Times*, the leading international financial daily newspaper.

http://www.fortune.com/
This is the home page for *Fortune* magazine.

http://www.businessweek.com/
This is the home page for *BusinessWeek* magazine. It is one of the most popular sources for domestic and international business news.

http://www.barrons.com/
This is the home page for *Barron's* weekly business newspaper.

http://www.money.com/money/
This is the home page for *Money* magazine. It is of primary interest for personal finances.

http://www.smartmoney.com/
This is the home page for *Smartmoney* magazine. It is of primary interest for personal finances.

http://www.kiplinger.com/
This is the home site for *Kiplinger's*, a widely read source for personal finances and economic forecasts.

3. ACCOUNTING AND FINANCE ASSOCIATIONS

Although the primary purpose of a trade association is to serve its members, many finance and accounting associations have a wealth of useful information for nonmembers as well. Listed below are some of the most important sites.

http://www.taxsites.com/aicpa.html
This site provides a directory of tax and accounting Web sites from the American Institute of Certified Public Accountants (AICPA), the primary national association of CPAs.

http://www.imanet.org/

This is the home site for the Institute of Management Accountants, a professional organization devoted exclusively to management accounting and financial management.

http://www.aaa-edu.org/

This is the home site for the American Accounting Association, the primary association of accountants in academics.

http://www.afajof.org/

This is the home site for the American Finance Association, the primary association of finance academics.

http://afponline.org/

This is the home site for the Association of Finance Professionals.

4. TAX BASICS

The sites in this section provide tax information for personal and business taxes.

http://www.irs.ustreas.gov/index.html

This is the home page for the Internal Revenue Service. The site provides a wealth of useful information on all issues related to U.S. federal income taxes.

http://www.als.edu/lib/taxation.html

This Albany Law School site provides a nice summary of the Internal Revenue Code, tax treaties, Internal Revenue Service materials, court reports, and a "how to" guide for using basic tax publications.

http://www.taxresources.com/

A source of up-to-date information on taxes, as well as a number of other useful tax links.

http://www.usnews.com/

This is the home page for *U.S.News & World Report*. It often contains articles on taxation geared to a nonfinancial audience.

http://www.moneycentral.com/
This CNBC site often contains articles on taxation geared to a nonfinancial audience.

http://www.dtonline.com/taxguide/chap10.htm
At this site, the accounting firm of Deloitte & Touche provides a lay discussion of the Alternative Minimum Tax.

http://businessweek.findlaw.com/
At this site, *BusinessWeek On-Line* often provides articles on taxes for small businesses.

5. BUSINESS PLANS

A number of sites provide assistance in writing a business plan, as well as other information related to starting a new business. Some good sites are:

http://www.sba.gov/starting/indexbusplans.html
The government's Small Business Administration site provides a wealth of information on starting a business and developing a business plan.

http://www.businessplans.org/
The Center for Business Planning provides resources to help in creating a business or managing a business.

http://www.business-plan.com/
OUT OF YOUR MIND...AND INTO THE MARKETPLACE is a publisher focusing on business plan books and software.

http://www.planware.org/salepwb.htm
Business Planning Software—sophisticated package of business plan tools.

http://www.learn2.com/06/0603/0603.asp
This site contains an on-line book on how to write a business plan, a simple first look at business planning.

http://www.bplans.com/
Bplans.com provides a wealth of information for starting a business and developing a business plan. Sample plans, books, articles, and software are available through this site.

http://morebusiness.com/

The motto of Morebusiness.com is that it is a Web site by entrepreneurs for entrepreneurs. Chock full of articles, features, tools, templates, and other information for business plans and new businesses.

6. RAISING VENTURE CAPITAL

Raising venture capital is a difficult challenge for most new businesses. Listed below are the Web sites for a few venture capital organizations. We suggest that you also use a search engine and simply search for "venture capital" to identify additional organizations that are located in your geographic area. Also note that some venture capitalists will give you a better deal than others. It pays to shop around.

http://www.vcinstitute.org/

This is the home page for The Venture Capital Institute, a trade association for venture capitalists. Although not aimed at the general public, it does provide valuable information for someone starting out on the search for financing.

http://www.vfinance.com/

This Web site features the Venture Capital Resource Directory, a broad listing of venture capital firms.

http://www.concentric.net/~invernes/

Aabaar Capital provides purchase order financing. For a company with purchase orders in hand, this can provide the money needed to acquire the resources to fill the order.

http://www.avicapital.com/

AVI Management Partners is a family of venture capital partnerships specializing in seed and early-stage investments in high-technology companies.

http://www.alpineventures.com/

Alpine Technology Ventures is a Silicon Valley–based venture capital firm investing and working with early stage information technology companies.

http://www.brentwoodvc.com/
Brentwood Venture Capital has been an investor in Internet/e-commerce, communications and data networking, information technology, and health care.

7. BUDGETING

A number of vendors provide software and other assistance to help in the budget process. A few examples are:

http://www.comshare.com/
Comshare provides free on-line seminars in addition to their budgeting, consolidation, reporting, and business intelligence software applications.

http://www.srcsoftware.com/
SRC Software provides budgeting software for enterprisewide and Web-based budgeting and reporting.

http://www.epssoftware.com/
EPS Software provides budgeting, planning, forecasting, and management reporting software.

8. TIME VALUE OF MONEY

Time value of money is one of the most difficult aspects of financial management, but it is critical to financial decision making. If you want to explore this topic beyond the coverage in *Finance and Accounting for Nonfinancial Managers*, 3rd Edition, you might read the materials available at some of the following sites:

http://www.teachmefinance.com/
TeachMeFinance.com provides simple explanations of concepts: time value of money, present value, future value, annuities, bond valuation, internal rate of return, and more.

http://www.busadm.mu.edu/mandell/tvm.html
This site from Marquette University focuses on a mathematical presentation of time value of money concepts.

http://www.studyfinance.com/lessons/timevalue/index.html
A brief on-line course in time value of money concepts.

http://fisher.osu.edu/fin/811/opler/week3/index.htm
A graphical lesson in time value of money from Ohio State University.

9. WORKING CAPITAL MANAGEMENT

Discussion of working capital management may be found at the following sites:

http://web.utk.edu/~jwachowi/part4.html
This portal provides links to many sites providing information and assistance with working capital management.

http://www.studyfinance.com/lessons/workcap.html
Self-paced on-line course on working capital management.

http://www.mgt.smsu.edu/eworkcap/tsld001.htm
Graphic course in working capital management.

10. INVENTORY MANAGEMENT

There are numerous Web sites offering inventory management services. A few examples are listed below:

http://www.simba.org/
Web site of the Society for Inventory Management Benchmarking Analysis.

http://www.accurateid.com/
Accurate-ID is a provider of inventory management software.

http://www.effectiveinventory.com/
Effective Inventory Management provides articles, courses, and software for inventory management.

11. RATIO ANALYSIS

http://www.ventureline.com/entry/ratio_analysis.htm
VentureLine provides extensive discussions of ratio analysis at this site. Industry ratio analysis reports may be generated on-line.

http://www.studyfinance.com/lessons/ratioanal.html
A self-paced on-line course on ratio analysis.

12. PERSONAL FINANCE

http://www.ssa.gov/
Access to information on Social Security and Medicare benefits.

http://quote.yahoo.com/?u, http://quicken.com/, http://www.bloomberg.com/,
and http://www.multexpf com/pf/home.asp
Four examples of the excellent sites available for tracking your stocks,
getting research about specific stocks, and reading the latest business
news.

http://www.fool.com/
The Motley Fool exists to educate, amuse, and enrich the individual
investor; to prove to you that the best person to manage your money is
you. Many features to teach both novice and experienced investor.

http://www.finance-site-online.com/
Information on bankruptcy planning, mortgages and loans, interest rates,
auto loans, home loans, insurance, credit and debt management, retirement planning, on-line investing, stock research and quotes, banking,
estate planning, and tax planning.

http://www.vanguard.com and http://www.fidelity.com
Two of the nation's mutual fund powerhouses, each offering a broad range
of no-load funds. Vanguard is known for a focus on index funds and low
investment management fees. Both also offer discounted brokerage services.

http/www.law.indiana.edu/law/bizlaw.html
Discussion of many legal aspects of personal finance issues, such as credit
cards, bounced checks, lemon laws, and more.

13. TRAINING IN FINANCE AND ACCOUNTING
FOR NONFINANCIAL MANAGERS

A number of books, in-person, and on-line seminars are available for
those nonfinancial managers who want to study finance and accounting
further.

http://www.financialaccounting.com/
Financial Accounting Institute. Offers finance and accounting seminars with CPE and CLE credit for both financial and nonfinancial professionals in the public utility (electric, gas, water, and telephone) industry.

http://www.rctm.com/FinancialMedia.html
Financial management training programs from The Richardson Company. Training media include financial management books and audio tapes. Basic and intermediate courses on Finance and Accounting for Nonfinancial Managers. Courses on troubleshooting, business planning, cash flow, and more.

http://www.csom.umn.edu/WWWPages/EES/Courses/FIN.htm
Financial management training programs offered by the Carlson School at the University of Minnesota. Courses include Reading and Interpreting Financial Statements, Finance and Accounting for Nonfinancial Managers, and Financial Literacy for Administrative Staff.

http://www.microsoft-certification.com/microsoft_excel.htm
Microsoft Excel training and certification provided by Specialized Solutions, Inc. Course includes 3 interactive CD-ROMs or 3 video training tapes.

http://www.worldclasstrainers.com/
BizNiz provides software training in Excel, Database, Oracle, Microsoft, DBA, Access, Word, PowerPoint, and other programs. Provides manual with study guide, audiocassette, exercises, and technical support.

http://www.trainingtutorial.com/
Offers multimedia interactive tutorials for MS Excel 2000 and 97.

14. THE AUTHOR'S WEB SITE

Finally, you are referred to Steven Finkler's Web site at http://www.nyu.edu/classes/finkler for additional updated information.

INDEX